CAMDEN SOLDIERS OF KING & QUEEN 1788–1913

Janice Johnson

©Camden Historical Society Inc. 2020

All rights reserved. No part of this publication may be reproduced, stored in a retrieval system, or transmitted in any form or by any means electronic, mechanical, photocopying, recording or otherwise, without the prior permission of the publisher.

First published in 2020

ISBN 978-0-6485894-0-2

Published by the Camden Historical Society Inc.
40 John Street, Camden, NSW 2570
with funds from the Estate of the late Janice Johnson who died in 2017.

Front Cover: Corporal Reginald Sydney Smith in New South Wales Mounted Rifles Uniform – photo courtesy Camden Historical Society

Back Cover: Soldiers of Camden Mounted Rifles: L-R Front: Unknown; Sergeant John Martin Hawkey; Unknown; L-R Back: Unknown; Private Richard Sharpe; Private Henry Sharpe – photo courtesy Camden Historical Society

Contents

Introduction 1
British Regiments 3
    The Royal Marines: 1788 (First Fleet) 3
    The New South Wales Corps: 1790–1794 4
    73rd (Perthshire) Regiment of Foot: 1810 10
    48th (Northamptonshire) Regiment of Foot: 1817 11
    57th (The West Middlesex) Regiment of Foot: 1825–1826 14
    39th (Dorsetshire) Regiment of Foot: 1827 15
    17th (Leicestershire) Regiment of Foot: 1830 16
    The King's Own (Lanarkshire) 4th Regiment of Foot: 1831 16
    Royal Navy 17
    The Royal Regiment of Artillery: 1853 19
Soldiers From Europe 20
American War of Independence 21
4th Mysore War, India 23
    Battle of Seringapatam, India 24
Napoleonic Wars 25
Maori Wars 41
Crimean War 44
Sudan 50
Chitral Expedition, India 54
The North-West Indian Frontier 60
    48th (Northamptonshire) Regiment of Foot 61
The New South Wales Mounted Rifles 62
    4th Regiment Volunteer Infantry 62
Queen Victoria's Diamond Jubilee 82
Boer Wars 103
Boxer Rebellion 196
Federation 196
Death of Queen Victoria 197
Duke and Duchess of York's Visit 197
Coronation King Edward VII 197
Coronation King George V 198
Bibliography 199
Index 201

INTRODUCTION

> *This work is the result of research undertaken by the late Janice Johnson, who died in 2017. Janice made provision in her will to pay for the publishing of the book. Readers who wish to suggest corrections or additions should put them in writing and contact the Secretary of the Camden Historical Society, 40 John Street, Camden, 2570. (secretary @camdenhistory.org.au.)*
>
> *This Introduction was written by Janice:*

In March 2000 I began identifying those who were buried in the cemetery of St. John's Anglican Church Camden. This meant researching not only their date of death but their backgrounds, as far as possible, before they came to the colony of New South Wales. I was assisted by local families who shared their knowledge of their forebears and by Church burial records which provided additional insight.

By the time that listing was complete I had identified three men who had taken part in the Napoleonic Wars – including one who had served in the Royal Navy during the Battle of Trafalgar. At that time, I was satisfied that I had identified all the men that had participated in wars before arriving in the colony. As I continued with my database and to delve deeper into the histories of early burials in the Macarthur region, I identified others who had participated in not only the Napoleonic Wars but also other conflicts.

The article below appeared in the *Camden News* in July 1897, and sent me again delving into the history of Camden's early settlers.

Camden News
Thursday July 22 1897, page 1

The Sword and the Plough
EARLY MILITARY SETTLERS

It is not generally known that many of our earlier settlers were retired officers from the Army and Navy, but such was the case, and in the peculiar circumstances of the colony they were a most desirable class.

Before 1832 the land was given, by free grant, to all persons who could give satisfactory proof of having means of support, but, after that time, it was sold by auction. Retired officers of the Navy and Army being allowed remission in the purchase money proportioned to their service rank. They became fairly distributed about the country, and besides giving a tone to society, were useful as conservators of the peace, many being Magistrates, and all being accustomed to the management of bodies of men. The assignment system allotted prisoners of the Crown to all approved settlers, and these had a good share of them.

Amongst the retired officers in this the Camden district were

> *Capt. John Macarthur, of Camden Park*
> *Major Antill,[1] of Picton*

---

[1] Antill, Henry Colden, Major

> *Capt. Clark[2] and Capt. Forbes,[3] of Vermont*
> *Lieut. Woore,[4] of Harrington Park*
> *Capt. Hovell,[5] of Narellan Grange*
> *Commander Martin,[6] R N, of Camperdown*
> *Lieut. Shadforth,[7] of Ravenswood*
> *Colonel Breton[8]*
> *Post Capt. John Oxley,[9] of Kirkham*
> *Lieut. MacAlister,[10] of Clifton and*
> *Capt Molle,[11] of Molle's Maine*
>
> *A great many small grants, of the best lands, (called Veteran's grants), in batches along all the river frontages, were given to good service soldiers who desired to become settlers on leaving the army; so the military element must, at that time, have very much predominated. This was the germ of the frontier force which was established at New Zealand, the Cape, and other British possessions, as a protection against the attacks of the native tribes. It is difficult to realise that such military protection was actually needed at the Cowpastures.*

Following the completion of my work into *Camden's World War I Diggers* I looked further into the early colonists who had lived, and in many cases died, in the greater Camden area and had military connections. I identified other military men, and found that the *Camden News* was incorrect with respect to Captain Hovell's connection with Camden's military past.

William Hilton Hovell had been born on 26 April 1766 Yarmouth, Norfolk, England and gone to sea as a boy. By 1808 he was in command of a vessel trading with South America.[12] In November 1811 he applied for permission to settle in the colony of New South Wales but did not arrive until 9 October 1813 on the *Earl Spencer*. Shortly after arrival he applied for a 600 acre (243 ha) land grant in the Cowpastures at Narellan which he called Narellan Grove. The Deed was not issued until 1816.

Hovell is credited with discovering the Burragorang Valley in 1823, and in 1824, together with Hamilton Hume, explored the area between Lake George and Bass Strait, before settling in the Goulburn district.

Back in 2000, local resident Mrs. Shirley Rorke challenged me to look not only at prominent landowners, such as John Macarthur, but also the butchers, the bakers and labourers, and told me about her ancestor, Jesse Dunk. Jesse's story started me delving into the history of the ordinary people who had led extraordinary lives.

It has been a fascinating journey. Many of the early colonists who had lived and worked in the Camden district had connections with our military past. Some came in chains, others arrived as free settlers and others were part of the various military regiments that came to the colony. Undoubtedly there are many I have not been able to identify and so I apologise to any whose ancestors I have omitted.

---

[2] Clark, Ralph, Capt.
[3] Forbes, Charles, Capt.
[4] Woore, Thomas, Lieut.
[5] Hovell, William Hilton, Capt. Hovell wasn't a Naval Captain, rather the Captain of a merchant vessel
[6] Martin, Alexander, Commander
[7] Shadforth, Thomas (snr.), Lieut. Col.
[8] Breton, Henry William, Lieut.
[9] Oxley, John Joseph William Molesworth Capt.
[10] MacAlister, Lachlan Lieut.
[11] Molle, George James
[12] Perry, T. M., 'Hovell, William Hilton (1786–1875)', *Australian Dictionary of Biography*, National Centre of Biography, Australian National University, http://adb.anu.edu.au/biography/hovell-william-hilton-2202/text2847

BRITISH REGIMENTS

From the arrival of the First Fleet, 26 January 1788, there were various British Regiments who accompanied the convict and immigrant ships to the colony of New South Wales. Many of the men who arrived as part of a British Regiment settled in the colony and later moved to the Cowpastures.

THE ROYAL MARINES: 1788 (First Fleet)

Four companies of marines, comprising 213 men, commanded by Lieutenant Robert Ross under Governor Arthur Phillip, sailed with the First Fleet for Australia and remained in the colony until they were replaced by the New South Wales Corps in 1791.

CLARK, Ralph: *Rank:* (1) 2nd Lieutenant (2) Captain. *Unit:* Royal Marines. *Born:* 30 March 1872 Edinburgh, Scotland. *Parents:* George Clark and Ann Man. *Occupation:* Officer of the Marines, diarist. *Arrived:* 1st Fleet 26 January 1788 *HMS Friendship*. *Died:* 30 June 1874 West Indies. *Spouse:* Betty Alicia Trevan. *Married:* 23 June 1784 Stoke Demeral, Devon, England.

Clark was commissioned as a 2nd Lieutenant in the Royal Marines on 25 August 1779. As he had no intention of remaining in the colony, along with many other officers of the First Fleet he was not allowed to bring his wife and family with him. During his time in the colony he maintained a journal of the events that occurred and also wrote home to his wife. This journal remains one of the most comprehensive personal writings of the events occurring in Sydney. He was transferred to Norfolk Island on the *Sirius* on 4 March 1790 and lost most of his possessions when the *HMS Sirius* was wrecked.

It has been said: '*His only claim to importance is the diary he kept from 9 March 1787 to 17 June 1792, written up almost every day, sometimes at great length.*'[13] However, I believe the comment to be dismissive of Clark's contribution to the early colony. During his time in the colony Clark attempted to establish communication with the indigenous Australians, '*who seemed less afraid of him than of many others*'.[14] His name is commemorated by Clark Island in Sydney Harbour. Moreover, it is from Clark and other diarists from that period we learn of the lost cattle that would give the district the sobriquet of the Cowpastures.

On Monday, 28 January 1788 Lieutenant Philip Gidley King wrote: '*We landed only 4 mares and 2 stallions, 4 cows, 1 bull and 1 bull calf, ewes, a good stock of poultry, and 3 goats with hogs, which are the property of the Governor and Government.*'[15] On Thursday, 5 June 1788 Marine James Scott wrote: '*4 cows, 1 bull, with one bull calf was driven or strayed away from the Governor's farm.*'[16]

Surgeon-General John Scott reported an earthquake on Sunday, 22 June, which led to the return of escaped convict Edward Corbett: '*...he had been outlawed; and was supposed to have driven off with him four cows, the only animals of this kind in the colony. This, however, he declared himself innocent of...*'[17] Corbett was subsequently

---

[13] Janet D Hine, Clark, Ralph (1762–1794) *Australian Dictionary of Biography*, National Centre of Biography, Australian National University, http://adb.anu.edu.au/biography/clark-ralph-1898/text2239
[14] ibid
[15] Cobley, John. (1962). *Sydney Cove, 1788*. London : Hodder and Stoughton
[16] ibid
[17] ibid

hung for the crime of stealing clothes but continued to declare he was innocent regarding the disappearance of the cattle.

On Monday, 23 June Surgeon Charles Bouchier Worgan wrote:

We are just now under great tribulation about our bulls and cows, for they have been missing for some time. Many parties have been out in different directions, some said they thought they saw the print of the cattle's feet, and a man's near it. However, we have reason to fear they have strayed so far that they will never be brought back again. If they would but turn wild, they might still, perhaps, be of use to the country, but we fear that the natives will kill them, if they fall in with them.[18]

It was Collins, who reported in September, on the fate of the only cow that had not escaped, the one belonging to Lieutenant Robert Ross:

We had now given up all hope of recovering the cattle which were so unfortunately lost in May last; and the only cow that remained not being at that time with calf, and having since become wild and dangerous, the Lieutenant-Governor, whose property she was, directed her to be killed; she was accordingly shot at his farm, it being found impracticable to secure and slaughter her in the common way.[19]

THE NEW SOUTH WALES CORPS: 1790–1794

The New South Wales Corps replaced the Royal Marines, who had accompanied Governor Phillip on the First Fleet. The Royal Marines had objected to supervising convicts, and being part of the civil administration. The New South Wales Corps was raised to assume this role and to supervise the convicts whilst they performed public works, and guard them in transit within the colony. They also provided guards for Government House, the courthouse and the commissariat stores. The officers served as district magistrates, jurors and public servants, and the commanding officer of the regiment was second only to the governor. The New South Wales Corps were an essential and very influential force in the new colony.

The New South Wales Corps was also known as The Rum Corps, Botany Bay Rangers, Rum Puncheon Corps, Condemned Regiment but later became known as the 102nd Regiment.

Although the New South Wales Corps has often been the subject of controversy because of the position of power attained by many of the officers including Macarthur, the majority of the soldiers have been described as ordinary wage earners unable to find employment, who had been recruited from poor rural and urban labourers. In 1809 the New South Wales Corps was formed into the 102nd Regiment of Foot and recalled.

The final group of the New South Wales Corps arrived in Sydney on 14 February 1792 with Major Francis Grose, on the *Pitt* as part of the Fourth Fleet. At 775 tons the *Pitt* was the largest convict ship to have come to Australia and carried 410 convicts.

EUSTACE, Isaac: *Rank:* Private. *Unit:* (1) New South Wales Corps (2) Royal Veteran Regiment. *Born:* c.1766 Northumberland, England. *Died:* 7 May 1814 Appin, NSW. *Buried:* Liverpool Apex Park. *Spouse:* Catherine.

---

[18] Cobley, John. (1962). *Sydney Cove, 1788*. London : Hodder and Stoughton
[19] ibid

Private Eustace was killed at Appin on 7 May 1814 while reloading his musket; the time in which he was most vulnerable to attack.[20] Chopping his hand off was possibly done to prevent him from using a musket in his next life. By placing the blame for the hostilities on the *wild temperament of fury natural to the savage state of Man* the *Gazette* demonised the indigenous people within the framework of colonial discourse, with the authoritative tone of '*Repulsive measures we have had frequent necessity of resorting to, as the only means of self-defence*' strongly suggesting that punitive expeditions, both official and unofficial were frequent and under-reported.

The Sydney Gazette & New South Wales Advertiser
Saturday 14 May 1814, page 1

Our public duty once more lays us under the painful necessity of reporting violences between the natives and ourselves, which from the tranquillity and good understanding that for the last 5 or 6 years has subsisted we had entertained the flattering expectation were not again likely to occur. It appears from information received, that on Saturday last three privates of the Veteran Company, in the district of Appin, fired on a large body of the natives who were plundering the corn fields of a settler, and refused to desist, at the same time making use of every term of provocation and defiance, and in token of a determined spirit, menacing with their spears.

A native boy was unfortunately killed, and the small party was immediately attacked with a promptitude that put it out of their power to re-load. They were compelled to fly, and two escaped, the third, whose name was Isaac Eustace, was killed on the spot. This unhappy rencontre[21] took place on the grounds of one Milehouse,[22] contiguous to which lay the farm of a settler of the name of Butcher,[23] which being also reported to be attacked, a party of 14 went thither to prevent injury, if possible, to the persons residing on it. The mangled body of the deceased Eustace had been previously found, stripped, and one of the hands taken from the wrist. The party fell in with a group of the natives, and fired upon them; they fled, leaving a woman and two children behind them, dead. The next day they made an attack on a stock-keeper's hut belonging to Mrs. Macarthur, when the stock-keeper, Wm. Baker,[24] and a woman named Mary Sullivan,[25] generally called Hirburt, were both killed. Some other atrocities have this day been reported, but we have no present reason to treat them with any degree of confidence.

Without offering an opinion to which side the first act of aggression may justly be attributed, we feel confident in asserting that every effort will be used by Government in ascertaining the fact; and we have every hope that the measures judiciously acted upon will put a speedy termination to those evils to which the lonely settler is exposed from the predatory incursions of an enemy whose haunts are inaccessible, distant, and unknown, and who by surprise or stratagem accomplish every project they devise in a wild temperament of fury natural to the savage state of Man. The care of Government and the general disposition of the inhabitants to preserve a friendly intercourse with them had in former years

---

[20] *The Gazette,* of 25 February 1815 identified that Private Eustace was killed on 7 May 1814.
[21] i.e. meeting (Oxford Dictionary)
[22] Also known as 'Milhouse'
[23] No reference can be found to someone of this name at the time in question. Other references refer to the property as being Broughton's farm (William Henry Broughton) which is more likely.
[24] William Baker's death is reported to have taken place on 8 May 1814 near where the General Cemetery is located on Cawdor Road.
[25] ibid

seldom been disturbed, but at this identical season of the year when the fields of ripened maize were open to their pillage. Without property, or a wish to obtain anything by industry, they respected it not in others, and the slightest opposition they retorted with the bitterest hostility; which we may almost venture to affirm, was until within the last 6 or 7 years periodically repeated.

Repulsive measures we have had frequent necessity of resorting to, as the only means of self-defence, and we have always found a temporary banishment effect a speedy reconciliation, as those accustomed to live among us derived benefits from the intercourse which the woods of the interior could not replace. Those of the latter description, whose small tribes straggle about the part of the coast, are already coming in, as an evidence of their taking no part in the excesses of their brethren of the mountains who, on the other hand, are reported to have wholly disappeared from the settlements of the interior which they visited, but whether with a view to their own security, or for the purpose of alarming the yet more distant inhabitants, seems doubtful. In the present state of things with them, it would be advisable for settlers and travellers to be well upon their guard; to be ready to give assistance in every case of alarm, and to be cautious at the same time not to provoke or irritate them by ill treatment, but endeavour on the contrary to soothe them into a better disposition than their present seems to be. Travellers and more especially those who are but little acquainted with their manners, should in the meantime be very wary, as they are liable in a moment to be surprised and surrounded from the sides of the roads, and subjected to very ill, most likely barbarous treatment.

Events like the above eventually led to the Appin Massacre on 16 April 1816 when at least 14 indigenous people were shot and killed, whilst others were forced to jump to their deaths into a rocky gorge near Broughton Pass. The local Dharawal people had made friendships among several Appin settlers, but were in conflict with the more belligerent colonists. After the death of settlers at Bringelly,[26] Governor Lachlan Macquarie sent a military expedition to round up all the indigenous in the area. However, settlers like John Kennedy did their best to protect the Dharawal people from the military.

The diary of Governor Lachlan Macquarie, which is kept in the Mitchell Library, clearly details the orders Macquarie gave preceding the massacre:

Governor Macquarie's diary
10th April, 1816

I therefore, tho, very unwillingly felt myself compelled, from a paramount sense of public duty, to come to the painful resolution of chastising these hostile tribes, and to inflict terrible and exemplary punishments upon.

I have this day ordered three separate military detachments to march into the interior and remote parts of the colony, for the purpose of punishing the hostile natives, by clearing the country of them entirely, and driving them across the mountains.

In the event of the natives making the smallest show of resistance—or refusing to surrender when called upon so to do—the officers commanding the military parties have been authorised to fire on them to compel them to surrender; hanging

---

[26] Noonan, Timothy: killed Bringelly 1815 and Waxted, James: labourer for Hannibal Macarthur died of wounds 1815

up on trees the bodies of such natives as may be killed on such occasions, in order to strike the greater terror into the survivors.

This tragedy was in part fuelled by misunderstandings. Indigenous tribes were hunter gatherers and did not accept the white settlers' concept of ownership of land. Furthermore, the settlers' clearing of lands for farming and indiscriminate shooting of wildlife further decimated the indigenous food sources, when the long drought of 1814 was causing extreme hardship and the Gandangara tribe had strayed into Dharawal territory in search of food. It is most likely that it was the Gandangara (i.e. 'brethren of the mountains') who were involved in the death of Isaac Eustace.

The long drought also had a major effect on the economy of the colony:

Government Public Notice
Deputy Commissary General's Office, Sydney
Monday, 20th Dec. 1813

The severe distress suffered by the settlers in general, and most particularly by those in the middle and lower classes, from the late long continued drought, which has alike injured the livestock, and rendered the present harvest much less productive than was hoped for and expected, has induced HIS EXCELLENCY the GOVERNOR to rescind that part of the Public Notice given from this office on the 11th instant, as far as it extends to the limiting price of wheat at the respective Government Stores within this colony, and the same is accordingly rescinded.

HIGGINS, Robert: *Rank:* (1) Corporal (2) Sergeant. *Unit:* (1) 3 February 1791 New South Wales Corps (2) 102nd Regiment stationed Norfolk Island 1793–1794 (3) 24 April 1810 73rd (Perthshire) Regiment of Foot. *Arrived:* Third Fleet 27 September 1791 *HMS Queen. Born:* c.1792 Wiltshire, England. *Died:* 8 March 1843 Camden, NSW. *Buried:* St. Peter's Church of England, Campbelltown, NSW. *Spouse:* Lydia Farrell nee Blair. *Married:* 9 July 1810 St. Phillip's Church of England, Sydney, NSW.

Robert Higgins formed part of the detachment under the command of Captain Abbott who had been at Norfolk Island for several years. On 6 November 1794, the troops were ordered to return to Sydney, and Robert Higgins together with Lydia Farrell departed from Norfolk Island on the *Daedalus.*

In the early 1800s, Sergeant Higgins was part of Captain Abbott's detachment at Parramatta and was involved in the Castle Hill Rebellion in 1804. By 17 July 1809 he was living at High Street, Sydney leasing a small area of land near the army barracks. On 24 March 1810 he transferred to the 73rd (Perthshire) Regiment of Foot that had arrived with Lachlan Macquarie.

As part of his social reforms, Macquarie encouraged formal marriages to replace the casual relationships that were common in the colony. On 9 July 1810 Robert Higgins and Lydia Farrell were married by Samuel Marsden at St Phillip's Church of England Church. It was one of the first marriages in the church that had been completed that year. By the time of their marriage they had four children: Mary aged 15, Elizabeth aged 13, John aged 12 and Sarah aged 10.

Macquarie adopted a policy of establishing small farm developments and offered land grants to retiring soldiers if they stayed in the colony. In July 1811, Robert Higgins was granted 50 acres of land at Elderslie, east of Camden on the Sydney side of the Nepean River. He was also assigned a convict servant, Thomas Seymour, who arrived on the *Admiral Gambier* on 29 September 1811. By 1822 Robert and his son John were employed at the Camden Park Estate.

HUON de KERILLEAU, Gabriel Louis Marie: *Rank:* Private. *Unit:* New South Wales Corps. *Born:* 17 April 1769 St-Pol-de-Léon, Brittany, France. *Parents:* Jean Francois Huon, Seigneur[27] de Kerhillio-Lesguern en Plouvorn and Anne de Kersalliou. *Arrived*: 25 October 1794 *HMS Surprize. Occupation:* soldier, tutor. *Died*: December 1828 Bungonia, NSW. *Spouse:* Louisa Emanuel Renaud aka Le Sage. *Married*: 7 February 1801 St. John's R.C. Parramatta, NSW.

Huon joined the New South Wales Corps as Louis Huon believing his life was in danger in France because he was a nephew of a Comte and his father was a property owner. During the French Revolution the family had fled to England to escape the guillotine.

He was discharged from the New South Wales Corps in 1807[28] and until 1809 was tutor to James and William Macarthur, the younger sons of John and Elizabeth Macarthur, at Elizabeth Farm, Parramatta. In January 1810 he received a grant of 400 acres (162 ha) from Governor Macquarie at Narellan which he called Buckingham.

In 1823 Huon, together with his eldest son Paul and son-in-law Captain William Mitchell[29] received a ticket-of-occupation for 3000 acres (1214 ha) of land at Bungonia in 1823 and in 1825 went on to purchase 1000 acres at 5 shillings an acre at nearby Corrundaroo.[30] In the same year he sold Buckingham at Narellan to James Chisholm; the property was renamed Gledswood by Chisholm.

The exact date of his death is unknown. It is known that one Sunday mid-December 1828 he started to walk from his Bungonia property to Campbelltown to visit his son. He was carrying a book and during the walk was seen and spoken to on two occasions and directed to the correct road. Unfortunately, he again wandered from the track and became lost in the gullies of the Shoalhaven River and was never seen again.

LAYCOCK, Thomas William: *Rank:* (1) Ensign, (2) Lieutenant. *Unit:* (1) 102nd Regiment of Foot, (2) 98th (Prince of Wales) Regiment of Foot. *Born*: 1786 Bristol, Gloucestershire, England. *Parents:* Quarter Master Thomas Laycock and Hannah Pearson. *Arrived:* 21 September 1791 *HMS Gorgon. Occupation:* soldier. *Died* 7 November 1823 Bringelly, NSW. *Buried:* Devonshire Street Cemetery, Sydney, NSW and in 1842 removed to Sandhills Cemetery, Botany, NSW. *Spouse* (1) Isabella Bunker, *married* 1 June 1809 St. Phillip's Church of England, Sydney, NSW; *spouse* (2) Margaret Connell, *married* 8 July 1817 St. Phillip's Church of England, Sydney, NSW.

Laycock had arrived as a 9-year-old with the Third Fleet but as soon as he was of age, entered into service with the New South Wales Corps, later 102nd Regiment. On 30 December 1795 he was commissioned as an Ensign and by 1802 had obtained the rank of Lieutenant. After serving in Sydney and on Norfolk Island in 1806 he was

---

[27] Seigneur was the name formerly given in France to someone who had been granted a fief by the crown, with all its associated rights over person and property. It is the equivalent of Lord in English.

[28] The *Australian Dictionary of Biography* re Huon claims that 'his discharge from the army in 1807 had been ordered by the Duke of York at the instance of [his] Eminent Relation the Bishop of St Paul de Leon and the Most Noble the Marquis of Buckingham'. See G. P. Walsh, 'Huon de Kerilleau, Gabriel Louis Marie (1769–1828)', *Australian Dictionary of Biography*, National Centre of Biography, Australian National University http://adb.anu.edu.au/biography/huon-de-kerilleau-gabriel-louis-marie-2215/text2877

[29] Mitchell had married Elizabeth Broughton Huon de Kerilleau 16-12-1812 at 'Horatio Farm', Narellan. Captain Mitchell was formerly in the Kent Militia but had resigned his commission prior to arriving in the Colony on the *Providence* 2/11/1811 as a free settler.

[30] County of Argyle near Jerrara Creek

sent to Port Dalrymple, Van Diemen's Land, to serve under Captain Anthony Fenn Kemp.

When Port Dalrymple (later known as Launceston) was stricken with famine he was entrusted to convey dispatches for Lieutenant-Governor David Collins overland to Hobart Town. Whilst a journey into the island's interior had not previously been attempted, on 3 February 1807 Laycock set out with four other men carrying enough provisions to last three weeks. Despite the difficult terrain encountered, the men traversed the island in just over eight days, arriving in Hobart Town on 11 February 1807 only to be told that the town was also suffering from the famine. After resting for four days the men returned to Port Dalrymple.

Upon returning to Sydney, Laycock was appointed to the criminal court that tried John Macarthur for his involvement in the plot to overthrow Governor William Bligh. He was ordered to search Government House for evidence and in the process fell through a manhole and sustained injuries. He received a land grant of 500 acres at Bringelly as a reward for his discoveries in Van Diemen's Land.

On 18 March 1810 Laycock departed for England on *HMS Dromedary* with his wife, and when the New South Wales Corps disbanded he joined the 98th (Prince of Wales) Regiment of Foot whilst in England, and by September 1811 had been promoted to Captain.

As part of the 98th Regiment he was posted to Bermuda and New Brunswick for the 1812 War against the United States. This war is generally seen as part of the Napoleonic Wars when the United States continued to trade with France. However, this war resolved many issues left over from the American War of Independence. The war had been declared by the United States on 18 June 1812 not only as a result of the trade restrictions being enforced by Britain as a result of its war with France, but also because American merchant sailors were being press-ganged into the Royal Navy. In addition, Britain was supporting the native Indian tribes in their opposition to American expansion. America was also outraged over perceived insults to national honour after humiliations on the high seas, whilst Britain was intent on preventing America annexing British territory in what is today Canada.

Following the war, Laycock returned to England and sold his commission prior to sailing for Sydney with his wife and children aboard the *Fame*, arriving on 8 March 1817. With the funds saved from the sale of his commission, he set up a general store and hotel, and quickly became one of the biggest suppliers of meat to the Commissariat Store. By 1819 he had become involved in local affairs, and was one of the leading citizens in a public call for the right to trial by jury. He died at Bringelly on 7 November 1823.

MACARTHUR, John: *Rank:* (1) Lieutenant (2) Captain. *Unit:* (1) 68th (Durham) Regiment of Foot (2) New South Wales Corps (later 102nd Regiment). *Born:* 13 August 1766 Plymouth Dock, Devon, England. *Parents:* Alexander Macarthur and Catherine Campbell. *Baptised*: 3 September 1767 Plymouth Dock, Devon, England. *Arrived*: 28 June 1790 *HMS Neptune-Scarborough. Occupation:* soldier, pastoralist. *Died:* 10 April 1834 at Home Farm, Camden Park, NSW. *Buried*: Camden Park Private. *Spouse:* Elizabeth Veale. *Married:* 6 October 1788 St. Bridget's Bridgerule, Devon, England. In April 1788 Macarthur was an Ensign in the 68th Regiment (later Durham Light Infantry) stationed at Gibraltar. By 5 June 1789 he had dramatically enhanced his rank and

John Macarthur – photo courtesy Camden Park House

transferred as a Lieutenant to the New South Wales Corps, then being enlisted for duty at Botany Bay. He arrived with his wife and son with the Second Fleet.

In 1791 Macarthur was posted inland to the Rosehill settlement for four months. In 1792 he was appointed regimental paymaster, and in 1793 appointed Inspector of Public Works, which gave him extensive and crucial control of the colony's rudimentary resources.

In 1793 he received a grant of 100 acres (40 ha) at Parramatta which he named Elizabeth Farm, described as 'some of the best ground that has been discovered' and became the first in the colony to clear and cultivate 50 acres (20 ha) of virgin land. This earned him another 100 acre (40 ha) grant. Macarthur soon became one of the foremost landholders in the colony, selling produce to the government, which by 1794 returned £700 ($1400) per annum. He was promoted to Captain on 6 May 1795.

73rd (PERTHSHIRE) REGIMENT of FOOT: 1810

When Lachlan Macquarie was appointed Governor he brought his own regiment, the 73rd (Perthshire) Regiment of Foot to the colony. The Indian sub-continent is central to the history of the 73rd Regiment. It first served in India as part of the 2nd Battalion of the 42nd Regiment and in 1784 defended the fortress of Mangalore from Tippoo Sahib, the ruler of Mysore in South-East India. The 73rd Regiment received Mangalore as a battle honour and were famed for their performance there even though they were forced to surrender honourably when provisions ran out.

Commanders deemed the 'Highland' dress of the 42nd (Royal Highlanders) Regiment of Foot, from which the 73rd came, unsuitable for the conditions in India. Linen trousers replaced the kilt in 1799 and the 73rd Regiment continued to wear trousers throughout its history. Its battle honours include Seringapatam, Mangalore and Waterloo.

The 1st Battalion of the 73rd Regiment landed in Sydney on 1 January 1810.

CROWE, William: *Rank:* Private. *Unit:* 73rd (Perthshire) Regiment of Foot. *Born:* 1793 County Clare, Ireland. *Arrived:* 1 January 1810 *HMS Dromedary*. *Died:* 6 October 1835 Hokianga Harbour, NZ. *Burial:* St. John's Roman Catholic Church, Campbelltown, NSW (memorial only). *Spouse:* Eleanor (Ellen) Hayes. *Married:* 28 April 1809 Ireland.

Sydney Gazette
Saturday 16 September 1837, page 2

SHIP NEWS

The Brazil Packet, *Captain Bucknell, arrived on Thursday last from New Zealand, having sailed from Hokianga the 11th August. Captain Bucknell informs us that he experienced boisterous and bad weather the whole of the passage, which accounts for the length of time she has been coming up, five weeks. They saw no vessel from this port, with the exception of the* Nimrod, *Bennett, master, at Hokianga. This vessel was to sail in about a week after her, so that she may daily be expected. She saw a ship on the 20th August, steering east, but it was blowing a gale of wind at the time; it was not in the power of Captain Bucknell to get close enough to have any communication. The* Brazil Packet *sailed from Hobart Town about the 10th March last, under the command of the late Captain Crowe, the cause of whose death is enveloped in mystery, the following is all that we have been able to learn. On the 6th May last, the* Brazil Packet *was lying at Hokianga;*

at night Captain Crowe went to bed, and the first announcement of anything having happened, was given by Mrs Crowe, who missed her husband from her side in the bed when she awoke. Immediate search was made, but all enquiries were in vain till after a lapse of nearly a fortnight, when his body was picked up in a state of decomposition, the unfortunate man having been drowned; but how or in what manner, does not appear. The following are the names of the passengers who arrived in her: - Mrs Crowe, widow of the Captain, and child.......

William Crowe was discharged from the regiment in Sydney between 1814 and 1815, (it is possible he may have served with the regiment in Ceylon [Sri Lanka]) with the rank of private. He received a land grant at Windsor but was driven from there by the indigenous people, so he moved to Narellan. He later had a land grant of 80 acres at Appin between 1816 and 1821 and installed his brother-in-law Michael Hayes as a tenant farmer.

There is some doubt that he was actually buried at Campbelltown. The newspaper report above suggests that the body was recovered a fortnight after the event in a bad state of decomposition. If that was the case it was unlikely to have been returned to Australia. There is some suggestion that the coffin buried in Campbelltown contains only stones.

48th (NORTHAMPTONSHIRE) REGIMENT of FOOT: 1817

The 48th (Northamptonshire) Regiment of Foot was a regiment of the British Army and fought as part of the Duke of Wellington's army for the duration of the Peninsular War against Napoleon. The regiment's most famous battle honour was gained at the Battle of Talavera in 1809 but it also participated in the Battles of Douro (1809), Albuera (1811), Badajoz (1812), Salamanca (1812), Vittoria (1813), Pyrenees (1813), Nivelle (1813), Orthes (1814), and Toulouse (1814). At the Battle of Albuera it lost its colonel, George Henry Duckworth. From 1817 until 1824, the 48th Regiment of Foot was stationed in Australia.

MacALISTER, Lachlan: *Rank:* Ensign, Captain, Lieutenant. *Unit:* 48th (Northamptonshire) Regiment of Foot. *Born:* 1797 Strathaird, Isle of Skye, Scotland. *Parents:* Dr. Duncan Grant McAlister and Janet McAlister. *Arrived:* 7 August 1817 *HMS Matilda. Occupation:* soldier, mounted police officer, explorer, magistrate. *Died:* 24 December 1855 Clifton, Picton, NSW. *Buried* St David's Presbyterian Church, Campbelltown, NSW. *Spouse:* Christina MacInnes. *Married:* 1851 St Andrew's Scots Church, Sydney, NSW.

MacAlister (or Macalister) is known in the district mainly for his involvement with Picton and for his contribution to exploration in NSW. A 1933 article in a Melbourne newspaper provides an excellent summary of his career.

The Argus
Saturday 27 May 1933, page 4

**LACHLAN MacALISTER
A SCOTTISH OVERLANDER
by CHARLES DALEY**

Like so many of the Australian pioneers Lachlan MacAlister was of Scottish birth, the son of Duncan and Janet MacAlister, of Strathaird, in the Isle of Skye, West of Scotland. He was born in 1797. In 1815 by purchase of a commission, he became an Ensign in the 48th Regiment, Northamptonshire, which two years later was drafted for service to New South Wales. In the following year the regiment was transferred to the settlement at Port Dalrymple on the Tamar, in Van Diemen's Land. The regiment was recalled to England in 1818, but MacAlister remained in Australia. From 1820-1 he was at Newcastle, and about this time he became intimate with the two sons of John Macarthur, of Camden, the founder of the wool industry in Australia.

It was the period when extensive grants of land were freely made to approved persons. Each of the Macarthurs, James and William had the good fortune to obtain a block of 2,500 acres of fertile land at Taralga. A creek was the boundary line between the two properties.

Here, in addition to successful grazing, the Macarthurs laid the foundations of the vine-growing industry in Australia. MacAlister, who about this time was at Tarlo with William Macarthur, received from the authorities, a written promise of a land grant of 2,000 acres, which on January 25, 1824, was honoured by his acquisition of that area at Myrtle Creek, now Myrtleville, five miles from Taralga. Macalister's close friendship with the Macarthurs evidently induced him to take up pastoral pursuits, in which they had prospered. Some cattle and sheep for breeding purposes were purchased by Macalister from their well-known strains.

In 1826 MacAlister was appointed a magistrate. He had acquired a recognised position in public affairs as a leading grazier and a patron of sport. In 1827 MacAlister was made resident Magistrate and Officer-in-Charge of the Mounted Police at Goulburn Plains. Bushrangers were very troublesome and aggressive, especially a gang under the leadership of a ruffian called Donahoe. A capable leader, he was bold and fearless in his depredations, and skilful in evading the police. MacAlister concentrated his troopers in a strategic spot at Bringelly, and on the approach of the gang the troopers were instructed to dismount and attack under cover on foot.

After a sharp encounter Donahoe was killed by a well-aimed shot by Trooper Muggleston,[31] a former soldier. Thus a dangerous criminal's career was ended, and the band of outlaws broken up. MacAlister was wounded, but not seriously. In 1833 he was appointed to the command of the Mounted Police at Bathurst. He increased the extent of his estate by another grant of 4,000 acres by purchase at Myrtle Creek. By 1837 the Macarthurs had jointly acquired 18,440 acres; and Macalister 16,300 acres at Stathaird, to the south of Taralga.

MacAlister's favourite residence was at Clifton homestead, near Picton, on the Southern Road from Sydney. A period of severe drought set in in New South Wales, and MacAlister sent his kinsman, Matthew MacAlister, south-east in search of fresh pastures. He himself, impressed by Major Mitchell's favourable report, resolved to go overland to Port Phillip. With Thomas Walker, Dutton and Brown, MacAlister, in April, 1837, set out for the land of promise. On the overland route they passed the Mollisons from Miara, who a few months later settled near Mt. Macedon. Crossing the Murrumbidgee River, they reached the Hume River, and then followed Mitchell's track to a favourite crossing place at the junction of the King and Ovens Rivers. Thence they reached the Broken River, then Violet Ponds. Proceeding they crossed the Campaspe River, then the Loddon, and west of Mount Macedon pursued a course southward. MacAlister and Walker were anxious to be in Melbourne at the land sale on June 1, 1837, of which they had received information. On May 29 they rode on rapidly ahead of the party, reaching Melbourne on May 31.

---

[31] Muggleston, John – Trooper 39th Regiment

At the land sale next day MacAlister purchased allotment 6, of block 2, between Flinders, Collins, King, and William Streets; also lots 6, 7, and 9, of block 4, between Flinders, Collins, Queen and Elizabeth Streets. At this time Walker and MacAlister dined with Captain Lonsdale and his wife, and made a trip up the Yarra River, visiting another Mollison station, also that of Willis at the Plenty River, and then Gardiner's station. At Williamstown they sold their bullocks, horses, and tents, and then voyaged to Georgetown in Tasmania. MacAlister was impressed by the prospects of Port Phillip district, and later he purchased land at Geelong; also at Mitchelltown on the Goulburn at the first inland sale of land on May 9, 1839. This investment, owing to the almost immediate divergence of the Sydney Road to a more convenient crossing place of the Goulburn, near the present site of the town of Seymour, proved valueless.

In January 1838, there came to MacAlister, with a letter of introduction, a young Scotsman, Angus McMillan, a compatriot from Skye. MacAlister gave him employment, and McMillan soon gained the experience of an expert bushman. With the prolongation of the disastrous drought MacAlister decided in 1839 to send McMillan across the Snowy River through Monaro, where he had acquired pastoral interests, with the object of finding fresh pastures for stock. McMillan, accompanied by an indigenous person, in a few days reached Mt. Haystack (or McLeod), near Buchan, and satisfied himself that there were good prospects southward. Returning by way of Omeo plains, where settlement had already been made by MacFarlane and the Pendergasts, he reported favourably to MacAlister, who in 1840 again sent McMillan in charge of a party to explore the unknown south-eastern district. After many difficulties and delays this enterprise resulted in the discovery of the rich and fertile province of Gippsland, as it was afterwards called by Strzelecki, and the opening in 1841 of a track over Alpine ranges and permanent streams from the Monaro and Yass tablelands to the sea, at what is now called Port Albert.

On September 16, 1839 McMillan had formed a first station for MacAlister at Numblamunjie, now Ensay, and MacAlister lost no time in profiting by the discoveries. Commissioner Tyers, reporting to Superintendent Latrobe in July 15, 1844, upon the 'Heart of Gippsland', writes:–– 'A part of this country is in the occupation of the discoverer (sic) of Gippsland, Mr. MacAlister, who, I am informed, at the enormous expense of £2,000 and £3,000, opened a road across the ranges to this beautiful district through the Omeo country, prior to Count Strzelecki's journey.'

Beside the cattle station MacAlister acquired Boisdale, near the Avon River, which he retained from October, 1840 to May 1850; Clydebank and Marlaz Point, near Lake Wellington, from 1843 to 1844; Dargo from July 1846 to May, 1850; and Newburn Park, at Tinamba, with Dr. Arbuckle, from 1844 to 1847.

One of MacAlister's objects in this great undertaking, consummated by Angus McMillan, was to reach a seaport from which he could safely export his cattle to Tasmania. Malcolm McFarlane, who had occupied Heyfield station, was the first to send cattle to Hobart, where their prime condition ensured a ready sale. MacAlister's fat cattle from the Gippsland pastures were forwarded, in the Waterwitch, *and were quickly disposed of. The communication by sea at Port Albert, the convenient gateway into Gippsland, rendered the difficult overland route from Monaro by way of Omeo and the Tambo River almost unnecessary, and it became seldom used. MacAlister continued his interests and connection with Gippsland for many years. The MacAlister River, named after him by McMillan, fitly commemorates his activities. He died on December 24, 1855.*

57th (THE WEST MIDDLESEX) REGIMENT of FOOT: 1825–1826

This regiment started out as the 59th Regiment of Foot and was raised in Gloucester in 1755. In 1786 after the disbandment of the 50th Regiment of Foot and the 51st Regiment of Foot, it then became the 57th Regiment of Foot. The regiment took part in the American Revolutionary War (Siege of Charlestown, May 1776, New York Campaign 1776, and Halifax September 1783). In 1782, it was given a county connection, becoming the 57th (The West Middlesex) Regiment of Foot.

The 57th Regiment earned their nickname of 'The Die Hards' after their participation in the Battle of Albuera, one of the bloodiest battles of the Peninsular War, fought on 16 May 1811. The commanding officer of the 57th, Colonel Inglis, was struck down by a charge of canister shot which hit him in the neck and left breast. He refused to be carried to the rear for treatment, but lay in front of his men calling on them to hold their position and when the fight reached its fiercest cried, 'Die Hard the 57th, Die Hard!'

The 57th arrived in New South Wales during 1826 serving in Van Diemen's Land, Sydney, Victoria, South Australia and the Swan River Colony. The regiment was transferred to Madras in March, 1831.

During the period 1789 to 1881 it earned the battle honours: Mysore, Seringapatam, Peninsula, Albuera, Ciudad Rodrigo, Badajoz, Nive, Nivelle, Pyrenees, Vittoria, Alma, Inkerman, Sevastopol, New Zealand and South Africa. In the Crimean War (1854-1856) the 57th took part in the Battle of Alma (19 September 1854), Battle of Inkerman (5 November 1855) and Siege of Sevastopol (September 1854 to September 1855).

Members of this regiment settled in the Camden area including Thomas Shadforth (snr) who will be discussed under the Napoleonic Wars, and his son Thomas Shadforth (jnr) who will be discussed under the Crimean War.

Others known to have connection with this regiment include:

MARDEN, John: *Rank:* Major. *Unit:* 57th (The West Middlesex) Regiment of Foot. *Born*: 6 May 1803 Frosley Court, Maidstone, Kent, England. *Parents:* John Marden and Sarah Lake. *Arrived*: 12 January 1828 *HMS Elizabeth*. *Died*: 30 January 1858 Lomar, Werombi, NSW. *Buried:* Lomar, Werombi, NSW. *Spouse:* Sarah Munro. *Married:* 9 July 1836 St James' Church of England, Sydney, NSW.

Marden arrived as a soldier and was stationed at Regentville, and went on to attain the rank of Major. According to legend John was buried standing up, because 'as long as I am standing this is my property'.

SHADFORTH, Henry Tudor: *Rank:* Lieutenant. *Unit:* 57th (The West Middlesex) Regiment of Foot. *Born:* 1 January 1803 Bermuda, West Indies. *Parents:* Thomas Shadforth (snr) and Frances Hinson. *Arrived:* 22 August 1825 *HMS Minstrel*. *Died:* 21 September 1890 Redfern, NSW. *Spouse:* Mary Ann (Marianne) Stephen. *Married:* 10 March 1838 St. James' Church of England, Sydney, NSW.

Henry resigned his commission when the regiment was posted to Ceylon [Sri Lanka] in 1841. He was later the first Sergeant-at-Arms of the New South Wales Legislative Assembly (between 1856 and 1860) and was appointed Usher of the Black Rod of the Legislative Council on 29 June 1860.

39th (DORSETSHIRE) REGIMENT of FOOT: 1827

The regiment served on Malta (1805), Sicily (1810) and Albuera (1811) before Canada during the War of 1812. The regiment was sent to the Peninsula during the Napoleonic Wars. It fought at Vittoria (1813), Sorauren (1813), Nivelle (1813), Nive (1813), Orthes (1814) and Toulouse (1814). It then served in Canada during the War of 1812 (1812-1815). It resumed its single-battalion status in 1815, returning to Europe to join the occupying forces in France, before seven more years in Ireland from 1818. In 1825 the regiment guarded convicts in New South Wales, remaining there until a 13-year posting to India from 1832.

MUGGLESTON, John: *Rank:* (1) Private (2) Corporal. *Unit:* (1) 39th (Dorsetshire) Regiment of Foot (2) NSW Mounted Police. *Born:* 1804 Neilston, Levern Valley, Glasgow, Scotland. *Occupation:* groom, soldier, mounted police officer. *Arrived:* 17 October 1827 *HMS Champion*. *Died:* 13 January 1841 Newcastle Hospital, NSW. *Buried:* Christ Church Cathedral Cemetery.

Little is known of Muggleston other than he was born in a Scottish agricultural and cotton milling town and had worked as a groom. He is also known as Mugglestone[32], Muckelstone, and Muccleston and it was under the latter spelling his death is recorded. The Industrial Revolution of the early 19th Century had a disastrous effect on employment opportunities for those working in and around milling towns. On 19 December 1826 Muggleston enlisted in the 39th Regiment of Foot at Kelstow, Kent and embarked for the colony as a guard on the convict ship *HMS Champion*. He did a tour of duty on Norfolk Island before joining the Mounted Police in March 1829.

Muggleston is best known in the Camden area for shooting John (Bold Jack) Donahoe on 1 September 1830 at Bringelly.

Sydney Gazette
7 September 1830

Muggleston, who is reckoned one of the best shots, kept his eye steadily fixed on Donahoe, and when the latter peeped from behind his tree, shewing only his head and part of his breast, the wary soldier took aim, fired, and, though a hundred yards distant, in less than a minute the vaunting bravo was in eternity. Muggleston's piece contained two balls, one of which entered the left temple, and the other the neck; both remaining in the deceased.

Sydney Monitor
11 September 1830

John Mugglestone, a private of the 39th regt, now in the employ of the Mounted Police, stated to the same effect, with the addition, that his carbine was loaded with two balls, and that they found on the horse's back some flour, sugar, and women's wearing apparel, and that deceased had a watch in his pocket.

By the end of 1830 Muggleston was stationed in the Newcastle area and it is believed he was involved in the pursuit of the 'Jew Boy' gang which was led by Edward Davis, the only known Jewish bushranger. The 'Jew Boy' gang, which operated in the Hunter region, was captured in December 1840.

---

[32] 'He fought six rounds with the horse police' - the shooting of Bold Jack Donahoe by John Low, Blue Mountains Historical Society Inc.

WARBURTON, James: *Rank:* (1) Private (2) Trooper. *Unit:* (1) 39th (Dorsetshire) Regiment of Foot (2) NSW Mounted Police. *Born:* 1809 Walmsley, Lancashire, England. *Arrived*: 17 October 1827 *HMS Champion.*

Little is known of Warburton other than his involvement in the shooting of John (Bold Jack) Donahoe in September 1830. In 1832 he applied for a grant of 32 acres at Field of Mars.

17th (LEICESTERSHIRE) REGIMENT of FOOT: 1830

Originally the Leicestershire Regiment was a line infantry regiment of the British Army, with a history going back to 1688. In 1751 a Royal Warrant assigned numbers to the regiments of the line, and the unit became the 17th Regiment of Foot.

A further Royal Warrant dated 31 August 1782 bestowed county titles on all regiments of foot that did not already have a special designation, the regiment then became the 17th (Leicestershire) Regiment of Foot.

The regiment was increased to two battalions in 1799 and both battalions served in the Netherlands before the second was disbanded in 1802. In 1804 the 17th moved to India, and remained there until 1823. In 1825 the regiment was granted the Badge of a Royal Tiger to recall their long service in the sub-continent. The regiment was posted to New South Wales from 1830 to 1836.

FORBES, Charles: *Rank:* Captain. *Unit:* 17th (Leicestershire) Regiment of Foot. *Arrived:* 18 December 1830 *HMS Andromeda II. Born:* 1813 Devonshire, England. *Occupation:* Captain, Police Magistrate, farmer Vermont, Cobbitty, NSW. *Died:* 6 February 1853 Dawlish, Devonshire, England. *Spouse:* Adelaide Lydia Matilda Manning. *Married*: 1 August 1838 Christ Church St Laurence Church of England, Sydney, NSW.

Forbes was discharged in Sydney 31 August 1835 and married in Sydney in 1838. He was a farmer at Vermont, Cobbitty until he returned to Devonshire, England with his family on the *SS Tamar* on 8 June 1846.

THE KING'S OWN (LANARKSHIRE) 4th REGIMENT of FOOT: 1831

The King's Own Royal (Lanarkshire) Regiment was a line infantry regiment of the British Army. During the Napoleonic Wars, the regiment fought at Corunna, Badajoz, Salamanca, Vittoria, San Sebastian, Nive, Bladensburg, and Waterloo. The regiment later served in Australian colonies from 1831 until 1837, and was stationed during various periods in Van Diemen's Land, Sydney, Victoria, South Australia, and the Swan River Colony under the command of Lieutenant-Colonel John Kenneth MacKenzie.

BRETON, Henry William: *Rank:* Lieutenant. *Unit:* The King's Own Royal (Lanarkshire) Regiment 4th Regiment of Foot. *Born:* 7 January 1799 England. *Arrived:* 14 May 1831 *HMS William Glen Anderson. Died:* 22 July 1889 England. *Spouse:* Catherine Norton.

Portrait of Col. Henry William Breton held by The King's Own Regiment Museum, Lancaster

Breton was commissioned as an Ensign in 1815 and served with the King's Own in the West Indies 1821–1826, and Portugal 1826–1827. In the new colonies he saw service in Van Diemen's Land, Parramatta and Goulburn Plains. Breton was promoted to Colonel and commanded the regiment from 1834 at Parramatta and Sydney and then in India at Madras, Bangalore, Bellary, Secunderabad and Kamptee. He became Colonel of the 56th Regiment in 1854 and later rose to the rank of General. His memorial in the church register at the Royal Garrison Church, Portsmouth, England reads:

In Memory of General
Henry William Breton
(Colonel of the 56th Pompadours)
He served in France, Portugal, West Indies and Australia
Held numerous Staff Commands in India
Commanded this District from Feb'y 1854 to June 1857
and in Mauritius from 1857 to 1862
Born January 7th 1799
Died July 22 1889

The record in the church ledger is annotated with the words

This is a beautiful bronze, the lettering raised, the whole let into a splendid specimen of Red Italian Marble. This Genl. was called the Father of the Army. He was buried at Southsea. The annotation is signed *J.J. Francis, Sexton.*

His connection with Camden is unknown apart from the reference to him in the *Camden News.*

ROYAL NAVY

GREGORY, John Jervis: *Rank:* Lieutenant. *Unit:* Royal Navy. *Born:* 1799 Norwich, Norfolk, England. *Parents:* William Gregory and Mary Ann Suffield. *Died:* 3 February 1841 Appin, NSW. *Buried:* St. Mark's the Evangelist, Appin. *Spouse:* Caroline Ann Filmer.

It is not known when Gregory arrived in the colony but he died in 1841 at his property, Appin Lodge at Appin. Under King George II his father had been the British Consul to Mexico, Lisbon, Madrid and Barcelona and is also said to have been a British spy.

Gregory's widow married Captain Francis Liardet R.N. on 10 October 1842 at St. James, Paddington, London, England.

The Sydney Morning Herald
Thursday 11 February 1841, page 3

On Thursday, the 4th, instant, at Appin Lodge, J. Jervis Gregory, Esq., Lieut. R.N, and J.P., for the colony.

The Times (London)
10 August 1841

Death

On the 3rd of February, at his residence, Appin Lodge, near Sydney, NSW, aged 43, John Jervis Gregory, Esq., R.N., fourth[33] son of the late William Gregory, Esq.

OXLEY, John Joseph William Molesworth: *Rank:* (1) Master's Mate (2) Acting Lieutenant (3) Lieutenant (4) Surveyor-General. *Unit:* Royal Navy. *Born;* 1784 Kirkham Abbey, Yorkshire, England. *Parents:* John Oxley and Isabella Molesworth. *Baptised:* Bulmer, Yorkshire, England 6 July 1784. *Arrived*: (1) 14 October 1802 *HMS Buffalo* (2) 31 December 1808 *HMS Porpoise* (3) 25 October 1812 *HMS Minstrel*. *Occupation:* Naval Officer, Surveyor-General, farmer, explorer. *Died*: 25 May 1828 Kirkham, Camden, NSW. *Buried:* Devonshire Street Cemetery, Sydney, NSW. *Partner* (1) Charlotte Jane Thorpe (2) Elizabeth Marmon. *Spouse:* Emma Norton. *Married:* 31 October 1821 St. Philip's Anglican Church, Sydney, NSW.

Oxley joined the navy in 1799 as a Midshipman on *HMS Venerable*, and transferred in November 1801 to *HMS Buffalo,* in which as Master's Mate he sailed to Australia. Arriving on 15 October 1802 he engaged in coastal survey work including an expedition to Western Port in 1804 and 1805. In 1805 Governor Philip Gidley King appointed him Acting Lieutenant in charge of *HMS Buffalo*, and in 1806 he commanded *HMS Estramina* on a trip to Van Diemen's Land. He returned to England where he was commissioned Lieutenant on 25 November 1807 but returned to Sydney in November 1808 to take up an appointment as First Lieutenant on *HMS Porpoise.*

Captain John Oxley

Lieutenant-Governor William Paterson granted him 1000 acres (405 ha) near the Nepean River but Oxley had to surrender these in 1810. Governor Lachlan Macquarie then granted him 600 acres (243 ha) near Camden which he increased in 1815 to 1000 acres (405 ha) and called the grant Kirkham after his home in Yorkshire. Oxley was later appointed Surveyor-General.

WOORE, Thomas: *Rank:* Lieutenant. *Unit:* Royal Navy. *Born:* 29 January 1804 Londonderry, Ireland. *Parents:* Capt. Thomas Woore and Catherine Anne Darcus. *Occupation:* Naval Officer, surveyor, pastoralist. *Died:* 21 June 1878 Double Bay, NSW. *Buried:* St. Jude's Church of England, Randwick, NSW. *Spouse:* Mary Dickson. *Married:* 1 January 1835 Scots Church, Sydney, NSW.

Woore visited Sydney on a number of occasions firstly on *HMS Zebra* then on *HMS Crocodile* and finally on *HMS Alligator* which operated out of Sydney. He resigned his commission in 1834 due to ill health. After his marriage in 1835 he returned to Britain but returned to New South Wales in 1839. He was made a magistrate and bought a station, Pomeroy near Goulburn, where he built a charming house and became a leading pastoralist. Woore is also associated with Harrington Park where he was living when he made a sketch of the Cowpastures Bridge at Camden circa 1842.

---

[33] Headstone indicates 3rd son

In May 1846, at his own expense, he carried out a survey for a railway but his work was largely ignored by the government. Between 1867 and 1869 Woore was a member of the Commission on the water supply of Sydney and its suburbs and in his report recommended building a dam at Warragamba but was ignored even though in the 1870s he pressed for the scheme in two pamphlets.

Sketch of the Cowpastures Bridge Camden circa 1842 by Lieutenant Thomas Woore

THE ROYAL REGIMENT of ARTILLERY: 1853

The Royal Regiment of Artillery was formed in 1762 and by 1772 the numbers had risen into four companies when it merged with two independent artillery companies based at Menorca (Spain) and Gibraltar. The new unit was renamed the Royal Regiment of Artillery and was commanded by Colonel Albert Borgard. By 1757 the regiment had grown to 24 companies, divided into two battalions and including a Cadet Company.

From its formation the Royal Artillery was controlled by the Board of Ordnance and not the War Office until 1855 when the Board of Ordnance was abolished and the regiment then came under War Office control in line with the rest of the army.

SWAN, Charles: *Rank:* quartermaster sergeant. *Unit:* Royal Regiment of Artillery. *Born:* c.1828 England. *Parents:* John Swan and Isabella. *Occupation:* soldier, farmer. *Arrived:* 26 September 1853 *HMS Waratah. Died*: 21 December 1907 Bargo, NSW. *Buried*: St Mark's Church of England, Picton, NSW. *Spouse*: (1) Jane Hardy. *Married:* Agra, India. (2) Sarah Carter. *Married*: 1894 Picton, NSW.

Swan served in the Lahore and Punjab from the late 1840s until 1853 when he arrived in the colony.

The Picton Post
Wednesday 1 January 1908, page 4

The death occurred at Bargo on the 21st December of Mr. Charles Swan, at the age of 79 years. Deceased was the father of Mrs. Frank Sheil, of Picton. His remains were interred in the Church of England Cemetery, Picton.

SOLDIERS FROM EUROPE

Not all the soldiers who came to the colony were from Britain; they came from all over Europe even though Britain initially endeavoured to prevent that from happening. Immigrants from Europe had to have special skills that were required by the colony in order to be eligible.

ZGLINICKI, Maximilian von: *Rank:* chief lieutenant. *Unit:* Austrian Army. *Born:* 1827 Poznań, Poland. *Parents:* Count Boguslaw von Zglinicki and Henrietta von Fitzwitz. *Arrived:* Melbourne 23 December 1852 *HMS Peru*. *Occupation:* police sergeant. *Died:* 18 January 1898 Camden, NSW. *Buried:* St. John's Church of England, Camden, NSW. *Spouse:* Bridget O'Hare. *Married:* 21 January 1862 St Mary's Roman Catholic Cathedral, Sydney, NSW.

Zglinicki was born in Poznań,[34] Poland in 1827, the elder son of Count Boguslaw von Zglinicki and Henrietta von Fitzwitz. After Napoleon's defeat, Poznań had become part of Prussia and functioned as the capital of the autonomous Grand Duchy of Poznań. At the time of Maximilian von Zglinicki's birth Poznań was semi-autonomous, but by 1846 this autonomy had been revoked.

By the early 1840s Zglinicki was in active service in the Austrian Army, as was expected of young men of his social background, and had been promoted to Chief Lieutenant. However, he became involved in the political troubles which would lead to the first of the two uprisings in Poland in 1848. Zglinicki made some incautious political statements which brought him to the attention of the authorities and when warned by a faithful servant that he was to be arrested he fled to England. He worked in London for a period, teaching languages with some success, and then decided to come to Australia, arriving on the *Peru* on 23 December 1852. Zglinicki worked hard teaching French and German but had limited success in finding pupils. On 21 January 1862 he married Bridget O'Hare, from Newry, Ireland at St. Mary's Cathedral, Sydney. After his marriage he visited the gold fields of Victoria and 'there gained colonial experience'.[35]

Zglinicki was described as 'a man of great stature', and this, combined with his military training, induced him to join the Queensland police. Despite the high praise he received from the Queensland authorities, Queensland did not live up to his expectations and he returned to NSW.

The NSW police in Sydney immediately employed him as an interpreter with the rank of Sergeant. When troubles arose in the gold fields, he was sent to quell the trouble. On another occasion several prisoners were being conveyed from the Sydney Gaol to Berrima. One of the prisoners managed to undo the chains and leg irons fastening the prisoners in the coach in which they were travelling. The prisoners endeavoured to escape, and in the scramble one managed to grab a constable's revolver.

---
[34] From the 2nd partition of Poland from 1793 until 1806, Poznań was in South Prussia (part of Prussia). From 1806 to 1815, Poznań was part of the Duchy of Warsaw: 'History of Poznań' Wikipedia
[35] 'Obituary, the Late Mr. Max Zglinicki' *Camden News* 27th January 1898

Sergeant Zglinicki struggled with him and disarmed and recaptured him.

Zglinicki was then appointed to Camden and Picton, and later to Scone where he resided for five years, becoming Governor of the Port Macquarie Gaol. He was then promoted to oversee the gaol at Campbelltown, but after a prisoner escaped whilst en route to Sydney, he received a rebuff from the authorities. After this he was for many years a sergeant in the mounted police. On his retirement he was awarded a substantial pension for his meritorious service.

During the latter period of his life he resided in Camden where he was a well-known figure. He was one of the thirteen foundation members when Abbotsford Lodge[36] was consecrated on 10 August 1894. Zglinicki was the Registrar for Births, Deaths and Marriages in Camden and also Electoral Registrar until mid-1897. He died on 18 January 1898 and was buried at St. John's Church of England, Camden, NSW.

AMERICAN WAR OF INDEPENDENCE
19 April 1775–11 April 1783

The American Revolutionary War (1775–1783) was the military rebellion against Great Britain of thirteen American Colonies which joined together as the United States of America in July 1776. Originally limited to fighting in those colonies after 1778 it also became a world war between Britain and France, Netherlands, Spain, and Mysore. France signed an alliance with the new nation to revenge its 1763 defeat by Britain in the French Indian war (1754–1763). France's entry into the war escalated the conflict into a world war, with Britain also at war with Spain and the Netherlands. Fighting also broke out between the British East India Company and the French allied Kingdom of Mysore.

The war had its origins in the resistance of many American colonists to taxes imposed by the British Parliament, which they held to be unlawful. Acts of rebellion against British authority began in 1774 when the patriot Suffolk Resolves effectively abolished the legal government of the Province of Massachusetts Bay. The tensions caused would lead to the outbreak of fighting between patriot militia and British regulars at Lexington and Concord in April 1775. By spring 1776 the Patriots had seized full control in all thirteen colonies and on 4 July 1776, their Continental Congress declared independence.

FRYER, Richard: *Rank:* Private. *Unit:* New South Wales Corps. *Born:* 24 October 1754, London, Middlesex, England. *Parents:* Richard Fryer and Catherine. *Arrived:* 21 August 1791 *HMS Salamander. Died:* 28 March 1844, Pomarie Grove, Cobbitty, NSW. *Buried:* St. Paul's Church of England, Cobbitty, NSW. *Spouse:* Julia Elizabeth Bidwell (common law wife).

Richard Fryer was a veteran of the American War of Independence, who enlisted in the New South Wales Corps on 14 January 1790. He arrived in Australia with the Third Fleet on Sunday, 21 August 1791 aboard the convict transport *HMS Salamander.* In Sydney he served in Lieutenant John Townson's detachment and was later despatched to Norfolk Island on the schooner *HMS Francis.* He arrived on Norfolk Island on 9 March 1794 on what would be the first of several visits to the island.

---

[36] Abbotsford Lodge changed its name to Camden Lodge No. 217 in 1916. Rev. Cecil John King was also a member

Richard received a land grant, Lot No. 175, comprising 30 acres valued at 1/- (10 cents) per acre on 1 April 1794 in the Ermington, Rydalmere, Dundas area. He was discharged from the New South Wales Corps on 24 January 1800 whilst still on Norfolk Island. On 11 December 1800 he leased 24 acres and on 29 August 1803 purchased 14 acres.

He was described in the 1805 Muster as a 'man of stores' and over the next few years he supplied the government stores on Norfolk Island with swine flesh and maize. He departed from Norfolk Island for Sydney on 5 April 1809 together with his common law wife, Julia Elizabeth Bidwell, who had arrived as a convict on the *Surprize* on 25 October 1794 and a son John who was born on the island in 1809.

Fryer first settled at Parramatta before moving to Cobbitty, NSW where he died in 1844.

KNIGHT, Isaac: *Rank:* Sergeant. *Unit:* (1) 8th Portsmouth Company, Royal Marines (2) New South Wales Corps. *Born:* 1750 Ferney, Fermanagh, Ireland. *Arrived*: (1) First Fleet 26 January 1788 *HMS Alexander* (2) 11 March 1803 *HMS Glatton*. *Died*: 17 April 1842 Macquarie Grove, Camden, NSW. *Buried*: St John's Church of England, Parramatta, NSW. *Spouse:* (1) Mary Talbot. *Married:* 7 April 1794 England (2) Elizabeth White nee Marks. *Married:* 10 June 1802 Portsmouth, England.

Marine Sergeant Isaac Knight enlisted as a member of the 8th Portsmouth Company and fought for Britain during the American War of Independence. He was stationed on board the ship *Alexander* and it was on this ship he left England for Australia. Prior to this he served as a marine on board the guard ships *Ganges* and the *Eagle*. On board the *Eagle* he was discharged as a prisoner. It is understood that this was as a result of a misdemeanour as a fellow Sergeant, James Scott, noted in his diary on two occasions that Knight 'had stripes taken from him' once whilst he was at the Cape of Good Hope.

> James Scott noted that 'Serjeant [sic] Knight, who was suspended at the Cape of Good Hope, was ordered to his former duty Friday.'[37]

Following his arrival in Sydney he spent some time with exploration parties through Richmond Hill and the Hawkesbury. He returned to England on board the ship *Atlantic* in 1792, returning in March 1803 with his wife and one child on board the ship *Glatton*. He received a grant of land for 100 acres at Bankstown. He then received a land grant of 100 acres at George's River where he established his home. The house was lost to floods in January of 1809. Granted further land at Castle Hill of 100 acres and at Upper Minto of 100 acres, he died at Macquarie Grove in 1842.

Knight's obituary also indicates that he had previously served seven years under Lord Howe and had participated in the American War of Independence, and that in May 1791 he had accompanied Captain Watkin Tench and Lieutenant William Dawes, on their explorations which established that the Hawkesbury and the Nepean was a single river.

Sydney Morning Herald
Wednesday 27 April 1842, page 3

> *At Macquarie Grove, on Sunday, the 17th instant, Isaac Knight, in his 93rd year, he was one of the first who arrived in the colony under Governor Phillip, as Sergeant in the Royal Marines, and was seven years under Lord Howe, and served in the first American War. He was universally esteemed for his kindness*

---

[37] Cobley, John. (1962). *Sydney Cove, 1788*. London : Hodder and Stoughton

and generosity, and for the last 16 years was a resident in the family of Mrs. J. J. Howell, and it may truly be said of him 'his end was peace'.

The Sydney Gazette and New South Wales Advertiser
Thursday 28 April 1842, page 3

DEATH

Died, at Macquarie Grove, Cowpastures, on the 17th instant, after a residence of 17 years Mr. Isaac Knight, in his 92nd year. This distinguished gentleman has been an efficient officer in the Marine Service, in various parts of the world - first in the American contest, serving also in the Mediterranean; was one of the naval officers on the establishment of this colony. The subject of this notice occupied several important situations under government, until his advanced age rendered his retirement needful.

It may also be noticed that Mr. Knight gave the name to George's River, after the name of the officer of the New South Wales Corps, viz Colonel Johnston, who had also suffered greatly from original researches in the desert bush of this colony.

4th MYSORE WAR: INDIA

India was a central part of the British Empire in the 18th Century. Though the East India Company directed trade and largely controlled the region, the British Government's influence steadily increased. For this reason, the army's role became very important. There were four military confrontations (1767–1769; 1780–1784; 1790–1792; and 1799) in India between the British and the rulers of Mysore.

The 2nd Mysore War was between the British and Muslim Hyder Ali, who had made himself Sultan of Mysore. The war ended with the signing of the Treaty of Mangalore in 1784 with Hyder Ali's son Tipoo[38] Saib. The 3rd Mysore War began in 1790, when Governor-General Lord Cornwallis dropped Tipoo's name from the list of 'friends' of the British East India Company. Following two campaigns, Tipoo was checked at Seringapatam (now Shrirangapatna, Karnataka) in 1792 and forced to cede half his dominions.

The 4th Mysore War was undertaken by Governor-General Lord Richard Mornington (later Wellesley) when in 1798 Tipoo Saib was discovered to be in league with the French. The following year the British Governor General Wellesley sent two armies to Mysore. Tipoo retreated to his Fortress of Seringapatam and the British army besieged the palace. After a siege of fourteen days the British attacked and captured the fortress on 4 May 1799 killing Tipoo. The Kingdom of Mysore returned to British control.

---

[38] There seem to be several ways of spelling this name, i.e. Tipoo, Tippoo, Tippu

Sir David Baird Discovering Body of Tipoo Saib. Illustrated History of The British Empire in India and the East, 1878. Steel engraved print

BATTLE OF SERINGAPATAM: INDIA 5 April 1799–4 May 1799

ANTILL, Henry Colden: *Rank:* Major. *Unit:* 73rd (Perthshire) Regiment of Foot. *Born:* 1July 1779 New York, USA. *Parents:* John Antill and Margaret Colden. *Arrived:* 29 December 1809 *HMS Dromedary*. *Died:* 14 August 1852, Jarvisfield, Picton, NSW. *Buried:* Vault Hill, Picton, NSW. *Spouse:* Eliza Wills. *Married:* 8 October 1818 St. Phillip's Church of England, Sydney, NSW.

Antill arrived to take position as Aide-de-Camp to Governor Lachlan Macquarie. The 73rd Regiment fought in the right-hand column of the British forces at the Battle of Seringapatam. They lost 21 men and 99 suffered injuries. They also garrisoned the fortress after its capture. The 73rd Regiment received the battle honour Seringapatam. The Earl of Mornington wrote that the attack had 'raised the reputation of the British Army in India to a degree of splendour and glory unrivalled in the military history of this quarter of the globe'.

MOLLE, George James: *Rank:* (1) Captain (2) Lieutenant-Colonel (3) Brevet Colonel. *Unit:* (1) Scots Brigade (later 94th Regiment of Foot) (2) 46th (South Devonshire) Regiment of Foot. *Baptised:* 6 March 1773 Chirnside, Berwickshire, England. *Parents:* John Mow and Margaret Crow. *Occupation:* soldier, Lieutenant Governor of New South Wales. *Arrived:* 11 February 1814 *HMS Windham*. *Died:* 9 September 1823 Belgaum, India. *Spouse:* Catharine Brown. *Married:* London, England.

Molle was commissioned Ensign (Scots Brigade) June 1793, Lieutenant (Scots Brigade) 12 May 1794, Captain (army) 1 July 1795, Captain (Scots Brigade) 29 March 1798. He was wounded at Seringapatam, India on 27 April 1799.

He was commissioned Major (8th Battalion-Reserve) on 3 September 1803, transferred to 9th Foot on 2 June 1804, Lieutenant-Colonel on 2 September 1808, appointed Lieutenant-Colonel of 46th Foot on 3 June 1813. Molle obtained the brevet rank of Colonel on 4 June 1814.

George James Molle

Molle was appointed Lieutenant Governor of New South Wales in 1813 and arrived in the colony in February 1814 in command of the 46th Regiment which had been sent to relieve the 73rd Regiment. Molle had known, and served with, Lachlan Macquarie in India and Egypt during 1801–1802. Molle acted as Aide-de-Camp to Major General Sir David Baird at the same time that Macquarie was Deputy-Adjutant General in Baird's Expeditionary Army to Egypt.

He left his property Molle's Maine at Narellan to his son William. The Molle Islands in the Whitsunday Passage are named after him. The family had changed the spelling of their surname from Mow to Molle after the death of George's father in 1795.

NAPOLEONIC WARS
18 May 1803–20 November 1815

The Camden region had a number of residents with connections to the Napoleonic Wars. The wars were fought mainly in France, Spain and Belgium but also spread to involve the United States of America, Canada, the West Indies and Egypt.

Napoleon's grand plan included overrunning the Middle East and marching to India. However, this plan was abandoned after August 1798 when Lord Nelson destroyed the French fleet during the Battle of the Nile at Aboukir Bay on the Mediterranean coast off Egypt. Napoleon's lines of communication were destroyed, forcing him to abandon his army and retreat to France.

After the naval battle of 1798, Britain decided to crush the French army remaining in Egypt. The second battle of the Egyptian campaign, the Battle of Aboukir, was fought, near the Nile Delta on the Mediterranean coast, on 8 March 1801, by the British Expeditionary Force, under the command of Sir Ralph Abercromby.

DE ARRIETA, Jean (John) Baptiste Lehimas: *Rank:* not applicable. *Born:* abt. 1774 San Sebastian, Spain. *Parents:* Lehimas and Arrieta. *Arrived:* 3 April 1821 *HMS Duke of York*. *Died:* March 1838. *Buried:* Moreton Park, Douglas Park, NSW. *Spouse:* Sophia Spearing.

One of the more controversial and intriguing settlers was Jean Baptiste Lehimas de Arrieta, the first Spanish settler in the colony whose arrival aboard the *Duke of York* via Hobart Town was announced in the *Sydney Gazette* of 7 April 1821.

De Arrieta had been born in San Sebastian in the Basque region of Spain, the son of a French father and Basque mother, but by the time of his arrival in the colony had ceased to use the title Lehimas de Arrieta and was simply known as de Arrieta. In Britain he had claimed reparations for his services as a supplier, co-ordinator and spy for the British forces during the Peninsular War which he claimed had resulted in the loss of property to the value of £30,000 during the Siege of Badajoz. It was during that period de Arrieta became acquainted with Walter John Wilkinson, part of the Commissariat[39] arm of the Duke of Wellington's staff, and through him with James Stares Spearing and William Morton Pitt MP of Dorset. It has been suggested that in 1820 de Arrieta may have been one of the witnesses in King George IV's divorce case against Caroline of Brunswick, Princess of Wales.

De Arrieta came to the colony at the suggestion of Pitt who prevailed upon Governor Sir Thomas Brisbane to grant him 2247 acres in the Cowpastures. De Arrieta named the grant Morton Park in recognition of Pitt's assistance but the property was better known as Spaniard's Hill.

Governor Brisbane allocated de Arrieta 20 convicts but he was known as a hard task master with little regard for the plight of those working for him. A gardener who accidentally blasted his hand off whilst attempting to shoot a hawk was bundled into a cart for a tortuous nine-hour journey to Liverpool for medical assistance when de Arrieta's chaise could have completed the trip in three hours. De Arrieta had no sympathy for the servant, bemoaning the loss of the services of the gardener who had been responsible for tending his tobacco crop.

By 1825 de Arrieta was in financial difficulties, despite having what was regarded as prime farmland. He struggled to grow tobacco and vines and eventually was forced to mortgage his property to the notorious ex-convict Samuel Terry known as The Botany Bay Rothschild. He would eventually sell him the property in 1831.

In 1825 James Stares Spearing and his family, including his illegitimate daughter 16-year-old Sophia Jacob Spearing, arrived on the *Harvey* and stayed with de Arrieta for a period until Spearing received his grant of 2000 acres in the Illawarra area. During this time Sophia absconded with a convict youth, Lazarus Davey,[40] but the pair were quickly apprehended on the Liverpool Road and returned to Spaniard's Hill. When brought before a Magistrate, Sophia cited her resentment of Spearing's harsh disciplinary treatment as the reason for absconding. The wayward Sophia remained at Spaniard's Hill and on 12th February 1828 at the especially erected private chapel on Morton Park married de Arrieta; she was 5 months pregnant at the

---

[39] A system for supplying an army with food; i.e. the mobile kitchen
[40] Davey did not receive his Certificate of Freedom until 1841. Confusion over the spelling of his surname led to the suggestion that he had already received his Certificate of Freedom

time. A daughter, Louisa Sophia de Arrieta was born in June of that year; Sophia would give birth to a son Walter in 1830.

De Arrieta was by no means faithful to his wife and was a reputed womaniser. In December 1829 when 21-year-old Adelaide de la Thoreza de la Vega arrived as a convict aboard the *Lucy Davidson*, having been sentenced to seven years' transportation for the theft of linen, she was assigned to de Arrieta as a housemaid and nanny to Louisa. Within ten months, Adelaide was pregnant and was quickly transferred to the Female Factory at Parramatta where she gave birth to a son in July 1831. Perhaps this was the reason for the argument that is said to have resulted in Sophia smashing a prize pumpkin over her husband's head.

Robert Henry Antill related an incident told to him by his grandfather Major Henry Colden Antill to John Fairfax. Sophia was causing so much trouble to de Arrieta that he sought the Major's assistance, asking that he give her a lecture. Reluctantly, the Major spoke to Sophia on how to be a good and dutiful wife, which it appears she listened to respectfully until he had finished. Sophia is reported to have said, 'Thank you sir. Now might I make a suggestion?' When the Major asked her to go ahead, Sophia is reported to have said, 'Might I suggest, sir, you go back and look after your own wife?' The Major had no suitable reply.

De Arrieta protected his property, and his wife, by staking out vicious dogs at intervals around the house with lengths of chain that would only allow the dogs to lick each other's noses and to attack at hip level any intruder.

After the sale of Morton Park to Samuel Terry in 1831, de Arrieta leased the property and continued to farm the land with little success until his death in March 1838. There is some conjecture as to where he is buried. His burial record appears in St. Peter's Church of England records at Campbelltown, but it is believed he was buried near his private chapel on Morton Park. He stipulated in his will that his effects should be sold to contribute to the education and maintenance of his children until they reached the age of 21.

His wife Sophia did not long mourn his death. In December 1838, Sophia married William Walker and the couple had various inns and hotels in the district, possibly financed from the dower from the government given to widows of the time.

DOUGLASS, Henry Grattan: *Rank:* Assistant Surgeon. *Unit:* 18th (Royal Irish) Regiment of Foot. *Born:* 1 January 1790, Dublin, Ireland. *Parents:* Adam Douglass and Ann Edwards. *Arrived:* 18 May 1821 *Speke. Died:* 1 December 1865, Woollahra, NSW. *Buried:* St. John's Church of England, Camden, NSW. *Spouse:* Hester Murphy.

One settler who rose to prominence was Henry Grattan Douglass, born in Dublin, Ireland in 1790, the son of Adam Douglass, an apothecary,[41] and Ann Edwards. In 1809 Britain was engaged in war against Napoleon, and experienced surgeons were in short supply. The government employed young men who had completed the first stages of their medical studies and Douglass, a 19-year-old medical student, was appointed as an Assistant Surgeon with the 18th Regiment during the Peninsular War of 1809–1810[42] and in the West Indies in 1811.[43]

---

[41] Apothecary is an historical name for a medical professional who formulates and dispenses medicines to physicians, surgeons and patients — a role now served by a pharmacist. In addition to pharmacy responsibilities, the apothecary offered general medical advice and a range of services that are now performed solely by other specialist practitioners, such as surgery and midwifery.
[42] The Peninsular War began in August 1808. In 1809 the battle concentrated mainly in Portugal around Corunna, Oporto and Talverna.
[43] In 1811 the British Navy captured Guadeloupe, the last French Colony in the West Indies.

Whilst in the West Indies he contracted rheumatic fever and returned home. The date of his return was fixed upon his memory by the entrance of one of his sisters into his bedroom the morning after his arrival, to tell him Prime Minister Spencer Percival[44] had been killed by an assassin's bullet.

In 1812 Douglass married Hester Murphy, the daughter of Arthur Murphy the Chief of O'Murrough in County Wexford, and Margaret Rooney, and accepted a civil appointment as Medical Superintendent of the Fever Hospital and Infirmary at Cahir, Tipperary. In 1815 he was admitted as a member of the Royal College of Surgeons of England.

He returned to Ireland in 1817 during a typhus epidemic and later published a thesis which he submitted for the Doctorate of Medicine at Trinity College, Dublin. In 1819 he was licensed as a Physician at the King's and Queen's College of Physicians of Ireland and in June 1820 he was elected to the Royal Irish Academy.

Henry Grattan Douglass aged 22 - courtesy Camden Historical Society

About this time he became interested in prison reform. Among his friends were prominent Quakers—the Frys,[45] Hoares,[46] Gurneys,[47] and Allens—who had combined to improve the condition of prisons, and soften the rigor of the penal laws which sent a woman to the scaffold for stealing from a counter a few yards of calico, and consigned hundreds of human beings to a similar fate for a crime which would now result in a short term of imprisonment.

It was towards the end of 1820 that Douglass accepted a colonial appointment. With his wife, son and two daughters he arrived in Sydney on the *Speke* on 18th May 1821 with a letter of introduction from Earl Henry Bathurst (Secretary of State for the Colonies 1812 to 1827) to Governor Lachlan Macquarie. As Douglass had good connections at home and was very highly qualified, Governor Macquarie reported back to Earl Bathurst:-

> *I have just made necessary arrangements for placing Dr. Douglass in charge of the Colonial General Hospital at Parramatta (which particular station he prefers to every other) where he will have considerable private practice and other advantages besides being placed in the centre of a fine rich populous district. I intend immediately to appoint Doctor Douglass a Magistrate at Parramatta and to build him a good, comfortable barrack, the present one for the medical officer at that station being in a state of decay and almost uninhabitable. I shall consequently be under the necessity of hiring a good house in the meantime, for the residence of Dr Douglass and his family until a Government quarter can be built for them.*[48]

---

[44] Spencer Perceval, KC (1 November 1762–11 May 1812) was a British statesman and Prime Minister. He is the only British Prime Minister to have been assassinated.
[45] Within Britain, prison reform was spearheaded by the Quakers, and in particular, Elizabeth Fry during the Victorian Age. Her father, Joseph Gurney, was a partner in Gurney's bank. Her mother, Catherine, was a member of the Barclay family, who were among the founders of Barclays Bank.
[46] Quaker banker Samuel Hoare came over from Cork and set up home in Heath House in 1790. He was concerned with the anti-slavery movement.
[47] Joseph John Gurney was a banker in Norwich, England and an evangelical Minister of the Religious Society of Friends (Quakers). He was also the brother of Elizabeth Fry.
[48] From copy of letter in the *History of Parramatta Hospital to 1988*:
catalogue.nla.gov.au/Record/569670

Governor Macquarie left the colony soon after sending this letter but Douglass became very friendly with his successor, Governor Sir Thomas Brisbane, who arrived in November 1821 and became a regular visitor at the new Governor's residence. This association brought him into conflict with his senior colleagues on the Parramatta bench, but the friendship stood him in good stead in the troubles in which he became embroiled.

In 1822 Douglass received a grant of 800 acres being Portion 7, Parish of Camden, which he called Hoare as a compliment to his friend Samuel Hoare. The original grant had two of its boundaries on the Nepean River and Harris Creek and was registered in the name of his young son Arthur. When the rail line to Goulburn was constructed in the 1850s a small township named Hoare Town[49] was built on part of his property to house the construction workers.

Grave of Henry Grattan & Hester Douglass

The first clash between Douglass and his fellow magistrates – Rev. Samuel Marsden, Hannibal Hawkins Macarthur and Dr. James Hall – came in August 1822 over a convict girl, Ann Rumsby, who had been assigned to him as a servant. Dr Hall had been Surgeon Superintendent of the *Maria Ann* on which Rumsby had been transported and had met her again on a visit to the Douglass residence.[50] Misunderstanding a comment from Rumsby, he placed the matter before Marsden and Macarthur, alleging that Douglass was behaving improperly with her.

The three magistrates summoned Douglass to appear before them but when he failed to appear they had Ann Rumsby[51] arrested. When Rumsby denied the allegations against Douglass she was charged with perjury and sentenced to imprisonment at Port Macquarie. Governor Brisbane intervened, gave her a free pardon and threatened to remove the Parramatta magistrates who had not only refused to sit with Douglass on the bench but also called a secret general meeting of Justices to support their action, and complained to London.

Douglass could fend for himself. In April 1823 he brought an action for libel against Dr. Hall[52] claiming damages of £5000 ($10,000) but was only awarded £2 ($4) and costs. The following month, together with William Lawson, Douglass fined Samuel Marsden for allowing one of his convict servants to be at large. When Marsden[53] refused to pay, Douglass and Lawson had his piano seized and sold.

---

[49] The area was later renamed Douglass Park after objections from the local womenfolk. The dropping of the second 's' is thought to have been a clerical error.
[50] K. B. Noad, 'Douglass, Henry Grattan (1790–1865)', *Australian Dictionary of Biography, Volume 1*, Melbourne University Press, 1966, pp 314-316
[51] The problem had initially arisen when Dr Douglass insisted that Ann Rumsby marry William Bragge, despite her reluctance. After receiving her pardon Ann agreed to marry Bragge and they were married by Reverend Thomas Hassall at St. John's Parramatta on 3 February 1823 and they had 7 or 8 children. Ann is buried in the churchyard of St Anne's Anglican Church, Ryde
[52] Dr Hall was himself later found guilty of kissing female prisoners after having had them flogged, and was removed from office. Charles Bateson, 'Hall, James (1784–1869)', Australian Dictionary of Biography, Volume 1, Melbourne University Press, 1966, p. 503
[53] It is interesting to note that Samuel Marsden himself was known as 'the flogging parson'.

Marsden promptly sued him for damages of £250 ($500), but the court awarded him only the amount of the fine, which resulted in Marsden complaining to Charles James Lord, Bishop of London, that Douglass was preventing inmates of the Female Factory from taking their infants to church for baptism.

Marsden also connived with Hannibal Macarthur to send a letter to Sir Robert Peel at the Home Office charging Douglass with drunkenness, torture of prisoners and other disreputable official conduct. The letters, forwarded to the Colonial Office, brought orders for an inquiry which exonerated Douglass but provided a loophole for Hannibal Macarthur as foreman of the Grand Jury to publish further complaints against Douglass in the *Sydney Gazette*. Brisbane's reports extolled his virtues with increasing warmth after each attack and in February 1824 he nominated Douglass as Commissioner of the Court of Requests and sent him to London to consult the Colonial Office on the functions of the new court.

In addition, the Governor suggested Douglass be appointed as Clerk of the Legislative Council, but changed his mind when Douglass was censured for a gross breach of military discipline when it was revealed that he had left England in 1821 without permission from the War Office. Douglass was recalled for service in March 1825 but sailed for Sydney without apology or explanation.

In May 1828 Douglass again sailed for England. This led to Robert Howe, the Editor and proprietor of the *Sydney Gazette*, publishing an article on 9 May 1828 which, whilst not mentioning Douglass by name, made comments such as 'ex-civil officer' and 'to save his political reputation from being blasted in Downing Street' and made reference to 'inflicting illegal punishment on prisoners in the colony'. On 24 December 1828 a case of libel against Howe was held in the Supreme Court before Mr Justice Dowling. Despite Douglass not being present, the Jury found in his favour, Howe was found guilty of libel, and Douglass was awarded £50 ($100).

Later, Douglass heard that Governor Ralph Darling, who had arrived in December 1825, had cancelled his land grant at Narrigo on the Shoalhaven River. This land and his son's farm at Douglass Park had been leased in 1828 to William Charles Wentworth for three years. After the Douglass Park lease ended a small cottage was built on the site. This was used by his widowed sister Elizabeth Taylor and her children. Elizabeth looked after the family interests until her death in 1864.[54]

In 1839 Douglass sought compensation from the Colonial Office, but after long correspondence his claim was rejected, in spite of a letter of support from Sir Thomas Brisbane. Governor Sir George Gipps could trace no record of Douglass's authority to the Narrigo grant, although he did unearth proof of a 17-year-old debt to the Colonial Government of more than £700 ($1,400). Douglass remained in England until 1848. Records from 1835 indicate Douglass was a physician attached to King William IV's household, but shortly after, he left England for France. In Paris his knowledge of infectious disease was valuable during an epidemic of cholera, and his services won commendation and a medal from the government of King Louis Philippe the First. In a suburb of Le Havre, Douglass founded a Seamen's Hospital and directed it for twelve years.

He returned to Sydney in October 1848 as Surgeon Superintendent of the emigrant ship *Earl Grey*. The following year he became an Honorary Physician at Sydney Hospital and was one of the first teachers of clinical medicine in Australia. In 1854 he was appointed a Director of the hospital, but resigned after two years to take a seat in the first Legislative Council under responsible government.

---

[54] Elizabeth Taylor is buried in the churchyard but has no gravestone.

Dr. Douglass initiated, and followed up, several important reforms. He introduced into NSW, before it was adopted in England, the Law of Limited Liability in commercial partnerships. He also obtained the abolition of public executions which he hoped would lead to the abolition of capital punishment. One of his Bills was to regulate the qualifications of practitioners in medicine, surgery and pharmacy but this was laid aside in 1860. He also resumed his philanthropic activities, becoming a Vice-President of the Benevolent Society, and helping Charles Nicholson to revive the Philosophical Society, of which he was the first Secretary. This society was later renamed the Royal Society of NSW. He was also a member of the Royal Agricultural Society.

Douglass helped to introduce child welfare by sharing actively in forming a Society for the Relief of Destitute Children and in establishing an orphanage at Randwick for their care. There are few of our educational or charitable institutions in the organisation of which Dr Douglass had not a distinguished part, including in a project for taking better care of the blind.

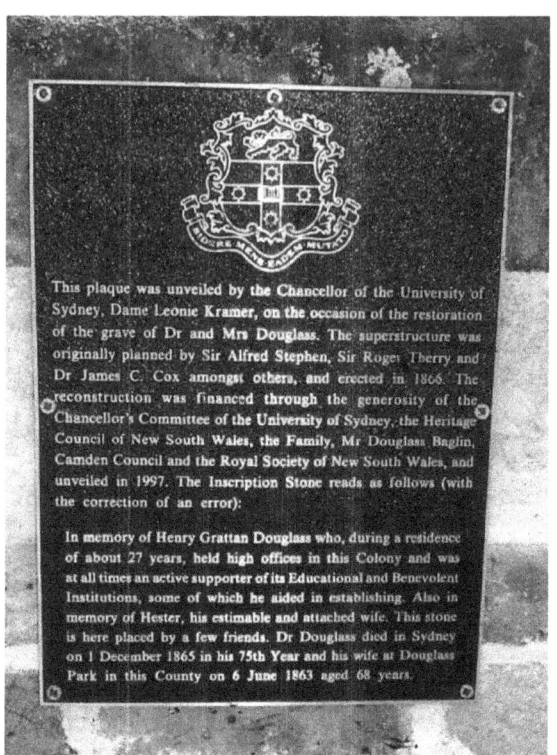

Plaque commemorating the restoration of the Douglass Grave in 1996 by Sydney University

He also played a part in the founding of Sydney University. In 1849 Douglass had badgered Francis Lewis Shaw Merewether, at the time Clerk of the Legislative Council and of the Executive Council, seeking his influence for the establishment of a University. Merewether advised Douglass to seek the assistance of William Charles Wentworth, who had already shown interest in such an establishment. Wentworth was successful in establishing the University, but Douglass was not appointed to the first university senate. He was, however, elected to fill a casual vacancy in 1853, and was a member of the Medical Faculty Committee and remained a senator until 1865.

Henry Grattan Douglass died at Woollahra on 1 December 1865 and is buried at St John's Church of England, Camden, NSW alongside his wife Hester, who had died on 6 June 1863. He is commemorated at Sydney University by his coat of arms in stone on the south side of the entrance to the Great Hall, and in a stained-glass window in the south porch of the main building. The university was also instrumental in repairing his grave in 1996.

DUNK, Jesse: *Rank:* Private. *Unit:* 39th (Dorsetshire) Regiment of Foot. *Born:* 22 April 1787 Battle, Sussex, England. *Parents:* John Dunk and Sarah Blunden. *Arrived:* 26 October 1839 *Florist. Died:* 15 June 1860 Cawdor, NSW. *Buried:* St. John's Church of England, Camden, NSW. *Spouses:* (1) Charlotte Martha Sellings (2) Susanna Silvaris (3) Sarah Hilder. *Honours:* Military General Services Medal 1848 with 5 bars.

Jesse Dunk was born in Battle, Sussex on 22 April 1787, the son of John Dunk and Sarah Blunden. He worked as a labourer but employment opportunities were scarce. In 1808 the Peninsular War against Napoleon began, so with the call to arms and the offer of regular pay, 22-year-old Jesse enlisted in 1809 in the 39th (Dorsetshire) Regiment of Foot.

Jesse Dunk and his medal – photo courtesy of Shirley Rorke

Jesse saw service in France and Spain at the Battles of Busaco, Albuera, Vittoria, Pyrenees and Toulouse. He was sent to Canada to take part in the War of 1812 which was fought between the United States and Great Britain (rising out of a dispute on blockading trade with France, as well as other issues). The war began in June 1812 and continued until 1815 although the Peace Treaty ending the Napoleonic War was signed in Europe in December 1814. The main land fighting of the war occurred along the Canadian border and also in the Gulf of Mexico. Jesse took part in the Canadian campaign and in the Chesapeake Bay campaign which culminated in the burning of Washington on 24 August 1814. However, by 1814 he was back in France, taking part in the Battle of Montmartre (Paris) 30–31 March 1814. Jesse was awarded the Military General Services Medal in 1848. This medal was not authorised until 1847 and then issued only to survivors living at that time who had applied for the medal.[55]

On 12 June 1816 Jesse was discharged and returned to Sussex. Now that the war was over, there was a large increase in the number of men seeking work so Jesse moved to Mountfield, a short distance away, where there was limited work available for labourers. On 6 June 1818 he married Charlotte Sellings at All Saints, Mountfield.

Sadly, Charlotte died on 24 March 1835 leaving Jesse to raise a young family of seven children aged 3 to 16. In 1836 he married Susanna Silvers, but with the industrial revolution threatening the family with hardship and the workhouse, decided in 1839 to take the opportunity of assisted immigration to Australia. The family sailed from Plymouth on 29 June 1839 on the *Florist* arriving in Sydney on 26 October 1839.[56]

Jesse at first found work with a Mr Manning of Sydney and later worked at Vermont[57] for William Charles Wentworth, later settling in Cobbitty where he had a clearing lease.[58] In later years he moved to Kenny's Hill, then to Elderslie, then to Camden Park before moving back again to Elderslie. The incessant shifting about proved very

---

[55] Some 25,650 applications were made for the medal. The reason for the delay in issuing the medal is said to have been due to the Duke of Wellington, who was opposed to the issue of a standard medal to all ranks – Orders Decorations and Medals [56] The shipping records list the family as Donk
[57] Grant of 1750 acres to William Charles Wentworth, near Greendale, west of Bringelly
[58] Obituary – Thomas Dunk – 23 April 1896

unfavourable to the education of the children, and they were never sent to school to learn to read and write. Susanna died without issue in 1853.

Five years later, on 4 March 1858, Jesse married Sarah Hilder, a girl of just 19. At this time he was 71, but the marriage records stated he was 54. Sarah, also from Mountfield, had arrived on the *Marquis of Hastings* on 4 February 1841 with her parents Eli Hilder and Mary Playford and grandparents Henry Hilder and Keturah Haines. Sarah was only 3 when her mother died, and on 10 August 1842 her father then married Sarah Piall. By the time she was 19, Sarah was desperately unhappy at home and marriage to Jesse gave her a reason to leave. Jesse was kind to her but died on 15 June 1860, less than two years after their marriage. Sarah married Robert George Britt on 19 June 1861.

HEPBURN, Robert William (James): *Rank:* Captain. *Unit:* 39th (Dorsetshire) Regiment of Foot. *Born:* abt. 1791 Omagh, Co Antrim, Ireland. *Arrived:* 23 August 1847 *Phoebe*. *Died:* 14 November 1875 Coleman's Creek, NSW. *Buried:* Coleman's Creek, Burragorang, NSW.

In September 1878 the *Australian Town & Country Journal* published an article written by Ellen Mary Martin: 'Another "Arcadia at Our Gates" –Burragorang'. This article was in response to many of a similar vein that had appeared in the Sydney newspapers during this period, each extolling their own Arcadia. In 1502 Jacopo Sannazaro had published his long poem 'Arcadia' describing it as 'a lost world of idyllic bliss'. Ellen, who had been born and raised in the Burragorang, was inspired to describe her birthplace as 'A veritable Arcadia of innocence and beauty – the home of all that is fair and lovely in rural nature! This charming valley – so little known and poorly appreciated'. There are many today who would agree with her; many who still mourn the loss of this valley to Warragamba Dam.

Within the article Ellen refers to a gentleman she knew, one who had been her teacher. A gentleman well respected in the valley but whose past remains a mystery to this day – 'Burragorang has for me an especial interest, containing the grave, the unmarked grave, of the truest gentleman and most finished scholar I ever knew; one whose whole life was a stirring romance.'

The gentleman in question was known in the Burragorang district as James Hepburn. Hepburn claimed he was formerly a Captain in the British Army, and to have fought under the Duke of Wellington. He claimed that he had served with distinction all through the earlier portion of the Peninsular War, and had been severely wounded at the storming of Badajoz. Some weeks later, he quit the British Army after a quarrel with his Colonel over a matter in which he believed he had been unfairly treated, and then joined the French Army under Marshal Soult. Under the French flag he took part in the Battle of Toulouse gaining distinction both for his strategical ability and bravery.

According to Hepburn his 'brilliant qualities' won him the patronage of the Empress Josephine and he received a personal commendation from the 'Little Corporal', the great Napoleon. During Napoleon's last campaign Hepburn was attached to the famous Imperial (Old) Guard, the most illustrious and formidable corps in the French Army. Hepburn fought at Liguey where the French, under Soult and Messina, forced back the Prussian, Hanoverian, English and Frenchy armies towards Waterloo.

At his own request Hepburn was transferred to Paris under the patronage of Marshal Soult's niece, a Duchess. After the restoration of Louis XVII, the last of the Bourbons to sit on the French throne, as a 'gentleman of culture' together with the influence of his patroness, he entered the Academy of Sciences in Paris as an English tutor, where he remained until the 1830 revolution. He arrived in New South Wales between 1835 and 1840 and found employment as a tutor to several families in the Burragorang district.

Hepburn is believed to have been born in Omagh, Co Antrim, Ireland in 1791. He died after accidentally falling from a cliff at Coleman's Creek, Burragorang on 18 November 1875, aged 84, and was buried in an unmarked grave near where he had died.

Hepburn's saga would have been lost but for an article in the *Camden News* in 1915 when Edward Robert Reilly told his story and begged the readers to subscribe to the Hepburn Memorial Fund. The intention was to re-inter Hepburn's remains in the Upper Burragorang Cemetery with a fitting memorial stone to mark the grave. Nothing seems to have happened after the plea from Reilly. News of what had happened at Gallipoli reached Camden, and Hepburn was again forgotten.

In 1928 Bob Gaudry, a member of the Royal Australian Historical Society, endeavoured to solve the mystery. He contacted the Secretary, Minister for War, in Paris and was advised 'Mr. Hepburn's name does not appear among those of the officers who composed the main army of Marshal Soult 1812–1815. Also this name does not appear in the records of my Department.'

Undeterred, Gaudry contacted the Public Records Office, London and was advised: 'A search has been made in the Army Lists 1808–1817 but James Hepburn does not appear to have served as a Commissioned Officer in the British Army during that period.'

Undoubtedly the mysterious Captain Hepburn had changed his name to avoid the wrath of the British Government and being tried for treason, or that his story has been exaggerated to impress his audience. The battle in which he claims to have been wounded, was the Siege of Badajoz, which took place from 16 March to 6 April 1812, whilst the Battle of Toulouse took place 10 April 1814. There appears to be no reference to any Englishman/Irishman having changed sides to fight for the French, which is surprising if the story were true.

There is no record of a James Hepburn arriving in the colony, but it is believed he was the Captain Hepburn who arrived as a passenger on the *Phoebe* on 23 August 1847. We will never know Hepburn's full story, as the deep waters of Warragamba hide his grave and those that knew him personally are long gone.

HOWE, William: *Rank:* Ensign. *Unit*: 1st Royal Scots Regiment. *Born*: 1776 Dumfriesshire, Scotland. *Arrived:* 22 July 1816 *Atlas. Occupation:* Police Magistrate, Justice of the Peace, settler, farmer, dairyman. *Died*: 1 August 1855 Glenlee, Menangle, NSW. *Buried:* St. David's Presbyterian Church, Campbelltown, NSW. *Spouse:* Mary Twentyman. *Married:* 21 September 1802 Calvertsholm, Annandale, Dumfriesshire, Scotland.

Howe joined the 1st Royal Scots Regiment in 1813 and was an ensign when he participated in the Napoleonic Wars. He resigned from the army in 1815 and the following year sailed to Australia with his family. Howe received a grant of 3000 acres (1214 ha) at Upper Minto in January 1818, which he named Glenlee. Whilst Macquarie regarded Howe as factious and dissatisfied, Samuel Marsden approved of him and recommended him to Commissioner John Thomas Bigge as a man of honour and practical experience in agriculture.[59]

---

[59] Parsons, V., Howe, William (1777–1855), *Australian Dictionary of Biography*, National Centre of Biography, Australian National University, http://adb.anu.edu.au/biography/howe-william-2207/text2859

MACARTHUR, Edward: *Rank:* Major General. *Unit:* (1) 60th (King's Royal Rifles) Regiment (2) 39th (Dorsetshire) Regiment. *Born* 18 March 1789 Bath, Somerset, England. *Died*: 4 January 1872 London, Middlesex, England. *Buried:* Brompton Cemetery. *Spouse:* Sarah Smith Neill. *Married:* 18 November 1862 England.

Sir Edward Macarthur obtained a commission in the 60th (King's Royal Rifles) Regiment and served at Corunna and in Sicily. As a Lieutenant in the 39th Regiment he took part in the Duke of Wellington's campaigns of 1812–1814 and was present at Vittoria, the Pyrenees and the battles in southern France. After brief service in Canada during the War of 1812 he joined the army of occupation in France.

MARTIN, Alexander: *Rank:* Commander. *Unit:* Royal Navy. *Born:* 2 September 1784 Portsea, Hampshire, England. *Parents:* John Martin and Mary. *Arrived:* 2 January 1832 *Caroline. Died:* 7 September 1868 Camden NSW. *Buried:* St. John's Church of England, Camden, NSW. *Spouses:* (1) Henrietta Maria Fullagher (2) Sarah Smith Fullagher.

Edward Macarthur

One retired naval officer was Commander Alexander Martin born in Portsea, Hampshire, England on 2 September 1784, the son of John and Mary Martin. Nearly all his relatives were connected with the Navy, or involved with the dockyards, or shipping; his father had also served in the Navy. He was 11 when in 1795 he joined the Royal Navy as a First-Class Volunteer on board *HMS Triumph 74*[60] serving under Captain Sir Erasmus Gower and later under Captain William Essington. Shortly after joining he was involved in a battle which became known as the Retreat of Cornwallis.

Admiral Sir William Cornwallis[61] and his fleet of four ships of the line and two frigates were cruising near Brest on 16 June 1795 when they were sighted by the French fleet of twelve ships of the line and several large frigates. Admiral Cornwallis was attacked from both sides, but turned to support his rearmost ship, the *HMS Mars*. This convinced the French that the Admiral had other ships within easy reach and they gave up the pursuit.

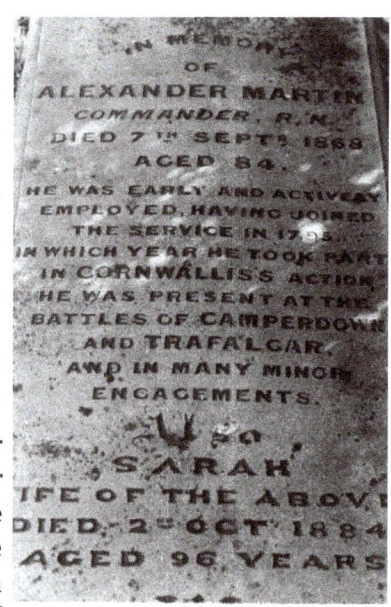

Alexander Martin's tombstone – courtesy Camden Historical Society

Martin also took part in the action near the Dutch coast off Kamperduin[62] (north of Haarlem and north-west of Alkmaar). The Battle of Camperdown was fought at 7:00

---

[60] A number after the name of the ship indicated the number of cannons on board
[61] Admiral Sir William Cornwallis was the brother of the 1st Marquis Cornwallis, General Charles Cornwallis. encyclopedia.jrank.org/Cor_Cre/Cornwallis_Sir_William_1744_181.html Sir William Cornwallis (1744–1819)
[62] Also spelt Camperduin and more popularly as Camperdown

am on 11 October 1797 and both the battle and victory were obviously important to him as he was to later name his property, near Theresa Park, Camperdown.

In January 1799 Martin transferred to *HMS Formidable 98*, under Captains James Hawkins Whitshed, Edward Thornbrough, and Richard Grindall. In that ship he served in the Channel, Mediterranean, and West Indies until September 1802 and towards the end of this period was promoted to Midshipman. He was with Captain Grindall again in 1808 on board *HMS Prince 98*, and was for about three years sailing in the Channel, and off the Port of Cadiz.

Aboard *HMS Prince 98* he was involved in the Battle of Trafalgar[63] which took place on 21 October 1805. This famous sea battle was fought between the British Royal Navy and the combined fleets of the French and Spanish Navies during the War of the Third Coalition (August–December 1805) of the Napoleonic Wars (1803–1815). The battle was the most decisive British victory of the war and was a pivotal naval battle of the 19th Century. Twenty-seven British ships of the line led by Admiral Lord Nelson aboard *HMS Victory* defeated 33 French and Spanish ships of the line under French Admiral Pierre Villeneuve off the south-west coast of Spain, just west of Cape Trafalgar. Martin was later awarded the Naval General Services Medal with clasps for Camperdown and Trafalgar but the medal was not authorised until 1847, and then only awarded where the recipient was still living.[64]

He later sailed on *HMS Glory 98*, under Captain William Albany Otway, and on *HMS Prince 98*, the flagship of Rear Admiral John Child Purvis, both stationed at Cadiz. In December 1807 he was promoted to Acting Lieutenant of the *HMS Terrible 74* under Captain Lord Henry Paulet, and was part of the force employed in the Mediterranean.

In February 1810, he joined *HMS Alacrity 18*, under Captain Nesbit Palmer. In May 1811 that vessel was captured by the enemy, but Martin at the time was absent from the ship as he was in charge of a Greek prize vessel. On 29 October 1811 he was promoted to Lieutenant and was from 2 November 1811 until 8 January 1815 employed on the Leith Station[65] in *HMS Nightingale 16*, under Captain Christopher Nixon.

After the end of the Napoleonic War most of the ships were out of commission, so Martin was compelled to look about for means of adding to his income. He leased a wharf at Chatham, Kent, engaged some Sunderland colliers, and started business as a coal merchant. On 2 September 1816 he married Henrietta Maria Fullagar, the daughter of John Smith Fullagar and Rachel Smart, in Chatham, Kent. Shortly after, the Navy informed him that it was against navy regulations for an officer to engage in business, so he was forced to close the business.

Having one relative in London who was a sugar refiner, and another who was a sugar planter, and member of the Legislature in Jamaica, he took to the sea again, this time trading to Jamaica and St. Kitts, in the West Indies. He next entered the employ of Green, of Blackwell, and was involved in transporting convicts to the colony. He placed his eldest son, Alexander Smart Martin, under the tuition of the Royal Engineers, to learn field surveying at the Brompton & Chatham lines, as his brother-in-law, Smart Fullagar, was a designer in the Chatham Dockyard and he hoped this profession would prove lucrative for his son in Australia.

---

[63] Commander Alexander Martin, RN: A Memoir; by one of his Sons, *Camden News* 25 August 1898 and 1 September 1898
[64] Litherland, AR & Simpkin, BT, *Spinks standard catalogue of British and associated orders decorations & medals with valuations*
[65] Leith Station was in the harbour in Edinburgh, Scotland

Martin and Henrietta had three sons between 1816 and 1821. Sometime prior to 1823 Henrietta died and Martin married her sister, Sarah Smith Fullagar on 23 June 1823 at St. Pancras, London. Their first child, Sarah Henrietta Maria Fullagar was born in Chatham on 26 October 1824, and their son Robert Jonathon Martin was born in Chatham in 1826.

Martin was favourably impressed with the colony, and, after one of his voyages on the *John* in September 1829 (when one of the passengers was Archdeacon, later Bishop, William Grant Broughton) he was given control of the Church and School Corporation whose offices were then in Macquarie Place, Sydney. As the paperwork needed urgent attention, the Archdeacon offered Martin a temporary position as a clerk. After he had completed his work he made Liverpool his headquarters. As the Courts of the time were composed of the military officers of the garrison and half-pay officers of either service, he was soon placed on the court list. He attended the Assize and Quarter Sessions Courts, but also travelled about to see the country as he intended in the future to apply for a grant of land.

After seeing much of the country and acquainting himself with the regulations respecting land grants, he returned to England to bring out his family, expecting to obtain 1000 acres (404.7 hectares) for himself and 640 acres (259 hectares) for each of his children on their coming of age, or marrying.

As there was very little commerce with NSW at this time, he had difficulty in obtaining passage. His delay in returning was further exacerbated when one of his sons was smitten with brain fever. The delays were to completely destroy any hope of his obtaining a land grant. He was finally able to secure a passage on the barque *Caroline* and sold off some property and effects. The family went into lodgings, awaiting notice to join the ship, but many weeks elapsed before they departed Gravesend in August 1831. Arriving in the colony on 2 January 1832 they learned that Governor Sir Ralph Darling had returned to England, and had been succeeded by Major General Sir Richard Bourke, who had arrived just a month before. They then realised the consequences of their having failed to arrive earlier, for an Order in Council had reached the colony with Governor Bourke, abolishing free grants and substituting sale by auction.

Martin appealed to the Governor, who promised to submit the matter to the Home Authorities. He also had his Navy agent in London, Mr. Stilwell, present a petition to the Secretary for the Colonies, showing that he had sacrificed everything in a bona fide effort to become a colonist, in full expectation of obtaining a liberal grant of land, which had been frustrated by the unexpected change. The reply to both petitions was that he had no valid claim as he had not given notice of his intention when leaving the colony, nor at Downing Street, before finally leaving England.

The family first resided at Parramatta, and later on their property of Camperdown, which Martin purchased in 1832. The property consisted of 640 acres (259 hectares) situated below Camden on the left bank of the Nepean River. The neighbouring properties were those of Hannibal Macarthur – Westwood,[66] James Terry Hughes – Theresa Park, and Alexander Macleay[67] – Brownlow Hill. Across the river was William Charles Wentworth's property Vermont.

Martin has been described as being of a cheerful and affectionate disposition. Bishop William Grant Broughton held him in high regard, and he was a frequent

---

[66] Hannibal Hawkins Macarthur (1788–1861), was a pastoralist, politician and businessman. He was born on 16th January 1788 at Plymouth, Devonshire, England, son of James Macarthur, the elder brother of John.
[67] Hon. Alexander Macleay MLC FLS FRS (24 June 1767–18 July 1848) was born on Ross-shire, Scotland, eldest son of William Macleay, provost of Wick.

guest with the Bishop and his family on his visits to Sydney. In 1837 the Bishop placed Martin in charge of the Female Orphan School at Parramatta.[68]

As Martin had not resigned his commission he was still in effect a serving naval officer and had to apply every two years for a fresh leave of absence. During the China Opium War[69] there were concerns that he might be recalled to service, but on 1 April 1853, he was retired on the rank of Commander. He died in Camden on 7 September 1868, aged 84.

SHADFORTH, Thomas: *Rank:* (1) Lieutenant (2) Captain (3) Lieutenant-Colonel. *Unit:* (1) 47th (Lancashire) Regiment of Foot September 1798 (2) transferred as Captain to 57th (The West Middlesex) Regiment of Foot, the Die Hards, May 1802 (3) promoted to Lieutenant-Colonel August 1819. *Arrived:* 23 February 1826 *Mangles*. *Born:* abt. 1771 Newcastle-Upon-Tyne, Northumberland, England. *Parents:* Henry Shadforth and Esther Giles. *Died:* 4 August 1862 Everleigh House, Redfern, NSW. *Buried:* St. Mark's Church of England, Greendale, NSW. *Spouse:* Frances Hinson.

Near the University Farms at Greendale is a monument relocated from the old cemetery of St. Mark's Greendale in November 1980. The inscription reads, *In memory of Thomas Shadforth. Formerly Lieut Colonel of HM 57th Regt who departed this life 4th August 1862 aged 90 years and of Frances his wife who died at Ravenswood 6th October 1850 aged 79 years*. Behind this simple inscription lies the story of a pioneer military family.

Thomas Shadforth was born in Northumberland, England c.1771. His father was a landed proprietor but as a younger son Thomas sought a military career and joined the 47th (Lancashire) Regiment as a Lieutenant in September 1798. He served for a period in the West Indies during the War of 1812 against America, over the blockade of France and other issues, during the Napoleonic Wars, and whilst stationed in Bermuda in 1801 met and married Frances Hinson. He was transferred to the 57th Regiment in May 1802 as Captain.

By 1805 his family was stationed at Gibraltar whilst he, as part of the 57th Regiment, fought Napoleon's forces in the Peninsular Wars. It was during the Battle of Albuera on 16 May 1811 the regiment was to earn the title Die-Hards. The 57th, outnumbered four to one fought bravely despite sustaining appalling casualties, with many of the officers and men killed or seriously injured. Thomas was injured, promoted to Major, and took part in the Battle of Waterloo in June 1815. He was promoted to Lieutenant-Colonel in August 1819.

In February 1826 Shadforth, together with his wife, and daughter Frances Esther, arrived on the convict ship *Mangles* which was carrying 199 male convicts and joined their sons Lieutenant Henry John Tudor and Ensign Thomas (jnr.) Shadforth of the 57th Regiment, who had arrived in August 1825. The youngest son Robert William, after completing his education in England, arrived in May 1834.

During this period, commissariat notes were creating a problem for Governor Sir Ralph Darling. These store receipts had been issued by the Government Store (the Commissariat) for local goods and produce with the intention that producers would accumulate them over a period of time before consolidating them for a single treasury bill; instead the notes were being used as currency. In June 1828 Darling appointed Shadforth president of the board to check and destroy the commissariat notes and

---

[68] Clancy, EG., *A Giant for Jesus: The Story of Silas Gill, Methodist Lay Evangelist* (Waitara, NSW, 1972)
[69] The First Opium War or the First Anglo-Chinese War was fought between the British East India Company and the Qing Dynasty of China from 1839 to 1842

plates from which they had been struck, a task Shadforth promptly and successfully undertook.

When the 57th Regiment was ordered to India in June 1828 Shadforth and his son Henry resigned their commissions. A newly married Thomas (jnr.) was exempted from the order and continued to live near Cobbitty. His son Henry purchased Eveleigh House, Redfern and Shadforth (snr.) purchased Ravenswood at Mulgoa and became a prosperous grazier and leader in the commercial life of Sydney.

In January 1833 Shadforth became Honorary Secretary of the Australian Subscription Library and in June 1833 a Director of the Bank of Australia, and was later appointed to several other important commercial institutions. In 1835 he was President of the Australian Wheat & Flour Co and the Australian Union Benefit Society; in 1836 Deputy-Chairman of the Australian Gaslight Co, and a Director of the Fire & Life Assurance Co and a Trustee of the Illawarra Steam Co, and in 1841 a Trustee of the Savings Bank of New South Wales. When an association was formed to seek permission to import labourers from India in 1842 Shadforth (snr.) was appointed a member.

In March 1843 the Bank of Australia failed, causing great distress and monetary difficulties for the whole colony including the Macarthurs, the Macleays and the Trustees for St. John's Anglican Church then under construction in Camden. Shadforth then retired from public life and settled down to life as a farmer at Mulgoa where his wife Frances was to die on 6 October 1850.

Memorial to Thomas & Frances Shadforth

Thomas Shadforth (snr.) died 'full of years and honours' *at* Eveleigh House, Redfern on 4 August 1862. His obituary reminded readers 'He received several wounds during the peninsular campaign, from which he suffered more or less to the day of his death.'

SHOOBRIDGE, William: *Rank:* Foot soldier. *Unit:* Unknown. *Born:* 23 July 1790 Rolvenden, Kent, England. *Parents:* Thomas Shoobridge and Mary Buss. *Arrived:* 20 February 1864 *Cornwall. Died:* 25 April 1894 Thirlmere, NSW. *Buried:* Upper Picton Church of England. *Spouses:* (1) Mary Ann Piall (2) Jane Kedwell.
Little is known of William Shoobridge other than he was a foot soldier at the Battle of Waterloo.

STARR, William: *Rank:* Foot soldier. *Unit:* 73rd (Perthshire) Regiment of Foot. *Arrived:* 4 April 1839 *Orient. Born:* 4 May 1800 Mountfield, Sussex, England. *Parents:* Thomas Starr and Ann Wood. *Died:* 18 July 1878 Menangle, NSW. *Buried:* St. John's Church of England, Camden, NSW. *Spouse:* Elizabeth Arnold. *Married*: 5 March 1832 Kensington, Middlesex, England.

Starr served under the Duke of Wellington through the Waterloo campaign. He arrived in the colony in 1839 with his wife and three children and resided in Market Street, Sydney, for a brief period before he purchased a cottage and two acres of land at St. Peters. He later purchased a wagon and team of bullocks and trekked to Menangle where he rented, and later purchased, a 100 acre farm owned by Ellen

Rosetta Hughes of Albion House, Surrey Hills, Sydney. There he built a slab house which stood for more than fifty years.

WHEELER, Jonathan: *Rank:* Foot soldier. *Unit:* unknown. *Arrived:* 19 January 1838 *Layton*. *Born:* 4 September 1791 Bisley, Gloucestershire, England. *Parents:* Nathaniel Wheeler and Sarah Fowler. *Died:* 19 May 1855 Camden, NSW. *Buried:* St. John's Church of England, Camden, NSW. *Spouse:* Jane March. *Married:* 4 January 1813 Bisley, Gloucestershire, England.

Wheeler was a foot soldier at the Battle of Waterloo and, according to the baptismal record for his daughter Hester, remained in the army until the end of 1815. Wheeler then returned to Bisley and worked as a weaver but when widespread destitution arose, as the small clothiers who employed spinners and weavers in their mills were replaced by cloth manufacturers and the factory system, Wheeler was among the many that were looking for a new beginning in the colony of New South Wales. On 21 June 1837 the Bisley Parish submitted a list of 68 people selected to travel to the colony on 8 September 1837 on the *Layton* as assisted immigrants.

The Wheeler family were amongst this group and spent approximately five weeks on board the *Layton* prior to their departure and were visited by James Macarthur; Wheeler was selected to work at Camden Park. The voyage was tragic for many when a measles epidemic broke out; the Wheelers' two youngest children were to die at sea. The *Layton* arrived on 19 January 1838 and the Wheeler family made the journey on foot to Elizabeth Farm at Parramatta before continuing the journey to Camden Park.

Jonathan Wheeler was employed at Camden Park as a sawyer, and his sons followed the same trade. He later opened a sawmill at North Cawdor on Mataylor Creek and it was here he cut the timber sourced from Crocodile and Monkey Creeks for the Camden Inn which was erected in 1841 at the corner of Argyle and Elizabeth Streets.

Jonathan felled the ironbark trees and shaped the timber used to construct the roof of St. John's Church of England Camden with the logs being brought from Bargo, The Oaks and Bob's Range. Jonathan and his sons each took a clearing lease of 100 acres (40.5 hectares) of land at Mount Hunter, each joining and bordering on Westbrook Creek. He died on 19 May 1855 after falling from his wagon whilst he and one of his sons were carting wheat to Junee.

WILD, John Henry: *Rank:* Quartermaster Sergeant, Quartermaster, Adjutant Ensign, Lieutenant Adjutant. *Unit:* 2/48th (Northamptonshire) Regiment of Foot. *Born:* abt. 1781 Laois, Ireland. *Arrived:* 30 August 1817 *Lloyds*. *Died:* 6 March 1834 Vanderville, The Oaks, NSW. *Buried:* St. Paul's Church of England, Cobbitty, NSW. *Spouse*: Mary Edwards nee Lynch. *Married* 16 May 1804 Mallow, Co. Cork, Ireland.

Lieutenant John Wild arrived in Australia as part of the 48th (Northamptonshire) Regiment of Foot, under the command of Colonel James Erskine, on 30 August 1817 on the *Lloyds*; with him were his wife, stepdaughter and son. He was promoted to Lieutenant on 3 March 1820.

John Henry Wild – copyright exempt

Wild's main task as the 48th's Adjutant was to ensure that all drills and manoeuvres were carried out under the strict military guidelines of the time. He was discharged from the regiment on 25 September 1822 and was appointed Principal Overseer of Government Stock at Cawdor. He was granted 2000 acres on Werriberri Creek near The Oaks which he named Vanderville.

Sydney Gazette
6 March 1834, page 3

Obituary
John Henry Wild

On Tuesday last, at his residence, Vanderville, after a long and painful illness, Lieutenant Wild, Adjutant of His Majesty's 48th Regiment – a gentleman of the strictest honour and integrity, deeply regretted by a large circle of relatives and friends.

WINTLE, Abraham Joseph: *Rank:* Foot soldier. *Unit:* unknown. *Born:* abt. 1798 Gloucestershire, England. *Parents:* Isaac Wintle and Hannah Moxley. *Arrived:* 26 September 1820 *Shipley*. *Died:* 15 November 1865 at The Oaks, NSW. *Buried:* Upper Picton – Anglican. *Spouse:* Ellen Bourne. *Married*: 13 May 1828 St. John's Church of England, Parramatta, NSW.

Wintle was a foot soldier at the Battle of Waterloo but following the war was unemployed due to the Industrial Revolution. He was convicted of theft and tried at the Monmouth Assizes on 10 August 1818 and sentenced to transportation. He arrived on 26 September 1820 as a convict and received his Certificate of Freedom on 18 August 1825. He later became a farmer at Glen Hill, The Oaks, NSW.

MAORI WARS
1845–1872

A series of armed conflicts took place in New Zealand from 1845 to 1872 between the New Zealand Government and indigenous Maori. Though the wars were initially localised conflicts triggered by tensions over disputed land purchases, they escalated dramatically from 1860 as the Government became convinced it was facing a united Maori resistance to further land sales and a refusal to acknowledge Crown sovereignty. The Government summoned thousands of British troops to mount major campaigns to overpower the Maori King Movement and also acquire farming and residential land for English settlers. Later campaigns were aimed at quashing the so- called Hauhau movement, an extremist part of the Pai Marire religion, which was strongly opposed to the alienation of Maori land and eager to strengthen Maori identity. From 1828 the 58th (Rutlandshire) Regiment of Foot spent 11 years in Ceylon (now Sri Lanka) and then in 1843 escorted convict ships from Britain to the colony of Van Diemen's Land. It remained in Australia for two years before a 14-year posting to New Zealand that included service during the First Maori War (1846–1847). Several men retiring from the regiment decided to stay in New Zealand when the 58th left in 1859, others returned to Sydney or England.

POOLE, John William: *Rank*: Private #551. *Unit:* (1) 58th (Rutlandshire) Regiment of Foot the Black Cuffs (2) 80th (South Staffordshire) Regiment of Foot (3) 99th (Lancashire) Regiment of Foot. *Born:* 1808 Carnew, Wicklow, Ireland. *Parents:* George Poole. *Arrived:* 30 July 1844 *Maria Somes*. *Died:* 1849 Sydney, NSW. *Spouse:* Susannah Richardson. *Married:* 14 June 1843 All Saints Church of England, Great Oakley, Essex, England.

Imperial regiments and colonial forces with Māori prisoners, Whanganui, 1867 – copyright exempt

John Poole enlisted in the 58th (Rutlandshire) Regiment of Foot (known as the Black Cuffs because of the facings on their uniforms). In 1843 it was decided that the 58th (Rutlandshire) Regiment should take over garrison duties in New South Wales from the 80th (South Staffordshire) Regiment of Foot which was going to Madras. The 58th Regiment provided the guards for nineteen convict ships that left London and Ireland for Van Diemen's Land in 1843 and arrived as part of the military detachment on the convict ship *Maria Somes* which arrived in Hobart Town, Tasmania 30 July 1844. As Poole had indicated he wished to remain in the colony, his wife Susannah was able to sail with him.

In May 1845 John was mustered with the main part of his regiment and left for New Zealand to take part in the First Maori War. He and Susannah arrived in Auckland on 28 March 1845 on the ship *Velocity*. Susannah must have been pregnant during this voyage as she gave birth to their son George on 30 June 1845 in Auckland. His regiment took part in the fighting at Okaihau, Ohaeawai, Ruapekapeka, Boulcott's Farm, Horokiri, and St. John's Wood.

Poole and his family returned to Sydney in April 1847 and he was then attached to the 99th (Lanarkshire) Regiment of Foot for the remainder of 1847 and during 1848 until he was placed on furlough awaiting his discharge. A son John William was born on 14 October 1849 in Sydney and Poole qualified for a military pension but died the same year. Susannah Poole then married James Butler in Camden on 24 March 1851 and died 15 July 1898 at Waterloo, Sydney and was buried at St. John's Church of England, Camden.

The 99th (Lanarkshire) Regiment of Foot also saw service during the Maori Wars 1845–1846. This regiment had arrived in Australia as a guard on ships transporting convicts to Van Diemen's Land. After serving some time in the Parramatta area and also Port Phillip, the regiment was sent to New Zealand in 1845 to fight in the Maori Wars and took part in the Hutt Valley Campaign at the Battle of Battle Hill. Following the capture of Te Rauparaha in 1846, the regiment returned to Australia, although

Non-commissioned Officers of the 58th Rutlandshire Regiment of Foot in New Zealand

detachments would be sent as needed to reinforce the British forces in New Zealand for the next few years. For its service in the First Maori War, the regiment earned its first battle honour: New Zealand.

In Sydney the 99th Regiment gained an unsavoury reputation and as a result became very unpopular and the 11th (North Devonshire) Regiment of Foot was brought to Sydney to keep it under control.

GIBSON, James: *Rank:* unknown. *Unit:* 99th (Lanarkshire) Regiment of Foot. *Born:* 1816 Dromore, Tyrone, Ireland. *Arrived*: 16 August 1842 *Kandahar. Occupation:* Chief Constable, Camden. *Spouse:* Margaret Birmingham. *Married* 5 February 1838 Ireland.

Gibson arrived in Hobart Town, Van Diemen's Land with his wife and young son as part of the 99th (Lanarkshire) Regiment of Foot on the convict transport *Kandahar* (also spelt *Candahar*). After disembarking the convicts, the ship travelled on to Sydney where Gibson settled his family in Parramatta. In 1845 he joined his regiment in New Zealand during the First Maori War and took part in the Hutt Valley Campaign at the Battle of Battle Hill.

After the regiment returned from New Zealand he resigned from the regiment and was appointed as the Police Constable in Camden. The family lived in Camden until 1858 before moving to Lismore.

CRIMEAN WAR
4 October 1853–1 February 1856

The Crimean War was a conflict in which Russia lost to an alliance of France, Britain, the Ottoman (Turkish) Empire and was fought mainly on the Crimean Peninsula. In January 1855 Sardinia also joined the alliance.

The conflict was caused by Russian demands to exercise its protection over members of the Orthodox Church who were subjects of the Ottoman Sultan. At the same time there was a dispute between Russia and France over the privileges of the Russian Orthodox and Roman Catholic churches in the holy places in Palestine, particularly Jerusalem and Bethlehem.

Britain supported the Ottoman Empire and together they took a firm stand against the Russians, who had occupied the countries on the Russo-Turkish border in July 1853. The British fleet was ordered to Constantinople (Istanbul) on 23 September and on 4 October the Ottoman Empire declared war on Russia.

On 1 February 1856 Austria threatened to join the alliance and Russia accepted peace terms.

CROSS, Ephraim Snr: *Rank:* Foot soldier. *Unit:* Cambridgeshire Militia. *Born:* 1834 Eli, Cambridgeshire, England. *Parents:* Philip Cross and Ellen. *Arrived:* 23 May 1856 *Robert Small. Occupation:* Brickmaker. *Died:* 18 December 1919 Elderslie, NSW. *Buried:* St. Thomas' Church of England, Narellan, NSW. *Spouse:* Fanny Foreman. *Married:* 25 December 1855 Eli, Cambridgeshire, England.

The Cambridgeshire Militia, originally raised in 1759, was a body of men who, after training, could return to civilian jobs but would attend annual training and be paid a small retainer and could be called up at times of national emergency. By the time of the Crimean War there was only one active battalion of the Cambridgeshire Militia remaining. It served in the Crimean from 1853 to 1856 and fought at many of the now infamous battles such as Alma and Sevastopol.

An article in the *Camden News* of 27 December 1919 gave a short biograph of Ephraim Cross. However, the Editor of the *Camden News* appears to have been unaware that Ephraim had died 18 December 1919, shortly before the article was published.

Camden News
Thursday 27 December 1919, page 1

General Information

Mr. and Mrs. Ephraim Cross, of Elderslie, who four years ago celebrated their Diamond Wedding, are still hale and hearty. Their respective ages are 86 and 84 years, they are natives of Eli, in Cambridgeshire, England, where they were married on Christmas Day, 1855. Shortly after their marriage they left for Australia by the sailing ship Robert Small, *650 tons. After a most eventful voyage, they arrived at Sydney, on 23rd May, 1856. From this it will be seen they have resided in this colony for 63 years, of this period 43 years have been spent in the district of Camden. Of the marriage there were 77 descendants, 65 of whom are living, made up of 3 sons, 5 daughters, 41 grandchildren, and 18 great grandchildren. This is a record that they should well be proud of. Four grandsons served the Country's call, one was a prisoner of war for two years, but all returned little the worse for their adventures.*

In the early days of their settlement they resided near Penrith, where Mr. Cross was engaged by the Government in constructing the main Western Line over the Mountains from Parramatta, and also the route from Parramatta to Blacktown. From here they went to Bega, where he started a brick kiln, this being his occupation, however, their sojourn there did not last long, six weeks elapsed before they saw a living soul. It was from there they came to this district, where, Mr. Cross again commenced manufacturing bricks. Many buildings can now be seen in and around Camden that are constructed from his production. Such works as the Menangle Railway Bridge, the late John Kidd's residence Campbelltown the late E.L. Moore's, Badgally, "Raby" Homestead, and the Campbelltown Grammar School, "Camelot" at Kirkham, Carrington Hospital, Masonic Hall and "Orielton" Narellan, (where his son Ephraim now resides). Perhaps, had Mr. Cross not started this enterprise many of these fine structures would not at present be within this district.

Mr. and Mrs. Cross are pioneers of the highest class, and can relate some very interesting history of the early days within this State, and nothing gives them more pleasure than to sit down and talk these matters over to anybody who is interested in such matters. In the course of an interview with Mr. Cross he states that he had on one occasion gone to Bathurst on business, there were of course no conveyances from Camden so he decided to walk, this he did and covered the journey in two-and-a-half days.

The French Fleet during the Crimean War – Copyright exempt

ONSLOW, Arthur Alexander Walton: *Rank:* Captain. *Unit:* Royal Navy – Baltic Squadron. *Born:* 2 August 1832 Trichinopoly, India. *Parents:* Arthur Pooley Onslow and Rosa Roberta Macleay. *Arrived:* Sydney 1864. *Died:* 31 January 1882 Camden Park, Menangle, NSW. *Buried:* Camden Park Private. *Spouse:* Elizabeth Macarthur. *Married:* 31 January 1867 St John's Church of England, Camden, NSW.

Arthur Alexander Walton Onslow first arrived in Sydney in 1838 and lived for a period with his grandfather Alexander Macleay. In 1841 he returned to England with the widow of Colonel Dumaresq and re-joined his family including his brothers Alexander Campbell Onslow and Francis Montgomery Onslow. Educated in Surrey and Nottingham, he entered the Navy in May 1847 as a midshipman on the *Howe* and served with the Channel and Mediterranean Squadrons, and in the suppression of the slave trade on the West African Coast. In 1852 he became a Lieutenant in the Baltic Squadron during the Crimean War and was at the bombardment of Sveaborg[70] 6 August 1855.

Captain Arthur Onslow – photo courtesy Camden Park House collection

From 1857 to 1861 he was on the ship *HMS Herald* during a survey of Shark Bay, Torres Strait and the Barrier Reef. He came to Sydney with the rank of Captain and retired from the Royal Navy in 1871. In 1874 he travelled with his cousin William Macleay to explore the New Guinea Coast.

SHADFORTH, Thomas (jnr.): *Rank:* Lieutenant Colonel. *Unit:* 57th (The West Middlesex) Regiment of Foot (the Die Hards). *Born:* 1805 Gibraltar. *Parents:* Thomas Shadforth and Frances Hinson. *Arrived:* 22 August 1825 *Minstrel*. *Died:* killed in action 18 June 1855 Sevastopol, Crimea. *Buried:* Cathcart's Hill, Crimea. *Spouse:* Eliza Powell. *Married:* 26 May 1831 St James' Church of England, Sydney, NSW.

Lieutenant Colonel Shadforth was killed in the attack on the Redan Fort in June 1855. He had originally joined the 57th Regiment in 1825 and had arrived in Australia on the *Minstrel* on August 22, 1825. Thomas, his brother Henry and his father were part of the 57th Regiment assigned to the colony.

During the attack on the Redan on 18 June 1855, command of the left column of assault fell to Shadforth almost immediately when Major-General Sir John Campbell was killed as soon as he left the trenches. Shadforth barely had time to give the order: 'Colonel Warre, you mind the right, I will take the left, and Major Inglis the centre', when he too fell dead. The attack quickly degenerated into a dismal failure.

His headstone reads:

> *Sacred to the memory of*
> *Lieut. Colonel Thomas Shadforth*
> *Commanding 57th Regiment*
> *Killed in action June 18th 1855*

Prior to his departure for the Crimea, Shadforth lived on the family property at Greendale (near Bringelly).

---

[70] Suomenlinna, Finland

Empire (Sydney)
Thursday, 22 November 1855, page 5

THE LATE COLONEL SHADFORTH OF THE 57TH

The following letter (says the Times August 10) from the Acting Sergeant Major of the 57th to the widow of Colonel Shadforth, who was killed in the attack on the Redan on the 18th of June, affords a most affecting testimony to the esteem with which the Colonel was regarded by his regiment, and the courage with which he led them to the assault:

Camp before Sevastopol, July 14.

Madam-I trust you will pardon me for presuming to address you while in the midst of such distress, but I consider it my duty to convey to you the deep regret of the non-commissioned officers and men of the regiment at the loss of our late Colonel. He was our father and friend, and watched over the regiment and its wants in a manner that gained for him the adoration of his men; and never did I see more genuine grief among a body of men than what was seen in the 57th Regiment for the poor Colonel, and the memory of his many acts of kindness, of his unflinching courage at the head of his own 'Die-hards', and of his glorious death, will long be a theme in the 57th Regiment.

Such are the feelings of the men of the regiment they have lost their best friend, but I have lost, if possible, more than any of them, for I never experienced such kindness as he invariably showed to me and my welfare. He lost no opportunity in advancing me in my profession, and not only did he look after my temporal, but my spiritual welfare, and if ever a man died a Christian he did.

I spoke to him a few minutes before he fell; the last words I heard him say were, 'Now, Colonel Warre, you mind the right, I will take the left, and Major Inglis the centre' -This was said amidst a shower of missiles of every kind, and he was then as cool and collected as if on parade. Poor Colonel it was the last order I heard him give, and the last time I saw him alive. He could not have suffered much pain from the nature of his wound.

I would have written to you before, but I did not like to intrude upon your grief. If there is any service I can do for you, or any information I, can furnish, I will do so with pleasure; and Boakes knows that if there is anything to be done which, he cannot properly manage I will give him all the assistance in my power.

In conclusion, I beg respectfully to assure you of my best wishes for the welfare of yourself and the young ladies, and I trust you will not consider me too forward in thus addressing you.

I remain, Madam, your very humble servant, GEORGE CUMMING,

Colour-Sergeant and Acting-Sergeant Major, 57th Regiment.

Lieutenant Colonel Shadforth standing 3rd from right – copyright exempt

The following letter from Lieutenant-Colonel Henry James Warre, of the 57th Regiment, is dated

Camp before Sevastopol, June 18.

My dear Mrs. Shadforth, I trust the report from other sources will have prepared you to receive the painful intelligence it becomes my duty, to convey to you.

When I look to the sincere regard all the officers and men of the 57th Regiment felt for our lamented Colonel, it is with unfeigned grief that I am obliged to inform you that he is no more. His gallant spirit fled while leading his men to the unfortunate and unsuccessful attack on the Redan this day.

As a soldier, his 30 years' service in the 57th Regiment has endeared him to officers and men, and the recollection of his devoted attachment to the regiment has spread a gloom through our camp, showing how beloved he was in life and how respected in death. His remains were brought up by his attached men, and they will be interred tomorrow in the cemetery attached to the division, where our late Colonel Goldie and Lieutenant General Cathcart already rest in a soldier's grave.

Pray accept my deepest sympathy and heartfelt condolence for your irreparable loss, and believe me your faithful servant,

HENRY J. WARRE,
Lieutenant-Colonel,
57th Regiment

Colonel Shadforth seems to have felt some presentiment of his approaching fate, for he took leave of his wife and children, the night before the assault, in the following terms:

Before Sevastopol, June 17, p.m.

My own beloved wife and dearly beloved children, -

At 1 o'clock to-morrow morning I head the 57th to storm the Redan. It is, as I feel, an awfully perilous moment to me, but I place myself in the hands of our gracious God, without whose will a sparrow cannot fall to the ground. I place my whole trust in Him. Should I fail in the performance of my duty, I fully rely in the precious blood of our Saviour, shed for sinners that I may be saved through Him. Pardon and forgive me my beloved ones, for anything I may have said or done to cause you one moment's unhappiness. Unto God I commend my body and soul, which are His; and, should it be His will that I fall in the performance of my duty, in the defence of my Queen and country, I most humbly say, 'Thy will, be done.' God bless you and protect you; and my last prayer will be, that He of His infinite goodness may preserve me to you. God ever bless you, my beloved Eliza, and my dearest children; and, if we meet not again in this world, may we all meet in the mansion of our, Heavenly Father, through Jesus Christ, God bless and protect you; and ever believe me, your affectionate husband and loving father,

THOMAS SHADFORTH

Her Majesty, with that anxious consideration for those who have suffered in her service which has always distinguished her, had already signed a warrant granting a pension of £200 a year to Mrs. Shadforth, and had intimated that she would take advantage of any future opportunity which may occur to manifest her appreciation of Colonel Shadforth's services. Colonel Shadforth had a hereditary connection with the 57th, his father, who was severely wounded at Albuera, having served in it for 32 years, and two of his brothers[71] being also officers in the same regiment.

SHARPE, George: *Rank:* Foot soldier. *Unit:* Royal Marines. *Born:* 1838 Bishop's Stortford, Hertfordshire, England. *Parents:* John Sharpe and Mary Miller. *Died:* 27 July 1919 Wickham Fields, Camden, NSW. *Buried:* Glenmore Uniting Church. *Spouse:* (1) Anna Loomes. *Married*: 12 January 1864 St John's Church of England Camden, NSW. (2): Sarah Latty. *Married:* 5 September 1878 bride's residence Greendale, NSW. *Honours:* Crimean War Medal with Sevastopol bar.

Camden News
Thursday 31 July 1919, page 4

GEORGE SHARPE, 85 years

Camden has lost another old and highly respected citizen, Mr. George Sharpe died on Tuesday, 29th inst. at his residence 'Wickham Fields' in his 86th year. Mr. Sharpe, with his many years of colonial life, was an Englishman to the backbone, and was the proud possessor of the Crimean War Medal with the Sevastopol bar, having served in the Royal Marines in that war in 1855; he was on his way with the Navy to the Baltic when peace was declared. His birthplace was Bishop's Stortford, England, but he gave his younger life to seafaring work, and after the war referred to, he journeyed with the British Navy to Rio de Janeiro. On returning

---

[71] Shadforth, John Tudor Shadforth (1803–1890) and Shadforth, Robert William (1810–1900)

thence to England he declared for a new life, and set out for Australia, still a young man.

His first place of labour in this country was at Raby with the late Mr. Edward Moore, and was mainly employed with travelling stock – on one occasion travelling as far as Melbourne by road and track. Leaving this roaming life he was employed by the late Robert Loomes at The Oaks, only later to start farming and dairying on his own account at North Cawdor, on the farm now owned by Mr. V. Thurn. Subsequently he became manager of 'May Farm' for the late Alfred Bennett; from thence he look up land at Mowbray Park in the Picton district, but only to come back to 'May Farm' and his present home nearby, where he resided the last 18 years of his life. The deceased gentleman was a staunch member of the Sons of Temperance, being the oldest member of the Camden branch.

He was twice married; his first wife was a Miss Loomes; his second Miss Latty, both local families. He had seven in his first family, and six in the second. He now leaves a widow, six sons and two daughters; these are Mr. James, Gore Hill; Mr. Alex, Taralga; Mr. Robert, Granville; Mr. Harry, Neutral Bay; Misses Martha and May; Mr. Thomas, and Mr. Benjamin of Camden. There are 17 grandchildren. Two of his sons, Messrs. Robert and Harry, served in the Boer War. The funeral takes place to-day (Thursday).

SUDAN

Mahdist Sudan was an unrecognized state that attempted unsuccessfully to break British rule in Africa. Developments in Sudan during the late 19th Century cannot be understood without reference to the British position in Egypt. In 1869, the Suez Canal opened and quickly became Britain's economic lifeline to India and the Far East. To defend this waterway, Britain sought a greater role in Egyptian affairs. In 1873, the British government therefore supported a programme whereby an Anglo- French debt commission assumed responsibility for managing Egypt's fiscal affairs. This commission eventually forced Khedive Ismail to abdicate in favour of his more politically acceptable son, Tawfiq (1877–1892).

After Ismail's removal in 1877 Major-General Charles George Gordon, who had appointed him in 1880, resigned his post as Governor General of Sudan. His successors failed to continue the policies Gordon had put in place, which led to unrest in the region.

When a serious revolt broke out Gordon was sent back to Khartoum in 1884 with instructions to secure the evacuation of loyalist soldiers and civilians. Gordon succeeded in evacuating 2500 British civilians and then remained in Khartoum with a small group of soldiers and attempted to broker peace with the Mahdists. Muhammad Ahmad, the leader of the Mahdists, laid siege to Khartoum with the siege lasting ten months before the Mahdists finally broke into the city on 26 January 1885 and slaughtered the entire population.

Britain had procrastinated about sending a relief column and it was not until 1 September 1884 that General Garnet Joseph Wolseley (later Lord Wolseley) was asked to head a relief mission which became known as the Nile Expedition or Gordon Relief Expedition. General Wolseley had seen service in the Crimean War, India, Canada, the Gold Coast and southern Africa. His Expedition was composed of two officers and 43 soldiers from each British Light Cavalry Regiment. Wolseley's expedition crossed the desert to Metemmeh (Ethiopia) by ascending the Nile River.

However, the relief column arrived too late as the massacre at Khartoum had occurred two days earlier.

Volunteers for the New South Wales Infantry Contingent for the Sudan at Victoria Barracks, Sydney, shortly before the contingent's departure on 3 March 1885 – photo courtesy Australian War Memorial A05137

Five men with links to the Camden and Picton area are known to have been part of the Sudan Contingent which departed Sydney on 3 March 1885. The Australian contingent did not reach Sudan's port in the Red Sea until 29 March 1885 when the war was almost over. Two other men were also involved as part of British regiments. Henry Beauchamp Lassetter, who had links to both Picton and Camden, was part of Wolseley's Expedition, whilst Walter George Davey was part of the Buffs (Royal East Kent).

CORNWELL, William Charles:
Rank: Gunner/Corporal #941. *Unit*: Artillery Colonial Military Forces (New South Wales Contingent). *Enlisted:* 13 November 1882. *Departed:* 3 March 1885 *SS Iberia.*
Returned: 23 June 1885 *SS Arab. Born:* 10 February 1857 Camden, NSW. *Parents:* George Cornwell and Elizabeth Stephenson. *Occupation:* butcher. *Died:* 5 May 1934 Belmore, NSW. *Spouse:* Margaret Rose. *Married:* 1889 Sydney, NSW.

Cornwell is shown as John Cornwall on his enlistment papers.

William Charles Cornwell – photo courtesy Australian War Memorial

DAVEY, Walter George: *Rank:* Private # S/798. *Unit:* Buffs (Royal East Kent) Regiment. *Born:* 1865 Bristol, Gloucestershire, England. *Parents:* Thomas Davey and Ann. *Occupation:* blacksmith. *Died:* 17 March 1949 Archerfield, Singleton, NSW. *Buried:* Whittingham Anglican Church, Singleton. *Spouse:* Rebecca Bartlett. *Married:* 1886 Robertson, NSW.

Davey also served in the New South Wales Lancers during the Boer War and was a member of the Camden Half Squadron New South Wales Mounted Rifles.

DIVALL, William: *Rank:* Private #28. *Unit:* Artillery Colonial Military Forces (New South Wales Contingent – C Company). *Enlisted:* 18 February 1885. *Departed:* 3 March 1885 *SS Iberia. Returned:* 23 June 1885 *SS Arab. Born:* 1865 Goulburn, NSW. *Parents:* William Divall and Elizabeth White. *Occupation:* labourer, railway guard. *Died:* 24 August 1935 Newcastle, NSW. *Buried:* Sandgate Cemetery, Newcastle, NSW. *Spouses:* (1) Kate Maxwell. *Married:* 1885 Goulburn, NSW. (2) Jane Neill. *Married:*1897 Newtown, NSW. *Honours:* Khedive's Star 1882–1891 (Sudan).

Khedive's Star

Divall served in E Company, New South Wales Volunteer Infantry (Goulburn) before serving in C Company of the Sudan Contingent in 1885. He was a railway guard in Campbelltown and served during the Boer War as a private in the 1st New South Wales Mounted Infantry and in World War I as a Corporal with the 6th Light Horse Regiment. For a short period he had been a member of the Picton Half Squadron New South Wales Mounted Rifles. He was well known in Campbelltown during the Boer War.

FIDDEN, Charles William: *Rank:* Private #330. *Unit:* Artillery Colonial Military Forces (New South Wales Contingent). *Enlisted:* 20 February 1885. *Departed:* 3 March 1885 *SS Iberia. Returned:* 23 June 1885 *SS Arab. Born:* 6 September 1864 Elderslie, NSW. *Parents:* James Joseph Fidden and Mary Hilder. *Occupation:* printer. *Died:* 3 December 1911 Waterloo, NSW. *Spouse:* Olive Matilda Thompson. *Married:* 1905 Newtown, NSW.

Fidden served as a Lance Corporal in the Army Medical Corps (NSW) during the Boer War.

HILDER, Henry: *Rank:* Bombardier #898. *Unit:* Artillery Colonial Military Forces (New South Wales Contingent). *Enlisted:* 11 August 1882. *Departed:* 3 March 1885 *SS Iberia. Returned:* 23 June 1885 *SS Arab. Born:* 17 December 1864 Camden Park, Menangle, NSW. *Parents:* John Hilder and Elizabeth Dunk. *Occupation:* labourer. *Died:* 1 March 1935 Summer Hill, NSW. *Buried:* Woronora columbarium. *Spouse:* Caroline Harriet Barnes. *Married:* 1891 Leichhardt, NSW.

LASSETTER, Henry Beauchamp: *Rank:* (1) Lieutenant (2) Captain (3) Major. *Unit*: 80th (South Staffordshire) Regiment of Foot. *Born:* 19 March 1860 Darling Point, NSW. *Parents:* Frederick Lassetter and Charlotte Hannah Iredale. *Died:* 17 February 1926 Sydney, NSW. *Buried:* South Head Cemetery. *Spouse:* Elizabeth Anne Antill. *Married:* 19 August 1891 St. Mark's Church of England, Picton, NSW. *Honours:* Nile Medal with clasp, Khedive's Star.

Lassetter served for a number of years in the British army, firstly in 1880 as a Second Lieutenant with the 38th (1st Staffordshire) Regiment of Foot. In 1881 he transferred to the 80th (South Staffordshire) Regiment of Foot as a Lieutenant and served under General Garnet Joseph Wolseley in 1884 as part of the Nile Expedition in the Relief of Khartoum. He was promoted to Captain in 1887 then returned to New South Wales in 1888 as a Major and raised and trained the New South Wales Mounted Rifles.

*The return of the Sudan Contingent, Circular Quay, Sydney, NSW 23 June 1885.
Photo taken by the Studio of Henry King*

ONSLOW, Harry Hamilton: *Rank:* Corporal #474. *Unit:* New South Wales Contingent Sudan, B Company. *Enlisted:* 23 February 1885. *Departed:* 3 March 1885 *SS Iberia*. *Returned:* 23 June 1885 *SS Arab*. *Born:* 15 July 1858 London, Middlesex, England. *Parents:* Charles Hamilton Onslow and Mary Douglas Onslow. *Occupation:* mining engineer. *Died:* 1899 London, Middlesex, England.

Harry, a cousin of Arthur Alexander Walton Onslow, was living at Camden Park prior to the Sudan conflict and continued to live at Camden Park for a time after his return from the Sudan. He was a mining engineer for a period after his return from the Sudan but 'lost the use of his right arm through an unfortunate accident and was given recuperation time at Camden Park'.[72] He went on to draw 'the beautiful plans of the orchard and the old dairy complex, which he drafted with his left hand after much practice'.[73]

Horatio Herbert Kitchener (later Lord Kitchener) became Commander of the Egyptian Army in 1892 and started preparations for the re-conquest of Sudan. Britain's aim was to establish control over the Nile to safeguard the dam planned for Aswan. In 1895 the British government authorised Kitchener to launch a campaign to reconquer Sudan.

---

[72] Macarthur-Onslow, A., From the Old to New South Wales: the life of Astley John Onslow Thompson, *Camden History: Journal of the Camden Historical Society Inc.* March 2015, Vol 3, Number 9 Special Edition, pp 304-331
[73] ibid

CHITRAL EXPEDITION: INDIA
3 March–20 April 1895

From 1813 there was rivalry between the British and Russian Empires for supremacy in Central Asia. The British Empire saw Russian incursions into Central Asia as a threat to their supremacy in the region and feared that the Emirate of Afghanistan might provide a staging post for Russia's invasion of India. In 1838 Britain launched the first Anglo-Afghan War in an attempt to force a puppet regime on Afghanistan, but in 1842 Britain was forced to retreat back to India.

Russia continued to press steadily forward into Central Asia and by 1868 had annexed Samarkand. British Prime Minister Benjamin Disraeli proposed that Russia should be forced back to the Caspian Sea and introduced the Royal Titles Act of 1876 which added Empress of India to Queen Victoria's titles. In 1878 Russia sent an uninvited diplomatic mission to Kabul, and Britain then demanded that Sher Ali, the ruler of Afghanistan, accept a British mission. However, the mission was turned back, so in retaliation Britain sent a force of 40,000 men into Afghanistan, thereby launching the second Anglo-Afghan War.

Britain was successful and placed Abdur Rahman Khan on the throne, who agreed to let the British control Afghanistan's foreign affairs, while he consolidated his position. Khan managed, with ruthless efficiency, to suppress internal rebellions bringing much of Afghanistan under central control. However, in 1884 Russian

Chitral Fort – London Illustrated News 1895 – copyright exempt

expansionism brought another crisis when they seized the Oasis of Merv and then fought the Afghan troops over the Oasis of Panjdeh. To prevent a war Britain accepted Russian possession of territory north of the Amu Darya as a fait accompli.

Both Russia and Britain failed to consult with Afghanistan when between 1885 and 1888 the Joint Anglo-Russian Boundary Commission agreed that Russia would relinquish territory captured in their advance but retain Panjdeh. However, in 1889 Russia entered Chitral territory as well as Hunza.

After the death of Abdur Rahman Khan the new ruler was Aman-ul-Mulk II of the Katoor Dynasty. When he died in 1892 one of his sons, Afzul-ul-Mulk, seized the throne and killed as many of his half-brothers as he could. However, the old ruler's brother, Sher Afzul Khan, secretly entered Chitral with a few supporters and murdered Afzul. Nizam-ul-Mulk, another of Khan's sons, who had fled to the British at Gilgit, advanced toward Chitral. Realising he was outnumbered Sher fled back to Afghanistan and Nizam took the throne with the blessing of the British.

Within a year Nizam was murdered by his brother Amir-ul-Mulk and Sher Afzul Khan re-entered the contest. George Scott Robertson, the senior British officer at Gilgit, moved into the fortress for protection which increased local hostility. Sher Afzul and an ally, Umra Khan, continued their march towards Chitral, while secret messengers were sent out requesting help.

The Chitral Fort was relieved by two expeditions, a small one from Gilgit under Colonel James Kelly and a large one from Peshawar under Major-General Sir Robert Low. Captain James William Macarthur-Onslow was part of the relief expedition under Major-General Low.

Captain James Macarthur-Onslow was one of four New South Wales officers, who at the behest of Major-General Edward Hutton, took up an offer to serve with units of the British Indian Army, including the 11th Hussars (Prince Albert's Own), the Royal Regiment of Artillery and 60th (King's Royal Rifles), to gain operational experience. Following the completion of his secondment, Macarthur-Onslow volunteered to delay his return and took part in the Chitral Expedition.

MACARTHUR-ONSLOW, James William: *Rank:* Captain. *Unit:* 60th (King's Royal Rifles) Regiment. *Born:* 7 November 1867 Camden Park, Menangle, NSW. *Parents:* Arthur Alexander Walton Onslow and Elizabeth Macarthur. *Died:* 7 November 1946 Camden Park, Menangle, NSW. *Buried:* Camden Park Private Cemetery. *Spouse:* Enid Emma Macarthur. *Married:* 15 December 1897 St John's Church of England, Darlinghurst,

James William Macarthur-Onslow in his King's Royal Rifles Regiment uniform – photo courtesy Camden Park House collection

Honours: Chitral Relief Force Medal including storming of Malakand Pass and Khar medal with clasp.

During the Chitral Expedition James William was part of the 60th (King's Royal Rifles) Regiment (a light mounted infantry regiment). This Regiment had been raised in North America on Christmas Day 1755 and continued to serve during WWII. The regiment formed part of the Chitral Relief Force under Brigadier-General A.A. Kinloch and distinguished itself in the battle of Malakand on 3 April 1895 and in action at Khar on the following day. Besides its Chitral honours this regiment also received honours at the Battle of Seringapatam, India in 1799.

Camden News
Thursday, 4 July 1895 page 3

From Abroad

Captain A.J. Onslow Thompson, of the Camden Mounted Rifles, has kindly handed to us for publication the following interesting extract from a letter received from Captain James Onslow, who is now on Active Service in India.

King's Royal Rifles' Camp
Birram, Swat[74]
20th May 1895

I am now going to write you some sort of account of my experiences in this campaign. Leaving Peshawar on 29th April, we had two days' march to Noushera,[75] which is the railway base for the expedition. The 1st Brigade, viz, the K. R. Rifles, Bedfords, 16th Sikhs, 37th Dogras, and two squadrons of the 11th Bengal Lancers, were to come together at Hoti-Mardau,[76] one day's march from Noushera. There were four brigades, the Divisional Cavalry and three mountain batteries, making nearly 20,000 men. The 1st and 2nd Brigades were to push on as fast as possible to relieve the Chitral Garrison, and so we took no tents, very little baggage, and only 20 days' rations. The 3rd was to follow in support, and the 4th to remain at the base at Mardau on Dargai[77] as a reserve. The 1st Brigade was to advance through the Shahkot Pass and the 2nd through the Malakaud.[78] That was the plan as given out in orders. What happened was as follows: –

We, the 1st Brigade, marched from Mardau to Sandiquar at the entrance of the Shahkot Pass. This was over the frontier, so we had outposts round the camp, with one of which I was. It rained hard all night and we had not even the shelter of waterproof sheet shanties, which we could have rigged up in camp. However, we had the satisfaction of seeing the mountains in front of us covered with little fires where the nigger [sic] tribes were encamped, and with whom we expected to fight in the morning. At daylight we looted a hedge made of dry thorn bush and had a bonfire to warm ourselves. To everyone's surprise the bugles sounded no parade and we did not move till some hours after the time we expected, and then instead of going to the

---

[74] The people of Swat are mainly Pashtuns, Kohistanis and Gujars
[75] Nowshehra or Naushera is a town and a notified area committee in Rajauri district in the Indian state of Jammu and Kashmir.
[76] A fort in Yusufzai
[77] On India's northwest frontier
[78] Another pass

Shahkot Pass we turned to our left and marched to Dargai at the foot of the Malakaud, where we joined the 2nd and 3rd Brigades again. Our two squadrons had in the meantime gone to make a demonstration of forcing the Shahkot so as to keep its defenders employed. We were up before daybreak on the morning of the 3rd April, and watched the 2nd Brigade, which was camped about a mile in front of us, marching off up the Malakaud and disappearing round a hill corner. Soon after we followed them and then halted at the entrance of the pass. About 10 o'clock the artillery were heard going hammer and tongs and about 12 o'clock we were ordered to advance. We soon got across two miles of rough Country and came in sight of the guns pounding at men waving flags on the hill tops at range of 2000 yards or so, and saw the guides and Sikhs climbing a hill which took them four hours to get up, under a desultory fire. Then we came to the other Brigade which soon after started up the hill, then came the order for us to go and shortly after the 16th Sikhs were ordered to follow us. We were some way up the hill when they started, and I shall never forget looking back and seeing them coming up fairly ramping with fury, the men waving their guns over their heads and yelling the Sikh war cry, and for us to go on. For lots of their friends and relations had been killed in the party which was cut up in Chitral, besides all the Pathans and Hill Mahomedans are their hereditary foes.

Of course we soon lost all formation; we could see the two Scotch regiments struggling up the hill to our right with the bag-pipes going hard. And then the poor Sikhs were recalled to their great disgust. About half way up we came on an old road which had been made ages ago by the old Buddhists inhabitants of the country; and it was a real godsend to us. Almost immediately after we came under fire. For the first few minutes bullets make a very nasty noise, but one soon gets used to it. We could only go at a walk and were being fired at from two sides as we were immediately under the big Sangar or stone breastwork; and the K.O.S. Borders could not get up the Spur on our right. Two men were shot alongside me. But as we could not get on without great loss, we got behind stones and any sort of cover there was. I was with the Colonel, the Adjutant, and about eight men behind a big rock. The Adjutant and I got wounded men's rifles and did a lot of shooting. By this time the guides had got on the top and were coming along the crest of the hill. This was what we had been waiting for, so we went up and the Swats[79] ran. Some of them shammed dead and tried to kill men as they went past, so after that there was a lot of bayonetting, which was rather beastly to see. And when we got into their main position it was rather nasty. Luckily there was some shade, for I was nearly dead from the sun and most of us had our tongues hanging out. The men had emptied their water bottles long before they were a quarter of the way up; I hadn't touched mine which was very foolish, as I ended in giving most of it away. But we soon found water on the other side of the pass where we went down and camped after the roll had been called.

We all went on; the Second Brigade went back to Dargai for the night. As the guns and ammunition transport had to come over there was no time to get the commissariat over too, so we got no supper and just lay down to go to sleep. Luckily, there was any amount of dry grass for beds. Some of the wounded men who were with us had a very bad time. Next morning the Khan of Dir who had been hunted out of his dominions by Umra Khan, came

---

[79] People from the Administrative District of Swat

in with 300 of his followers to offer his help. After parleying with Kinloch, our General, for some time he went off. Then about 12 o'clock our hearts were gladdened by seeing the commissariat people coming in. But just as our meals were cooked, back came the Khan of Dir to say that the Bedfords and 37th Dogras, who were some three miles further on—near Khar—were being attacked by 12,000 men and soon we could hear the firing, so off we had to go. The hills were like an ant heap that has been dug up by niggers [sic]. All the defenders of the Shahkot, disappointed of their fight, had come over thirsting for blood. They tried to rush the Bedfords and Dogras again and again, and the volley firing was almost continuous; sometimes one man would rush down by himself and sometimes fifty. Then they tried to get round our flank and rush the baggage. So we (the KRR[80]) had to form between them and the long string of mules and ponies, but unfortunately they never came nearer than 1000 yards to us. The Dogras and Sikhs got into a tight place round a low spur of the hills which hid them from our view, where they used nearly all their cartridges. However, a squadron of the Guides Cavalry rounded the comer quietly and caught the enemy in the open and soon chased them up the hills, meantime the mountain guns gave them a fearful bashing on the hill tops where they stood waving flags and yelling their war cry. I saw a group of flags knocked down by bursting shells five times in succession, and each time more men stood out to wave them. By this time the baggage was pretty well all through and packed out on the plain, so we formed a strong rear guard and went after it. We had been baggage guard or gun escort the whole day, so did not have much fun except sitting still while men fired at us from about 1000 yards, all their shots fell about 50 yards beyond us. We spent the whole night in a square with our arms by our sides as it was expected there would be a night attack, and in fact their scouts did crop up, but finding we were ready did not come on. It was the most miserable night I ever spent, being hungry, cold and very tired, expecting an attack hourly. Next day we heard we were not to go on to Chitral, but to garrison the Swat Valley,[81] and protect the line of communication. We heard the firing of two more fights in the next two days, and were ordered to go forward to one, but it was over before we got there. Since then we have been making forts and roads, and some of us have had the luck to be sent reconnoitring.

***Camden News*
Thursday, 12 March 1896, page 4**
Menangle

FROM OUR OWN CORRESPONDENT

A lecture was delivered in the local hall on Friday last by Major Onslow on his late experience with the British forces during their march to the relief of Chitral, a fort situated in North West India. Mr John Hickey was voted to the chair. Major Onslow on appearing was received very cordially by a large audience, some of whom had come a considerable distance to hear his address, which was listened to throughout with marked attention.

On commencing the Major appeared a trite nervous, but before many minutes had elapsed he was perfectly self-possessed and had put himself on good terms with his audience. The opening remarks of the lecture detailed the cause of the trouble,

---

[80] King's Rifle Regiment
[81] The Swat River rises in the Hindu Kush range

which in this case was a not uncommon one amongst savage races, a chief had died and there at once sprung up a number of claimants to the governorship of the district, no sooner had one relative of the late chief got hold of the reins of government, than along came another who thought he had more right to the throne, seized the first claimant, cut his head off, and then started to rule the country in his own way, only to be turned out and beheaded in a short time himself, and so things went on until at last Umra Khan forced himself into prominence, by acting on the advice of Russian agents and Mahomedan Priests and ordered the British out of the country. He started by investing Chitral, a fort then held by a nephew of his own under the guidance of Dr. Robertson as British resident. The Indian Government then sent out two relief forces, the one under Colonel Kelly and the other commanded by General Low, to the latter of which was attached the 60th Rifles and to this corps Major Onslow was appointed as a volunteer.

The lecturer described the departure of this column from Peshawar and in doing so gave great praise to the native regiment of Sikhs, for their soldierly and martial appearance. After describing the country through which the forces had to pass, and portraying several acts of bravery by the various divisions of the relieving force, the Major told how news was received that the column under Colonel Kelly had destroyed Umra Khan's army and saved Dr. Robertson at Chitral, and thus put an end to all strife for the time being. Major Onslow has undoubtedly gained useful military knowledge by personal experience of the hardship and danger of a soldier's life, and this knowledge would be of great service to him in the event of Australia being forced into war by any foreign power.

A vote of thanks was carried by acclamation to the gallant Major for his excellent and interesting address, and to Mr. Hickey for presiding.

Camden News
Thursday 16 January 1896

A Complimentary Picnic will be given by the No. 2 (Camden) Coy, Mounted Rifles to Capt. Macarthur-Onslow, on his return from active service in India, at Camden Park, near the Cricket Ground, on Saturday the 18th inst., from 3 to 7 p.m.

Picnic at Camden Park, Captain James William Macarthur-Onslow standing centre

THE NORTH-WEST INDIAN FRONTIER: 1897–1898

The North-West Indian Frontier which includes the present-day Khyber Pakhtunkhwa region of the Indian Empire was of strategical and military importance during the late 19th Century and remains the western frontier of present-day Pakistan. The two main passes on the North-West Frontier during the 19th Century were the Khyber and Bolan.

The Government of British India had given a subsidy to the local Afridi tribe in return for the safeguarding of the Khyber Pass. This included the Punjab Frontier, Samana and Tirah. This arrangement had been in place for sixteen years before the tribesmen suddenly rebelled and captured all the posts in the Khyber held by their own countrymen, and attacked the forts on the Samana Range near the city of Peshawar.

Apart from an obituary to George Lewis little is known of the involvement of Walter Jones or George Lewis apart from the archives of the 48th (Northamptonshire) Regiment of Foot but they were not part of the Division of twelve men led by 2nd Lieutenant A.H. Macintyre who were killed 9 November 1897 as part of the Saran Sar battle.

The Brisbane Courier
Monday 15 November 1897

**INDIAN FRONTIER
THE NORTHAMPTONSHIRE REGIMENT
AN HEROIC DEFENCE,
A MESSAGE FROM THE QUEEN
FURTHER OPERATIONS
SECOND SUCCESSFUL
RECONNAISSANCE
A QUEENSLAND OFFICER**
(By Cable Message)

LONDON, November 12.

Further particulars from the Indian frontier regarding the men of the Northamptonshire Regiment (which formed the rear-guard of the British force when the latter retired after the reconnaissance at Saran Sar), who were at first reported as missing, and were afterwards found to have died fighting to the last, show that the bodies were stripped by the enemy, but were not in any way mutilated.

48th (Northamptonshire) Regiment of Foot at Saran Sar – Copyright exempt

Great courage was displayed by the British troops in retiring as, owing to the difficult nature of the country, and the harassing attacks of the tribesmen, the retreat was terribly trying even to the most experienced troops.

A movement is on foot in India for the erection of a monument to commemorate the gallantry displayed by the Sikh troops who have lost their lives in the recent fighting on the frontier.

General Gaselee has made a second reconnaissance at Saran Sar, with successful results, the enemy's defences being destroyed.

LONDON, November 13.

General Lockhart,[82] Commander-in-Chief on the Indian frontier, has informed the Orakzal tribesmen, who have been treating for peace, that the only terms of peace that will be accepted are the surrender of 300 breech-loading rifles, the surrender of the arms and property that have been looted by them since the outbreak of hostilities, the payment of a fee of 35,000 rupees, the forfeiture of the subsidies hitherto paid to them by the Indian Government for keeping open the passes, and the formal submission of the tribesmen at a durbar[83] to be held a fortnight hence.

It is announced that General Lockhart will visit every part of the disturbed country as a friend of the enemy.

Her Majesty the Queen has sent a cable message to the Earl of Elgin,[84] Viceroy of India, stating that she is much distressed at the losses that have been sustained in the fighting on the Indian frontier, and expressing her admiration of the heroism displayed by the troops.

Later reports regarding the death of the men of the Northamptonshire Regiment in the retreat from Saran Sar state that Lieutenant McIntyre and his men refused to desert the wounded, and fought so gallantly that the enemy were afraid to rush them, but they were all eventually shot down at close range.

Captain R. Gordon, of Queensland, has been attached to the Gordon Highlanders, who form part of the force now operating against the Afridi stronghold at Tirah.

48th (NORTHAMPTONSHIRE) REGIMENT of FOOT

The 48th (Northamptonshire) Regiment of Foot was a line infantry regiment of the British Army that existed from 1741 to 1960. The regiment received battle honours for actions in the North West Frontier Province and the Second Boer War.

JONES, Walter: *Rank:* Private #3190. *Unit:* 48th (Northamptonshire) Regiment of Foot. *Buried:* Camden General – Anglican. *Honours:* India Medal with clasps Punjab Frontier 1897–1898, Samana 1897 and Tirah 1897–1898. He also saw active service with this regiment during the Boer War. The burial records for St. John's Church of England, Camden list him as 'an Imperial Soldier – old age pensioner'.

LEWIS, George: *Rank:* Private 4476. *Unit:* 48th (Northamptonshire) Regiment of Foot. *Born:* 1875 Kingsthorpe, Northhampton, England. *Parents:* Edward Lloyd Lewis and Mary Wall. *Died:* 27 June 1930 Camden Hospital, Camden, NSW. *Buried:* Camden General – Anglican. *Spouse:* Emily Kate Wilson. *Honours:* India Medal with clasps Punjab Frontier 1897–1898, Samana 1897 and Tirah 1897–1898.

Lewis also saw active service with this regiment during the Boer War before arriving in Australia in 1921. An obituary for George Lewis can be viewed under his Boer War record.

---

[82] Lockhart, General Sir William
[83] The court of an Indian ruler
[84] Bruce, Victor Alexander – 9th Earl of Elgin; 13th Earl of Kincardine – Viceroy of India 1894–1899

THE NEW SOUTH WALES MOUNTED RIFLES: 1888–1913

Following the withdrawal of British forces, a regular defence force was enrolled in 1870. In 1874 the land orders for volunteers were abolished, and a direct system of partial payment introduced. However, all the volunteers were gradually disbanded, or merged in the partially-paid forces.

New South Wales subsequently sought advice from Britain and Sir William Francis Drummond Jervois, Major General in Her Majesty's Army visited the colony and provided a report.

The Sydney Mail and *New South Wales Advertiser*
Saturday 9 June 1877

THE DEFENCES OF THE COLONY

The following is the preliminary report by His Excellency Sir W. Jervois,[85] RE, CB, KCMG, on the defences of the colony, and which was laid before Parliament last evening:

> *Sydney, 4th June, 1877. Sir, — In accordance with the request of the Earl of Carnarvon, that I should report upon the military defences of the Australian colonies, whose Governments had asked his Lordship to name an officer of the Royal Engineers to advise with reference thereto, I commenced my investigation in this colony at the beginning of last month, accompanied by Lieutenant-Colonel Scratchley,[86] R.E., who was nominated by Lord Carnarvon[87] to assist me in this duty.*
>
> *Since that time I have inspected the works already constructed for the defence of Port Jackson, — the country between the Hawkesbury and Wollongong, — the harbours, bays, and coast between the latter place and Broken Bay, and I have visited the Port of Newcastle. I have received much information from gentlemen well acquainted with the country, especially from the officers of the several departments of Government concerned in the object of my inquiry, and 1 have much pleasure in acknowledging the ready assistance thus afforded me.*
>
> *As my visits to the other colonies must occupy some months, and as it will therefore be a considerable time before I can furnish a general report, I now submit a preliminary memorandum respecting the defences of New South Wales in order that your Excellency's Government may be informed at once of the conclusions at which I have so far arrived.*
>
>
>
> *I have the honour to be, Sir,
> Your obedient humble servant,
> Wm. F. Drummond Jervois*
>
>

4th REGIMENT NSW VOLUNTEER INFANTRY

In 1868 the military force was reorganised under the Volunteer Regulation Act, passed towards the close of the previous year. To stimulate volunteering in the colony the Legislature had recourse to a novel method. For continuous and

---

[85] Jervois, Sir William Francis Drummond - a British military engineer and diplomat
[86] Scratchley, Lieutenant-Colonel Sir Peter Henry – military engineer & Colonial Administrator
[87] Herbert, Lord George – 5th Earl of Carnarvon

efficient service for five years each man received a grant of 50 acres of land. This rule continued in force until 1874. This appears to have answered its purpose for while it prevailed the force reached a strength of 2884. On the abolition of land grants a system of partial payment came into place, and in 1878 a further reorganisation of the volunteer troops of the colony took place in accordance with a plan drawn up by Sir William Jervois, and the force served under the Act of 1867 as amended in that year. A corps of Naval Artillery Volunteers, who were to receive no remuneration, but only an allowance for instruction and incidental expenses, was raised in 1882, and it was followed a few years later by numerous bodies of military reserves on the same footing, but all were gradually disbanded or merged into the partially-paid forces of the colony. For many years, in fact until the end of 1895, the Sydney Scottish Rifles were the only effective Volunteer Corps in the colony. In the beginning of 1896, there was an outburst of patriotism and military enthusiasm in Sydney which resulted in the subsequent organisation of the St George's Rifles, the Irish Rifles, the Australian Rifles, and the National Guard. The 4th Regiment NSW Volunteer Infantry was formed in 1877; it had originally been established in 1855 as the Newcastle Volunteer Artillery and Infantry Corps and renamed, in 1860, the Newcastle Volunteer Rifles. In 1893 it was one of four partially-paid regiments in the colony comprised of ten companies, each with a small permanent staff.

PEGUM, Stephen: *Rank:* Captain. *Unit:* 4th Regiment NSW Volunteers. *Born:* 1844 Co Limerick, Ireland. *Occupation:* school teacher, farmer. *Died:* 27 July 1914 Camden, NSW. *Buried:* Camden Catholic church. *Spouse:* Helena Ann Gorman.

Pegum is listed on the Teachers' Rolls for 1869 to1908 but little is known of him apart from his obituary.

Camden News
Thursday, July 30 1914

OBITUARY

STEPHEN PEGUM, JP, ÆAT 71

We deeply regret to announce the passing away of Captain Stephen Pegum, JP of Brownlow Hill. He died on Monday afternoon the 27th inst, after only a short illness. Some weeks ago he injured one of his fingers, and despite surgical and medical attention blood poisoning ensued, and so in the end this well-known gentleman had to respond to the 'Last Call' of the trumpet. Mr Pegum was born at Bally, Neety, Limerick, Ireland and came to Australia 42 years ago. Shortly after his arrival, and after many trials and adventures, he settled in the Burragorang Valley. Prior to the period named he became one of the soldiers of the 4th Regiment (Volunteers) NSW, and ultimately became the Captain of the Regiment. Years afterwards he retired from active service, this was some 26 years past, on a pension well and worthily earned, a big tribute to his manhood and worth. The deceased gentleman was highly educated, a student in Greek, Latin and French languages. His prominent mark was made in agricultural pursuits, a keen student in this vast, nay, most important art – almost even now in Australia not at its limit, for there is no limit to agricultural knowledge. Whether Capt. Pegum was a financial agriculturalist is not known; enthusiasts in any sphere of life or avocation are not men who seek riches quickly. Mr Pegum had the fluent pen of an educated Irishman, who are born writers as well as orators, a significant fact. Mr Pegum, after leaving the Burragorang Valley, leased a farm at Camperdown, Brownlow Hill, on the rich flats of the Nepean River; he gave full vent to his experience and practical knowledge. He could use the plough arms as well as reaping his crops. Mr. Pegum was a writer in magazines, short pretty stories, full of facts; indeed he was an idealist, a most frequent contributor to the Camden News, which were received with thanks and again without price. Mrs. Pegum survives her husband; there are two daughters and one son: Misses Mary and Helena and Mr. George. The funeral took place on Tuesday at the North Cawdor Cemetery; the officiating clergyman being the Reverend Father Hogan, Mr W Peters conducting all the arrangements necessary.

The New South Wales Mounted Rifles were enrolled in 1885 as a partially-paid body, and were strengthened by the inclusion of a large part of the Light Horse. The *Government Gazette* of Friday 13 June 1885 approved the formation of a Volunteer Corps in Camden:

VOLUNTEER CORPS: The Governor has given authority, under the 5th section of the Volunteer Force Regulation Act of 1867, for the formation of volunteer corps at the following places (to be under the reserve System):- Camden : Infantry to be attached to the 1st Regiment West Maitland Mounted Infantry.

Shortly after this announcement Frederick William Arthur Downes of Brownlow Hill, Camden was appointed Captain of the Camden Reserve Corps of Volunteer Infantry and Arthur George Eagar was appointed First Lieutenant.

At the end of 1892 the rifle companies were disbanded, and civilian rifle clubs formed.

DOWNES, Frederick William Arthur: *Born:* 6 March 1855 Greystanes, NSW. *Parents:* Jeremiah Frederick Downes and Sarah Ann Kirk. *Occupation:* bank clerk, farmer, alderman. *Died*: 3 December 1917 Brownlow Hill, Camden, NSW. *Buried*: St Paul's Church of England, Cobbitty, NSW. *Spouse:* Caroline Frances May Thomas. *Married*: 12 April 1883 St Paul's Church of England Cobbitty, NSW.

Downes attended Macquarie Fields School and The King's School in Parramatta before becoming a bank clerk. Later he was a wheat and dairy farmer in the Camden area and became active in the local farmers' union. From 1885 to 1888 he was a Captain in the Camden Reserve Corps of Volunteer Infantry. In 1904 Downes was elected to the New South Wales Legislative Assembly as the Liberal member for Camden and served as a backbencher until his retirement in 1913.

The Volunteer Corps was absorbed into the Camden Reserve Rifle Company formed on 26 November 1888. Richard Benson Warren was appointed Honorary Captain on 15 February 1889 and held the position until he resigned on 9 March 1891 and was replaced by WR Cowper.

WARREN, Richard Benson: *Born:* 10 October 1855 Buckinghamshire, England. *Parents:* Latham Coddington Warren and Harriett Davidson. *Died:* 31 July 1891.

Little more is known of Warren other than he was a member of the Camden Reserve Corps of Volunteer Infantry when it was formed. He does not appear to have died in New South Wales.

COWPER, William Robert: *Born:* 6 May 1858 Sydney, NSW. *Parents:* Charles Cowper and Mary Copeland Lethbridge. *Occupation:* Manager, Commercial Banking Company, Camden. *Died:* 3 November 1925 Bowral, NSW. *Buried:* Bowral Church of England. *Spouse:* Ada Medora Elliott.

In 1914 'A Short History of N.S.W. Mounted Rifles 1888–1913' was published (authors unknown). This publication is now out of print, and copyright, but it was probably written by an Officer of the Mounted Rifles who was part of the Jubilee Contingent. The Australian Light Horse Studies Centre has a handwritten first draft which is titled 'Historical Records 2nd A.L.H.R. Coy Mounted Rifles'. Whilst the draft is in some instances identical to the published History there are a number of significant differences.

As the history ends in 1912 after the resignation of Astley John Onslow Thompson it is possible he was one of the authors. Another possible contributor was Richard Charles Holman, as it is only in the handwritten history that he is mentioned as the first recruit.

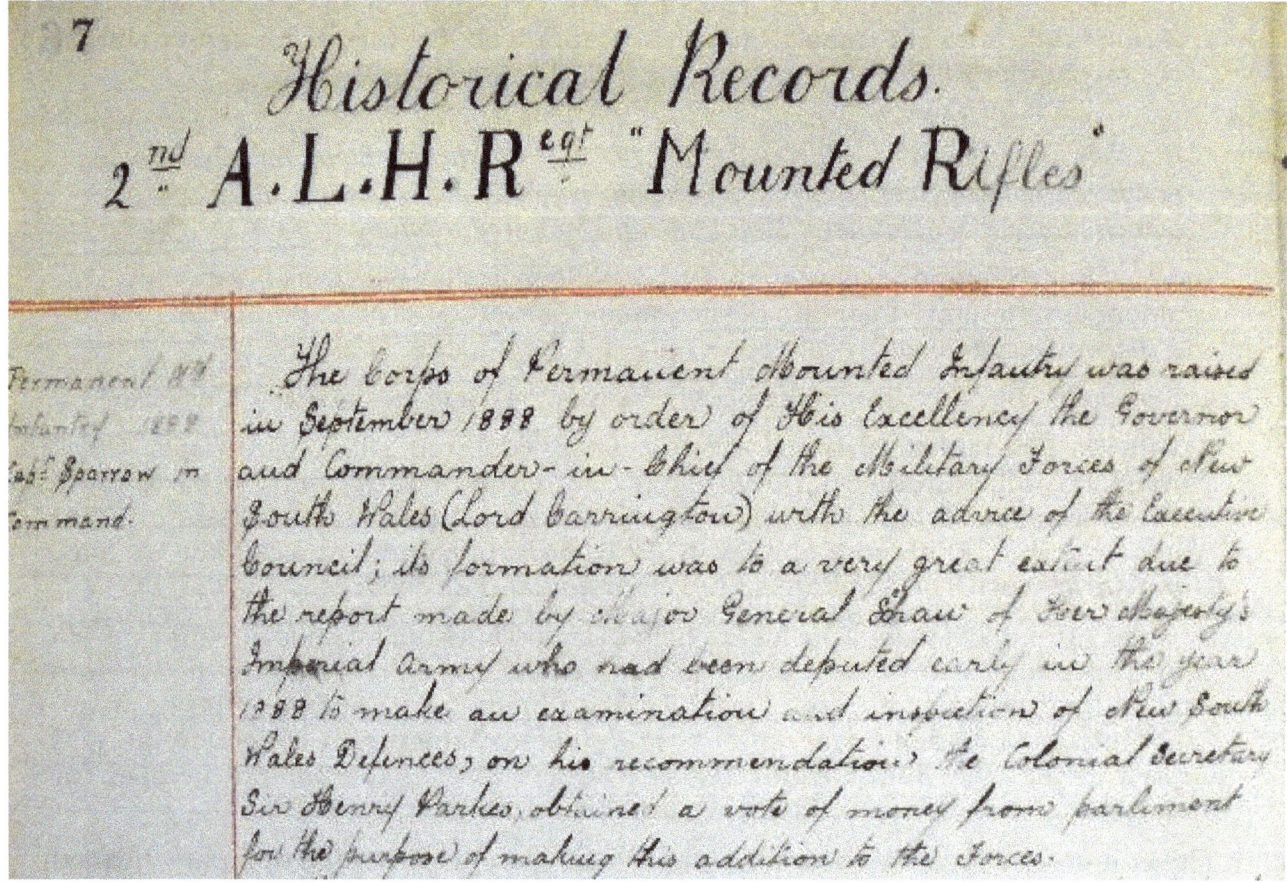

The Short History is reproduced here as it gives the most accurate description available of the formation of the Mounted Rifles and its involvement in Queen Victoria's Diamond Jubilee celebrations. I have, however, separated the basic history from the Jubilee Contingent and included it in a separate chapter.

Where additional information is provided in the handwritten record it has been included but the text is shaded.

History of the Regiment

Formation

The Corps of Permanent Mounted Infantry was raised in September, 1888, by order of His Excellency the Governor and Commander-in-Chief of the Military Forces of New South Wales (Lord Carrington),[88] with the advice of the Executive Council. Its formation was to a very great extent due to the report made by Major-General Schaw,[89] of Her Majesty's Imperial Army, who had been deputed early in the year 1888 to make an examination and inspection of New South Wales defences, and on his recommendation the Colonial Secretary, Sir Henry Parkes, obtained a vote of money from Parliament for the purpose of making this addition to the Forces.

Commanding Officer

The Officer appointed to command the Corps was Captain Henry Glendower Bodycham Sparrow, who was transferred from the Adjutancy of the 'Northern Reserves'.

Object of the Corps

The Corps was intended to supply men and horses for instructional purposes to the Officers of the mounted branches, and to form the nucleus of a regiment to be distributed by companies throughout the colony.

Recruiting commenced on the 11th September 1888, at Victoria Barracks, Sydney, the first enrolment being Richard Holman (now Warrant Officer and Regimental Sergeant Major of the New South Wales Mounted Rifles); a large number of the men presented themselves for attestation; each candidate was required to pass a successful trial of horsemanship before enlistment, and none were accepted below the height of 5 feet 7 inches, with a minimum chest measurement of 34 inches.

Establishment

The establishment consisted of one Captain, one Sergeant and thirty men.

The establishment having been speedily obtained, the men were grounded in the rudiments of foot drill, and gymnasium work until December 1888, when the horses arrived from Neotsfield Station, they were handled and broken by a selected number of men for duty in the ranks.

The Corps was employed chiefly on escort, orderly and guard duties, its first public appearance being in February 1889, when by command of His Excellency, the Governor, Lord Carrington, they were inspected by him at Government House. The first guard furnished was at Government House in July 1889. The Corps was popular with the inhabitants of the city, and gained much distinction by the particularly smart appearance of its members, and their good conduct.

Captain Lassetter to Command, 1889

Early in January 1889, Captain Henry Beauchamp Lassetter of 'Her Majesty's 80th Regiment of Foot', and a native of the colony, arrived in Sydney to take command of the Corps, and to perform in addition, the duties of Adjutant to the Lancer Regiment. During the first few weeks that Captain Lassetter occupied this dual position he spared neither time nor energy to promote and encourage his new Military factor, with the result that before Easter 1889, the Upper Clarence Light Horse, the Field Battery of Artillery at Bega and the companies of Reserves at Queanbeyan, Picton,

---

[88] Carrington, Baron/Lord Charles Robert – Governor 12 December 1885–3 November 1890
[89] Schaw, Henry (Major-General)

Campbelltown and Inverell were selected to form together with the Permanent Company stationed in Sydney, an administrative regiment under the partially-paid system, with Major Lassetter as Commanding Officer, and Captain Sparrow as Adjutant, the latter officer being also in command of the Permanent Company.

Each of the partially-paid companies consisting of 3 officers and 47 rank and file, who received an annual allowance of pay according to rank, which was paid for attendance at drill and training, the maximum a private could earn was £12/-/- per annum at the rate of 10/- per day.

Description of Clothing and Equipment

The following is a brief description of the clothing and equipment worn by the regiment. The buttons and mountings of the permanent company were brass, and those of the remainder white metal,

> Jacket: - Drab[90] tweed, with four outside pockets, two at breast and two at waist, with flaps, red cloth shoulder straps. The permanent company wore the regimental badge on shoulder strap, and the partially-paid men the letter of their company.
> Riding Pants: - Drab Bedford cord, fitting tightly.
> Hat: - Drab soft felt, turned up at side, enclosing a white pungaree and plume of black cock's feathers, the brim fastening back with the regimental badge.
> Leggings: - Brown leather, laced at side.
> Overalls: - Drab tweed, with ½ inch red welt down leg.
> Cap: - Drab tweed, piped with red of field service pattern.
> Gauntlets: - Brown leather, with buff tops.

The equipment was of brown leather throughout, and consisted of the following articles:

> Waist belt and frog, carrying long sword bayonet.
> Bandolier, for 50 rounds, worn over left shoulder.
> Haversack: white ordinary infantry pattern.
> Water bag: white canvas, carried on saddle.
> Clasp knife and lanyard, as used in the navy.
> Saddle: ordinary bush pattern, and supplied by men. Numnah,[91] brown felt.
> Valise: worn at rear of saddle.
> Great coat: black cloth, of infantry pattern.
> Breastplate, head collar, Pelham bit,[92] and two reins.
> An artillery pattern carbine, carried in a leather bucket on the saddle, and a cavalry pattern mess tin completed the equipment.

Regimental Badge

Southern Cross surrounded with wreath of waratahs, having a crown on top, and lion rampant in the centre of cross.

First Encampment

On the 19th April, 1889, the regiment assembled for the first time, and marched to the National Park to participate in the annual maneuvers of the troops at Easter, extending over nine days. The inauguration of the regiment met with so much approval on all sides, and was commented upon in such glowing terms by the press,

---

[90] Drab tweed is olive in colour
[91] A Numnah is a felt saddle cloth
[92] A Pelham bit has elements of both a curb bit and a snaffle bit. In this respect a Pelham bit functions similar to a double bridle, and like a double bridle it normally has 'double' reins: a set of curb reins and a set of snaffle reins.

that shortly after the conclusion of the training, numerous applications, memorials, and petitions were made or raised throughout the colony, and presented to Parliament, praying for an extension of this branch of the service.

The *Sydney Morning Herald*, in a leading article, dated 22nd April, 1889, says:

> *One of the most hopeful of our land forces is the Mounted Infantry, which has been established lately, and in a few years should give us a force of men most valuable in case of war.*

Writing of the camp in general, the same contemporary of the same date says:

> *The great feature of the camp is the M.I. in their smart uniform, under the command of Major H. B. Lassetter, of the 80th (South Staffordshire) Regiment, whose appointment was gazetted at the beginning of the year. A finer body of men would be difficult to get together. In some instances the men rode 60 to 85 miles to the railway station. The regiment marched into camp 185 strong, exclusive of the Bega and Queanbeyan companies, which have not gone under canvas owing to their equipment being incomplete.*

The same paper of April 24th 1889, says:

> *The special feature of the day's work was a sham fight, arranged by Major Lassetter, of the Mounted Infantry. It was viewed from start to finish by the General Officer Commanding and his Staff, who exhibited the deepest interest in the movements of Major Lassetter's handsome little corps.*

> *This corps must prove a tower of strength and usefulness in any, and every, conflict in which they may take part in the far, or near, future.*

> *The work done on the previous day was magnificent in every respect, and everybody, after hearing of the daring ride, was anxious to come and look on to-day, and to follow the brilliant little horsemen as best they could.*

> *Major General Richardson[93] exhibited the keenest interest in the proceedings, and congratulated Major Lassetter upon his fine force; indeed it is impossible to bestow upon them too much praise.*

> *The companies stationed at Bega and Queanbeyan were fully clothed and equipped in June 1889, and marched to Moore Park, Sydney, together with the Permanent Company for a twelve days' course of training. The training was conducted under Major Lassetter who kept all ranks hard at work up till the last day; the camp broke up on the 16th June 1889.*

Speaking of the Bega men, the *Sydney Morning Herald* of June 8th 1889 says:

> *The hardships which men undergo in coming into camp are seldom understood by the public, and rarely realised by any but the men themselves. The Bega men left home at 7am on June 5th, with a fifty-mile ride before them to Nimitybelle. The country was in a dreadful state from wet weather, and bad enough to prevent the progress of the most daring horsemen, but the men were determined at all hazards to reach Sydney and so they forced their way along most difficult and almost impassable roads, climbing up 7 miles to pass over a mountain 4,000 feet above the sea level.*

His Excellency, the Governor visited the camp on June 11th 1889, and was entertained by the officers; during the afternoon a programme of Military Sports was

---

[93] Richardson, Major-General John Soame

carried out in the presence of His Excellency, who was much pleased with the feats of Horsemanship.

Second Annual Encampment

On April 4th 1890 the regiment marched to the National Park, and took part in the Easter manoeuvres, the splendid horsemanship of the men excited so much attention that His Excellency the Governor ordered a display to be made before him and the public. As a special mark of her favour, Lady Carrington presented the regiment with a silver bugle. Speaking about the operations of April 5th 1890, a daily paper says:

> *The tactics were carried out with few mistakes, the whole being an evidence of the great strides recently made by the Mounted Infantry, it would be impossible to speak too highly of this new and valuable arm of the service, as they turned out on Saturday.*

On April 12th 1890, the *Sydney Morning Herald* said:

> *Captain Antill and his Picton Company had ridden 10 or 11 miles over terrible country on the right flank with a view to stopping the Infantry, and after a journey of the most dangerous description in crossing bogs, creeks and descending the fearful cliffs overhanging the river, they swam their horses through the stream, rode forward on the camp side of it by means of a beaten track, and sent a fire into the Infantry, that not only startled them, but set them wondering how such a force could have got ahead of them. Captain Antill did a magnificent piece of work.*
>
> *A force composed of men of this stamp is a valuable element in any Military Service.*

Permanent Company Disbanded

July 3rd 1890, saw the disbandment of the Permanent Company, on account of the great expense in maintaining the horses; at this time there was much distress throughout the colony, and a great deal of commercial depression, and as no immediate necessity appeared to exist for the maintenance of the company, Parliament decided to disband it with a gratuity of six months' pay to each man.

There are at present three members of the original Permanent Company of Mounted Infantry, serving in the military forces of the Commonwealth; viz., Major R. C. Holman, D.S.O., A. and I. Staff, W. Officer H. N. Lacey and S. S. Major T. Richards, Instructional Staff.

Maritime Strike

Owing to the excited state of the strikers during the great maritime disturbance in 1890, the Campbelltown and Picton companies were invited to take up the duties of special mounted constables. The instructions were telegraphed on Sunday, September 21st, 1890, and a few hours after the message had been received, officers commanding these two companies, assisted by the prompt action of the railway department, reached Dawes' Battery, Sydney, with 95 out of a total of 100 men.

The following day work commenced in earnest, and the troops, who in the meanwhile had been sworn in as 'Specials' and fitted with mounted constables' uniform and equipment, were told off in reliefs for patrol duty in the city and suburbs. This duty continued from 6 a.m. until midnight, and the men by their good judgment prevented a good deal of trouble. For this duty they were paid their usual regimental rates of pay, as well as receiving rations and forage.

The work of patrolling continued until October 30th, 1890 when the strike was practically settled. On this date the Premier, Sir Henry Parkes, held a review of the troops in Moore Park, and on behalf of the Government and the people of New South Wales, thanked all ranks for the work they had performed.

Regimental Band

On the 16th January 1891, a Regimental Band of 17 musicians was added to the establishment, and was raised at Camden.

On the 27th March 1891, the regiment assembled and marched into camp at Campbelltown to participate in the Annual manoeuvres at Easter, extending over nine days.

On conclusion of the Camp, the following letter was received from the Officer Commanding the 4th Infantry Regiment.

> *My Dear Major Lassetter*
> *Allow me to thank you for sending your band to play the 4th Regiment to the Railway Station on 4th inst; also to express my appreciation of the most valuable service rendered to my attaching column by the Mounted Infantry, it would be impossible for any men to work better, or to exhibit more readiness or intelligence. I consider it a most valuable force and the work they did reflects the greatest possible credit upon their instruction. The road we came along was so bad in many places that I sent my force back to camp, as did all my mounted officers, for we did not care to risk valuable animals, how your men managed to steal along quite surprised me.*
>
> *(Signed) C F Stokes, Lt Col.*

On the 1st October 1891, the establishment of the Mounted Infantry Regiment was further increased viz: from 327 to 427, by the enrolment of 50 men at both Camden and Liverpool.

Early in March 1893[94], the Regimental Headquarters of the Mounted Infantry Regiment was transferred from Sydney to Campbelltown.

The Commanding Officer, Major H. B. Lassetter, was granted 12 months' leave of absence from the 25th March 1893 and Lieutenant Colonel M. M. McDonald was appointed to temporary command of the Mounted Infantry Regiment in addition to the New South Wales Cavalry Regiment from the 16th June 1893.

Change in Designation

On 1st August 1893, the New South Wales Cavalry Regiment, and the Mounted Infantry Regiment, were constituted in a Mounted Brigade, which will be styled "The New South Wales Mounted Brigade".

And from the same date the regiment was named the New South Wales Mounted Rifles.

Colonel M. M. McDonald was appointed Colonel and Commandant of the Brigade.

The Mounted Infantry Regiment will from the same date be styled the 'New South Wales Mounted Rifles'.

---

[94] 1 March 1893

Colonel M M McDonald, was appointed Colonel and Commandant of the Brigade.

Commanding Officer Major H B Lassetter
Adjutant   Captain Sparrow.

No. 1 Company	(Captain Lloyd)		
		Liverpool	2 Divisions
		Campbelltown	2 Divisions
No. 2 Company	(Captain Antill)		
		Picton	2 Divisions
		Camden	2 Divisions
No. 3 Company	(Captain Bland)		
		Bega	2 Divisions
		Queanbeyan	2 Divisions
No 4 Company	(Captain Chauvel)		
		Tenterfield	2 Divisions
		Inverell	2 Divisions

Captain Chauvel[95] assumed command of the Mounted Rifles during the absence of Major Lassetter on leave.

Duff Challenge Cup and Hutton Shield

The first competition for the Duff Challenge Cup and Hutton Shield took place at Randwick Rifle Range on the 16th and 17th October 1893.

The Duff Challenge Shield was won by a section from No. 2 Picton Half Company, commanded by Sergt. Farrier Hill, the Mounted Rifle Regiment securing the first six places in the competition.

The Hutton Shield was also won by the regiment, the successful team being from No. 4 Tenterfield Half Company, commanded by Lieutenant Thomas. The first three places were filled by representatives from the regiment.

The Duff Challenge Cup was open to sections of four men; points being given for turnout and general appearance, riding, shooting and the Hutton Shield was open to teams consisting of one Officer, one Sergeant and 12 men. Points to be allotted the same as in the Duff Competition, course about two miles. This competition was won by the Mounted Rifles. In November 1893[96], the Headquarters of the Mounted Rifles was transferred from Campbelltown and located on the premises of the Headquarters, Mounted Brigade, Sydney.

Captain Sparrow, Adjutant of the Mounted Rifles was appointed Acting Staff Officer to the Mounted Brigade, in addition to his duties as Adjutant of the New South Wales Mounted Rifles from 1st October 1893.

On the 1st October, 1894, Captain H. B. Sparrow, Adjutant of the Regiment and Acting Staff Officer to the Mounted Brigade, resigned his commission, and Captain J. Antill, Acting Adjutant of the 1st Infantry Regiment was appointed Acting Adjutant.

---

[95] Chauvel, Henry George (Harry)
[96] 1st November 1893

Dress, Mounted Rifles, 1894 – Officers

The following alterations as regards 'Dress' for the Mounted Rifles, took effect from 1st January 1894.

Jacket:
Drab tweed. Collar stand and fall with 2 hooks and eyes, fall edged round base and front with ½ inch black mohair braid, traced inside with mohair Russia forming eye in corners. 5 small buttons on inside for white linen collar. Yoke with four 1-inch pleats down centre of back. Two breast patch pockets (5½ inches wide by 6½ inches deep) with box pleats, corner square at top, and slightly rounded bottom. 5 large plated buttons down front. White linen square cornered stand up collar, buttoning to inside of jacket, and showing ½ an inch above it, to lap over in front. Cuffs pointed with one bar of ½ inch black mohair, point 6 inches from button of sleeve, traced inside and out with black mohair Russia, forming eye under point, and Austrian knot on top. Officers above the rank of Lieutenant have cuffs with two bars of ½ inch black mohair. Field Officers have a row of braided eyes below the lace on the collar; braided eyes on the sleeve above and below the bars for Colonels and Lieutenant Colonels, and above the bars only for Majors. Shoulder straps of rifle green cloth, badges of rank in gold.

Additions for Full Dress
Epaulettes and aiguillettes of silver round cord of special pattern. Epaulettes to have woven into them one silk cord of same colour as facings. This addition to above constituted full dress.

Facings
Rifle green in place of primrose.

Waist Belt for Levees and State Ceremonies
Waist belt of 1¾ inch Waratah silver lace, fastened with regulation clasp. Slings of 1-inch Waratah silver lace.

Overalls
As at present, substituting for scarlet welt, double black mohair stripes ¾ inch wide, ¼ inch apart down each side of seam, to fasten at bottom with strap and buckle.

Pants
Bedford cord, made tight below the knee, but loose upward to the waist, strapped inside of knee only.

Hat:
As at present, with drab leather chin strap, silver embroidered badge on rifle green foundation.

Puggaree[97]
Dark green silk, three-fold, (2½ inches at sides, 2 inches at front and back) ⅓ inch red silk piping between each fold of green.

Forage Cap:
Drab tweed, with 1¾ inch silver Waratah lace, silver netted button on crown, surrounded by a special device of silver Russia tracing.

---

[97] The hat band of the Australian slouch hat is called a 'puggaree'. It has previously been spelt 'pugari', 'puggery' and 'puggari'. It is from an Indian (Hindi) word 'paggari' or 'pagri' which translates into something like small turban.

Boots
Brown leather knee, square at top, spur blocks.

Spurs
With knee boots - steel, swan necked, strap and foot chain, fasten with buckle. With overalls - steel, swan necked box.

Dress, Mounted Rifles, 1894 - NCOs and Men

Jacket
As in the case of Officers, except the back will be made with single pleat 2¾ inches wide, extending full length of Jacket, and no black mohair Russia on collar or cuffs. White celluloid collar in place of linen. Shoulder straps of rifle green cloth, with letters MR and number of company above, in white metal. Jacket for trumpeters to be piped with black on seams at back and sleeves.

Full Dress
As in the case of Officers, except that epaulettes and aiguillettes will be of black worsted cord; epaulettes to have woven into them one cord of red worsted.

Overalls
As in the case of Officers.

Pants
As in the case of Officers.

Hat
As in the case of Officers, but with white metal badge.

Puggaree
As in the case of Officers, but cashmere in place of silk.

Boots
As per sealed pattern.

Leggings
As per sealed pattern.

Spurs
Steel, swan necked, strap and buckle.

Mounted Corporal at Onslow Park (Camden Showground)

Captain Sparrow resigns, 1 October 1894

On the 1st October 1894, Captain H B Sparrow, Adjutant of the Mounted Rifles and acting Staff Officer to the Mounted Brigade, resigned his commission.

Captain J M Antill appointed Adjutant, 1 October 1894

On the same date, Captain JM Antill, Acting Adjutant of the 1st Infantry Regiment, was appointed Acting Adjutant to the Mounted Rifles Vice-Captain Sparrow resigned.

And on the same date, Captain G Lee, Adjutant of the Cavalry Regiment, was appointed Acting Staff Officer to the Mounted Brigade in addition to his duties as Adjutant to the Cavalry Regiment.

Duff Challenge Cup and Hutton Shield

Early in November 1894[98] the Duff Challenge Cup and Hutton Shield were again competed for on the Randwick Rifle Range; with the following results:

The Duff Challenge Cup competed for on the 2nd November was won by a section from No. 4 Inverell Half Company Mounted Rifles; commanded by Quartermaster Sergeant R H Fraser, R.H.

The regiment securing the first seventeen places in the competition. In all, twenty-eight teams from the Mounted Brigade competed.

The following day, 3rd November, the Hutton Shield was competed for, and won by a team from No. 4 Inverell Half Company led by Lieut. A A McLean. On this occasion the regiment annexed the first four places.

Campbelltown Disbanded

No. 1 Campbelltown Half Company was disbanded on 1st February 1895.

The regiment was further strengthened by the transfer of H (Molong) Company 3rd Infantry Regiment, with Captain Claude Smith in command, 1st July 1895.

No. 1 Liverpool Half Company was disbanded on the 30th June 1895.

Formation of Bathurst Half Company formed 13 August 1895

A half company was raised at Bathurst on August1 1895[99] with Captain Machatti in command, which was to form part of No. 1 Company, vice Liverpool disbanded.

On the 12th October 1895, the Commanding Officer Major H B Lassetter was promoted to the rank of Lieutenant Colonel.

Duff Challenge Cup and Hutton Shield

For the third time the Duff Challenge Cup and Hutton Shield were competed for on the 25th and 26th October 1895, at the Randwick Rifle Range. The former was won by a section from No. 3 Bega Half Squadron commanded by Quartermaster Sergeant Underhill. The first six places in the competition being secured by teams from this regiment.

The Hutton Shield was won by a team from No. 4 Tenterfield Half Company, in charge of Captain Thomas, the Shield thereby becoming the property of No. 4 Company. The regiment were successful in securing the first five places in this competition.

---

[98] 2 and 3 of November 1894
[99] 13 August 1895

Camp 1896

On the 25th January, 1896 the Mounted Brigade marched into camp at Campbelltown for a four days' course of continuous training, the whole of the Mounted Rifles going under canvas, with the exception of No. 4 (Tenterfield-Inverell) Company, the expense being too great to convey them to the place of concentration for such a short period.

Col. Hutton Appointed Hon. Colonel

Colonel E'I' Hutton, CB, ADC to Her Majesty Queen Victoria, and formerly Major-General Commanding the Military Forces of New South Wales, was appointed Honorary Colonel to the regiment on the 13th June, 1896.

At the beginning of September 1896, the headquarters of the regiment were transferred from Sydney to Camden.

Duff Challenge Cup and Hutton Shield

Once more the annual competition for the Duff Challenge Cup took place at the Randwick Rifle Range on the 23rd October 1896, the Cup being won this year by a section from No. 2 Camden Half Company under Sergt. Small, the winning section of last year's competition being beaten by one point only.

The next part of the History refers to the Jubilee Detachment and can be found in the chapter dealing with Queen Victoria's Diamond Jubilee.

Members of the Camden Unit at camp Rookwood in 1899
L-R Back Row: Alfred Sharpe; Alfred Maurice Dowle; John Beatson Huthnance; Frank William Ferris; Walter Vincent Nethery; Charles New; Herbert Thomas English; William Stanton; John Joseph Gillespie; William George Gunn – photo courtesy Camden Historical Society

During the absence of Lieut.-Colonel Lassetter with the detachment in England, Capt. and Hon. Major AS Menzies assumed temporary command of the regiment.

Major JW Macarthur-Onslow having returned from England took over the temporary command of the regiment from Capt. AS Menzies.

The Duff Challenge Cup was again competed for at the Randwick Rifle Range on the 30th October 1897, and was won by a section from No. 3 Bega Half Squadron.

Col. Lassetter Resigns

Lieut.-Colonel Lassetter returned from England on the 1st November, 1897, and assumed command of the regiment, and four months later the regiment lost this commanding officer, who had done so much to bring the regiment up into the position that it held then, and still retains.

Major J. W. M. Onslow Appointed C.O.

Lieut.-Colonel Lassetter, on his severance from the regiment, was placed on the Reserve of Officers, and his place was filled very ably by Major JW Macarthur-Onslow, who on taking over the command was promoted to the rank of Lieut.-Colonel.

On the 7th April 1898 the regiment marched into camp at Rookwood for eight days' continuous training, the camp terminating on the 16th April.

The annual competition for the Duff Challenge Cup in the year 1898 was won by a section from No. 2 Camden Half Squadron, commanded by Sergt. Small.

Queanbeyan Disbanded

On the 30th April 1898, the No. 3 Queanbeyan Half Company was disbanded.

Half Company Raised at Forbes

A half company of Mounted Rifles was raised at Forbes on the 6th June 1898, in lieu of the half company disbanded at Queanbeyan.

Camp 1899

On the 31st March 1899, the regiment went into camp for eight days' continuous training, under the mobilisation scheme, the Picton and Camden Half Companies being stationed at Middle Head and Botany respectively, the remainder of the regiment going under canvas with the Field Force at Rookwood. On Wednesday, 5th April 1899, the Picton and Camden Half Companies marched from their respective stations, and joined the remainder of the regiment at Rookwood.

The following is an extract from remarks by the GOC on Easter Encampment, issued with GO -48/99: *The GOC notes with satisfaction the conduct of Picton-Camden Company, of Mounted Rifles, on 5th April, when their hired transport broke down, and their arrival in camp was delayed till 2 a.m.*

The annual competition for the Duff Challenge Cup took place on the Randwick Rifle Range, and was won by a section from Bathurst Half Company, under Sergt. W. Barham.

First Contingent to South Africa

At the end of October 1890, a squadron from the regiment assembled at the Royal Agricultural Grounds, Sydney, for active service in South Africa. Capt. JM Antill commanded the contingent, his duties as Adjutant being carried on during his absence by Capt. AJ Onslow Thompson.

Capt. JM Antill and Lieut. AA McLean and 70 non-commissioned officers, and men of the contingent, embarked on the *SS Aberdeen*, the remainder took their departure from Newcastle by the *SS Langton Grange*, on the 14th November.

A draft of 25 NCOs and men accompanied the latter contingent to South Africa and joined the first contingent at Poplar Grove, Orange Free State, in March 1900.

The squadron took part in the relief of Kimberley, and in the Battles of Paardeberg, Driefontein, Johannesburg, Diamond Hills, and Wittebergen, besides numerous minor engagements, returning to Sydney on the 8th January 1901, after an absence of about 14 months.

During the early part of the war the Commanding Officer was attached to General Tucker's staff, whilst several other officers accompanied various contingents to the front.

During the South African struggle, the vanguard of the troops that captured General Cronje was led by a detachment of the regiment under the command of Lieutenant AJ Onslow (since retired) who received the white flag from Cronje, the Lieutenant being the first man to enter his laager. He was afterwards shot and wounded, and while a prisoner in the hands of the Boers at Heilbron where he was placed in hospital and well treated, his orderly was able to secure the Town Hall Boer flag, which he brought to Australia.

Canterbury Half Squadron Raised

In June 1900, the Canterbury Half Squadron was raised under the Volunteer Reserve System, and in December of the same year a regimental band was formed at Bathurst.

Commonwealth Celebrations

In the early part of January 1901, the regiment participated in the Commonwealth Celebrations at Sydney, and in the following March a contingent left for South Africa. Although Colonel Lassetter commanded this contingent, and most of its officers were officers from the regiments, it was not representative of the latter.

Duke of York's Visit

On the occasion of the Duke of York's visit, and the opening of the Commonwealth Parliament, in April 1901, a detachment of two officers and 50 NCOs and men proceeded to Melbourne to take part in these celebrations.

Camp 1901

In May of the same year the regiment went under canvas on the Old Paddington Rifle Range for six days, during which period they participated in the celebrations on the occasion of the Duke of York's visit to Sydney.

On the 1st July 1901 Capt. WWR Watson of the 1st Infantry Regiment was attached as Acting Adjutant. Vice Capt. AJ Onslow Thompson relinquished the position at his own request. In the following December Major Antill returned from South Africa, and resumed his duty as Adjutant to the regiment.

Reorganisation 1903

Under the reorganisation scheme of July 1903, the half squadrons at Inverell, Tenterfield, and Bega were lost by the regiment, and in their place we gained Dubbo, Wellington, and Mudgee Half Squadrons, and Rylstone Troops; Ulladulla and Canterbury Half Squadrons (Fortress Troops) were attached for administration.

Under this scheme Captain JM Arnott was appointed Militia Adjutant. The designation of the regiment was changed to 2nd Australian Light Horse Regiment (NSW Mounted Rifles).

King's Colours

The King's Colours were presented to the regiment in November 1904, by the Governor-General in Melbourne. The Colours were received by Col. JWM Onslow, WO Holman, and RQM Sergt. Wardrobe who formed the escort.

Gulgong Raised

On the 7th April 1906, Gulgong troop was raised to complete No. 2 Squadron, and in December of the same year the Rylstone troop of No. 2 Squadron was disbanded on account of not being able to get suitable men infused with the necessary enthusiasm.

Major Thompson Takes Command

Major AJ Onslow Thompson took command of the regiment in December 1907, from Col. JM Onslow, who was appointed Brigadier of the 1st Light Horse Brigade.

Hutton Shield

Molong Half Squadron was successful in winning the Hutton Shield in the competition held in 1907, at the same time that the Prince of Wales' Cup was competed for, and won by the NSW Lancers.

On 30th June 1908, the Ulladulla Half Squadron was transferred to the 1st ALH Regiment (NSW Lancers) for administration.

Pom-Pom and Machine Gun Section Formed

A Pom-Pom and Machine Gunn section were formed in December 1908 at Sydney. Lieut. DWA Smith was appointed to command the Pom-Pom section, and Lieut. AL McLean to command the Machine Gun section.

American Fleet Visit

In August 1908 a camp of continuous training was held at Liverpool extending over a period of 11 days, on the completion of which the regiment marched to Sydney, and went under canvas at Moore Park for a further period of five days, during which they participated in the celebrations on the occasion of the visit of the American Fleet, which were being held at that time.

Mudgee Raised

In October 1909 the Gulgong Troop of No. 2 Squadron was disbanded, and the full squadron of four troops raised at Mudgee.

Kitchener Camp

In January 1910, the regiment went into camp at Liverpool for eight days' continuous training, during which Field-Marshal Lord Kitchener inspected the military forces of the State of New South Wales.

Major Onslow Thompson Resigns

On 30th June 1912 Major AJ Onslow Thompson relinquished the command of the regiment, having completed over 20 years' commissioned service in the regiment, besides several months in the ranks, during which time he had never missed a parade, and had been awarded the Colonial Auxiliary Forces Officers' Decoration and the Colonial Auxiliary Forces Long Service Medal. He was tendered a dinner by the officers, present and past, of the regiment, who made a presentation of a plate to him.

Capt. Onslow Takes Command

Captain GM Macarthur-Onslow assumed command of the regiment from 1st July 1912.

Reorganisation 1912

On 1st July 1912 the designation of the regiment was changed to 9th Light Horse (NSW Mounted Rifles). The Canterbury Half Squadron was transferred to the 28th Light Horse (a new regiment formed under the scheme of reorganisation), and the Pom-Pom section was absorbed into the Machine Gun section, the section being issued with two maxim guns.

According to Herbert Thomas English (as reported to Annette Macarthur-Onslow) the Drill Hall at Onslow Park was designed by Astley John Onslow Thompson for the Mounted Rifles. The plans had previously incorrectly been attributed to Sir John Sulman; however Ms. Annette Macarthur-Onslow has been able to confirm that the plans are definitely the work of Onslow Thompson.[100]

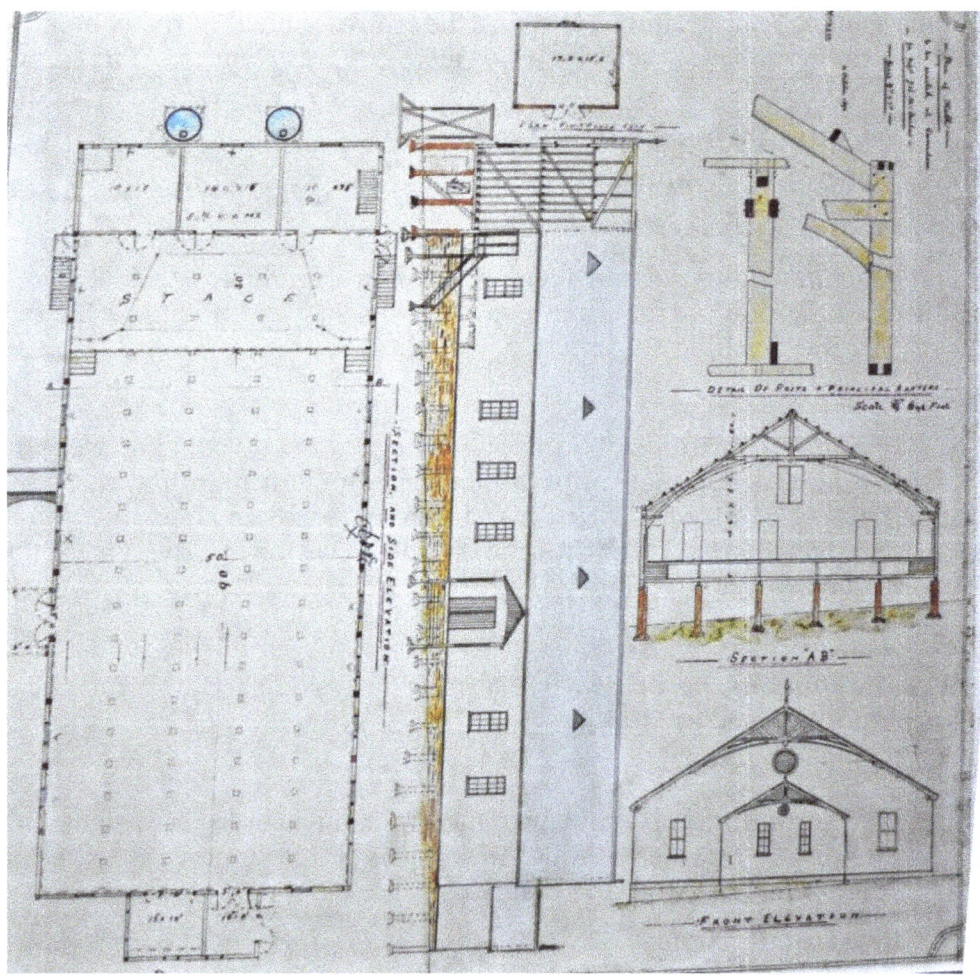

This building is still in use today as the hall for the Camden Agricultural Society. The hall was sturdily built, and also built to last under the guidance of Camden Park

---

[100] Macarthur, A., From the Old to New South Wales: the life of Astley John Onslow Thompson; *Camden History: Journal of the Camden Historical Society Inc.* March 2015, Volume 3, Number 9 Special Edition.

carpenter builder James Joseph English. In 1895 there were frequent references to the hall as being the Onslow Assembly Hall. However, an article in the *Camden News* quickly corrected the error:

Camden News
Thursday, 19 September 1895

The Mounted Rifle Drill Hall has of late been designated as the Onslow Assembly Hall, the latter is incorrect. The Hall was built for the purpose of the Mounted Rifles - as such should be henceforth known.

Known Members of the Camden Mounted Rifles

Antill, John Macquarie
Axam, Francis William
Bollard, Albert John
Brasher, James
Brookes, Frederick James
Bugden, William Henry
Burke, Michael Joseph
Burne, Frederick Henry
Butler, Arthur Albert
Campbell, Donald
Campbell, Robert Bruce
Childs, John William
Cowper, Cecil Spencer
Cowper, Frederick Robert
Cranfield, Arthur John
Curran, John Joseph
Daniels, Edward James
Davey, Walter George
Devlin, Arthur Ernest
Divall, William
Dobson, Edward William
Donaghy, James William Alexander
Donaghy, Thomas
Doust, Arthur John
Dowle, Alfred Maurice
Dwyer, Thomas John
English, Herbert Thomas
Farindon, Henry Charles
Ferris, Frank William
Ferris, George Chester
Ferris, John Dabinett
Furner, George Frederick
Furner, Walter Charles
Gillespie, John Joseph
Grigg, Robert Henry
Gunn, William George
Hanger, Joseph Henry
Hawkey, Frederick Joseph
Hawkey, John Martin
Hawkey, William Thomas
Hazelwood, Walter John

Hill, Farrier Sergeant
Hindes, Richard George
Hogan, M
Holman, Richard Charles Frederick
Hopson, William
Huthnance, John Beaston
Johnson, Charles
Kelloway, John Thomas
Kelly, Joseph Horatio
Kenny, Edward Francis
Kowald, Francis Christian
Landrigan, Michael John
Larkin, Willie
Learmonth, Charles
Liggins, Arthur James
Liggins, Reginald Charles
Linn, Thomas Henry
Little, Alfred Denison
Longhurst, James Patrick
Longley, Arthur John
Macarthur-Onslow, Arthur James
Macarthur-Onslow, Francis Arthur
Macarthur-Onslow, George Macleay
Macarthur-Onslow, James William
Marlow, Albert
Marlow, Percy Charles
Maxwell, John Cornelius
May, Percy Withers.
McEwen, James Fraser
Mills, George
Moore, Alfred Ernest
Moore, Henry
Moran, Harold Shaw Fleming
Nethery, Robert John
Nethery, Walter Vincent
New, Charles
Parsons, Archibald Arthur

Payne, William C
Pegum, Callahan George
Percival, M T
Poole, Alfred Cecil
Poole, James William
Potter, John Alexander
Potts, Pembroke
Preshaw, Charles Ernest
Rapley, William
Rixon, Kirwan
Rudd, Eugene Hay
Rudd, Harold Isaac
Saile, Thomas
Sharpe. Henry
Sharpe, Robert
Shoemark, Frederick
Shoemark, Henry (Harry)
Small, E
Small, James
Small, W
Smart, Charles
Smith, Reginald Sydney (Rex)
Smith, Walter
Stanton, William
Taplin, Henry Edwin
Thompson, Astley John Onslow
Varlow, William Henry
Vaughan, Arthur Ernest
Veness, John Edward
Veness, William Ernest
Viles, Edwin Ernest
Viles, Norman
Wasson, John James
Waterworth, James Edwin
Waterworth, Oswald Ernest
Wheeler, Robert John
Wignell, William
Young, A

James William Macarthur-Onslow in Mounted Rifles uniform
– photo courtesy Camden Park House collection

QUEEN VICTORIA'S DIAMOND JUBILEE

Detailed preparations were made to ensure the efficiency and success of the contingent chosen for the Jubilee celebrations. The strenuous timetable before they embarked for England provides a testimony to the workload imposed on man and beast.

The Queen's Jubilee Detachment was comprised of seven officers including four from Camden and Picton:

> Lieutenant-Colonel Henry Beauchamp Lassetter
> Major James William Macarthur-Onslow
> Captain Astley John Onslow Thompson
> Lieutenant Arthur John Macarthur-Onslow

There were also seven Non-Commissioned Officers including Warrant Officer Richard Charles Holman.

Twenty-six privates were also chosen including eight from the Camden and Picton Half Companies.

> Albert John Bollard
> Edward James Fairley
> John Dabinett Ferris
> John Martin Hawkey
> James Small
> Henry Edwin Taplin
> Caleb Francis Vacchini
> Alfred Edward Vaughan

Another who appears to have formed part of the contingent, although his name does not appear on the list, was Thomas John Dwyer.

Camden News
Thursday, 31 December 1896

New South Wales Mounted Rifles
REGIMENTAL ORDERS
The Camden Encampment

A detachment of the regiment consisting of — officers, to be hereafter detailed: 1 Company Sergt. Major, 1 Sergeant, 2 Corporals, 2 Lance-Corporals, 1 Bugler, 26 privates, will embark for the United Kingdom, at Sydney, on Monday, 15th February, on board the SS Gulf of Martaban for the purpose of attending the celebrations to be held in honour of the completion of the sixtieth year of the reign of Her Most Gracious Majesty, the Queen, of taking part in the summer training and manoeuvres of the Imperial troops, and also of competing at the Royal Military Tournaments at Islington and Dublin. Officers commanding half companies will at once forward for the approval of the commanding officer, the names of the four rank and file whom, they may recommend to proceed with the detachment. Great care is to be taken that only men will be selected who by their soldierly conduct, general smartness and efficiency, will be thoroughly representative of the regiment. The non-commissioned officers forming the detachment will be selected by the commanding officer—those who may in his opinion be best fitted for the positions—the remainder who may be non-commissioned officers will temporarily revert to the ranks. Each mounted rifleman forming part of the detachment should realise that in being chosen to represent his Corps in the United Kingdom, a high honour is inferred upon him. The detachment will be brought under the review of Her Majesty the Queen, and be keenly criticised by the leading Imperial soldiers; but the commanding officer feels confident that they will do credit to the regiment and to himself.

Horses – In order to avoid delay all horses must be ready for inspection on the receipt of a telegram from headquarters. All horses embarking with the detachment are accepted on the following terms, viz: — brought to headquarters at regimental expense. Used by the detachment prior to embarkation. Passage and insurance (about £20) (i.e. $40) advanced by the regiment. Provided with forage. On completion of the training, to be sold in England at the discretion of the commanding officer, and the proceeds of the sale, less passage, insurance, and a commission of ten per cent to the soldier who attends to them, will be handed to the owner.

The expenses in connection with the dispatch of the detachment are estimated as follows: —

Deck fittings for horses, £200 ($400); ditto for men; £50 ($100) saddlery; £285 ($570) forage; £685 8s 4d ($1,370.84) rations; £305 16s ($610.16); passage £693 ($1,386); kits, necessaries, extra (rations etc.) £300 ($600); pay, £925 ($1,850).

Training at Camden - Pay £95 5s ($191); rations £93 15s ($186.30); probable cost of transport, working material, labour, railway fares and incidental expenses, £500 ($1,000); freight on horses, £760 ($1,520). Total - £4,843 4s 4d ($9,686.48).

The contributions towards this amount are of £4,843 4s 4d, will be raised as follows: — 8 half companies at £320 ($640) each £2,560 ($5,120); HM Imperial Government £500 ($1,000); HM NSW Government £500; by officers and private sources (£750 ($1,500) recoverable on horses) £1,283 4s 4d ($2,566.88); Total £4,843 4s 4d. The contributions from the various Half Companies at the rate of £80 ($160) per man will be lodged to the credit of the Mounted Rifles 'Special Service Fund' at the head office of the Commercial Banking Co. of Sydney, Limited, George Street, Sydney, on or before 10 January. The Detachment will assemble in marching order for preliminary training at the Regimental Headquarters, Camden, on Friday, 15th January as follows: —

Molong   Jan. 14
Bathurst   " 14 arrive Camden 11:35
Picton   " 15 arrive by road
Camden   " 15 2 pm parade drill hall
Bega   " 15 local arrangements
Queanbeyan   " 14 arrive Camden 8:30 am
Tenterfield   " 14 by rail
Inverell   " 14 by rail

No civilian clothes of any kind are to be brought by the various parties.

Major J. Macarthur-Onslow will command the detachment during the preliminary training and be directly responsible for the discipline and instruction of the detachment. Regimental Sergt. Major Holman will be attached as instructor and receive his orders from the officer in command.

Captain AJ Onslow Thompson will perform the duties of Paymaster and Quartermaster, and will be held responsible that all payments made are strictly in accordance with, the following scales: —

Scale of pay per day. — Colour-Sergt Major, 4s 6d ($0.52); Sergeant, 3s 0d ($0.60); Corporal, 2s 8d ($0.28); Lance-Corporal, 2s ($0.20); Private 1s 9d ($0.19).

Scale of rations - in NSW 11d ($0.10) per diem; - in England, 1s 1d ($0.11) per diem.

Scale of forage - in NSW 1s 3d ($0.12) per diem; - in England 2s ($0.20) per diem.

The estimate of the expenses of an officer accompanying the detachment — return fare to London, passage for servant, freight on horse and insurance, forage for eight months, messing for five months, uniform, mufti, travelling expenses, incidental expenses is £316 10s ($632.10).

Preliminary training at Camden, January 15 to February 10.

Dress - Morning stables, evening stables, foot parades and stable picket — fatigue dress.

Mounted parades - drill order. — Midday stables same dress as morning parade with jumper.

Gymnasium - Fatigue dress and Sand shoes.

Walking out - Pants and leggings.

Detail - 5.30 a.m. reveille; 6 to 7.15a.m. morning stables; 7.15 a.m. stableman; 7. 30 am breakfast; 9 to 11 a.m. morning parade; 11.30 to 12.45 a.m. midday stables; 1 p.m. dinner; 2.15 to 4 p.m. afternoon parade; 4.30 to 5.45 p.m. evening stables; 6 p.m. supper; 7.15 p.m. picquet;[101] 7.30 to 8.45 p.m. gymnasium; 9.30 p.m. first post; 10 p.m. last post; 10.15 p.m. lights out.

Synopsis of work - January 15; assemble, issue of kits, numbering horses, permanent groups lecture detail of duties, synopsis of work, duties of NCOs and group leaders, object of service.

January 16: 9 to 11 a.m. detachment, squad drill, dismounted.

January 17: — a.m. Church parade.

January 18: 9 to 11 a.m. first division, riding school. Second division, squad drill, dismounted. 2.15 to 4 p.m. first division dismounted. Second division riding school, 7.30 to 8.30 p.m. gymnasium.

January 19: Same as the 18th January.

January 20: 9 to 11 a.m. first division, manual firing. Second division, swords dismounted. 2.15 to 4 p.m. first division, tournament work. Second division, field firing. 7.30 to 8.30 p.m. lecture. January 21, 9 to 11 a.m. first division, squad drill, dismounted. Second division, manual and firing. 2.15 to 4 p.m. detachment, squad drill, mounted. 7.30 to 8.30 p.m. gymnasium.

January 22: 9 to 11 a.m. first division, squad drill, dismounted. Second division, target practice. 2.15 to 4 p.m. first division, target practice. Second division squad drill, dismounted.

January 23: 9 to 11 a.m. first division, field firing. Second division, tournament work.

January 24: — a.m. Church parade.

---

[101] In modern military terms it refers to a soldier or small group of soldiers maintaining a watch.

January 25: 9 to 11 a.m. field practices, dismounted with ball ammunition. 2.15 to 4 p.m. tournament work.

January 26: General holiday.

January 27: 9 to 11 a.m. swords, mounted. 2.15 to 4 p.m. first division, swords dismounted. Second division, target practice, mounted. Field firing.

January 28: 9 to 11 a.m. first division, squad drill, dismounted, with arms. Second division, swords, dismounted. 2.15 to 4 p.m. first division, swords, dismounted. Second division, squad drill, dismounted.

January 29: 9 to 11 a.m. detachment, division drill, mounted. 2.15 to 4 p.m. first division, physical and bayonet exercises. Second division, swords dismounted.

January 30: 10 a.m. detachment, whole day parade with No. 2 Company.

January 31: — a.m. Church parade.

February 1: 9 to 11a.m. first division, tournament work. Second division, field firing. 2.15 to 4 p.m. detachment, foot drill.

February 2: 9 to 11 a.m. detachment, division drill, mounted 2.15 to 4 p.m. foot drill.

February 3: 9 to 11 a.m. first division, field firing. Second: division, tournament work. 2.15 to 4 p.m. detachment, manual, firing and swords.

February 4: 9 to 11 a.m. first division, riding school. Second division, foot drill. 2.15 to 4 p.m. first division, foot drill. Second division riding- school.

February 5: 9 to 11 a.m. detachment, division drill, mounted. 2.15 to 4 p.m. detachment, swords mounted.

February 6: Display.

February 7: — a.m. Church

February 8: 9 to 11 a.m. display. 2.15 to 4 p.m. swords, dismounted.

February 9: 9 to 11 a.m. division drill, mounted. 2.15 to 4 p.m. swords dismounted.

Special memorandum issued for the guidance of men joining the draft for service in England during the year 1897. To be in possession of each man:
    a To be carried on the man or horse
    b To be brought as baggage in a corn sack
    c To be supplied on or after assembly

Articles to be carried (a):

Clothing: — Boots Cossack: One pair, new or in good condition, to be worn, no other boots to be brought; one pair supplied at Camden. Caps f's Under centre cloak strap. Great coats: On saddle, special cloaks served out at sea. Gloves: One pair, purchased by the man; one pair free at Camden. Hats: One, further issue at Camden. Jacket: One New pattern. Leggings: One pair to be in good condition and repaired if necessary by individuals locally. Pantaloons: One pair in good condition. Jack spurs: One pair.

Arms: — Bayonet and scabbard, one. Revolver, one if necessary to be withdrawn from group leaders for the service. Rifle and sling, one. Sight protector, on rifle. Jag, in pocket of pantaloons. Note: company quartermaster sergeants will be armed with rifle and bayonet and send swords with baggage.

Equipment: — Belt waist bandolier and frog: one, and thirty-five rounds of ball ammunition per belt from half company's store, deducted from efficiency allowance for current year. Haversack: one (with towel, soap, and oil bottle). Lanyard revolver: one as per revolver. Pouch revolver: one as per revolver: Nose bags: one thoroughly bleached. Breastplate: one properly fitted. Bridle: one properly fitted. Numnah: one properly fitted. Head ropes: one. Saddle: one. Mess tin and strap: one.

To be brought as baggage (b):

Clothing: — Forage cap: packed in a cardboard box. Overalls, one pair thoroughly clean. Pantaloons: one pair fairly good for drill and practice. Aiguillettes: one set.

Arms: — Cavalry swords: 2 per half company from the supply issued for tournament practices. Cavalry swords: company quartermaster sergeants chosen for service will carry rifle and bayonet, the swords to come with baggage.

Equipment: — One picketing peg. One picketing rope.

Necessaries: — Drawers: two pairs by men accustomed to use them, at individual expense.

Articles supplied (free) on or after assembly (c):

Clothing: — One pair of Cossack boots, one pair of gloves, one hat, one jumper, one pair of fatigue trowers,[102] one whip all at Camden; one pair of Wellington boots, one jacket, one pair of pantaloons, one spur box at sea.

Equipment to be issued at Camden: —

One water bottle, one pair of shoe cases, one sheepskin fleece, one pair of wallets, one knife clasp with marling spike and lanyard, one hoof picker.

Necessaries carried in haversack: —

Towel, soap, oil bottle, two flannel shirts, one set boot brushes, one set of shaving brushes, one set horse brushes, one worsted cap, 6 1bs sheeting horse rubbers, one hair comb, one knife, fork and spoon, one grease pot, one hold all, one kit box, two pairs of socks, one razor, one pair of braces, one fitted housewife,[103] one worsted jersey, one curry comb, one kit bag, present one to be returned to half company's store, one pair spare laces, one tin blacking, one pocket ledger.

The following items of interest are published for information: —

Clothing etc. will be carried in the kit bags and kit boxes only, no other bags or portmanteaux will be allowed under any consideration.

All letters for the detachment during the preliminary training will be addressed 'Mounted Rifle Barracks, Camden'.

Men will be supplied with one pint of beer daily and two ounces of tobacco per week on board ship.

No matches or explosives of any kind are to be taken on board.

All ranks are strictly prohibited on taking beer or spirituous liquors on board.

Men must provide wire guards for their pipes, and smoking on board will only be allowed at certain times and in certain places.

---

[102] i.e. trousers
[103] A sewing kit for repairs

Camden News
Thursday 4 February 1897, page 4

The NSW Mounted Rifles
THE CAMDEN ENCAMPMENT

Very great interest has been centred in the doings of the Mounted Rifles now in camp at the Onslow Park. Daily the park has been crowded with visitors from all parts of the district, who highly appreciated the drills of the men. Except for one or two slight mishaps there have not been any serious casualties to report, the men as well as their horses are in good health and make the town very lively. In addition to the detachment chosen to go to England, the camp has been added to by the Camden and Picton half companies, the men arrived in camp at the latter end of last week and left for their homes on Sunday afternoon. The band of the NSW Permanent Artillery also came to Camden on Friday and remained in camp until Monday morning; during portions of the day and during the evening mess of the officers in command and their guests, played a very choice selection of music and which the residents took advantage of by attending in large numbers and showed their appreciation of the treat provided them. Major-General French, commander of the forces in NSW was in camp on Saturday and made his annual inspection of the Camden and Picton companies, as well as an inspection of the detachment which goes to England.

Addressing the officers and men on Saturday, at the conclusion of his inspection, he said he was delighted with the way the men had turned out, also with their work. He reminded them that they belonged to a fine regiment, and must do all in their power to keep up its high reputation. He conveys his personal thanks to Colonel Lassetter and Major Onslow, together with all the other officers, for their part in maintaining the regiment. Colonel Lassetter had taught the men the elementary part of the work, and had practically made the Mounted Rifles, while Major Onslow had taken an enthusiastic interest in his men, and helped them on wonderfully. To these two officers he (the Major-General) was especially grateful. A regiment like that could not have attained anything approaching its present efficiency but for such men at the head.

The sham fight at Razorback on Saturday was a great success, and many ladies and gentlemen joined there to witness the manoeuvres. On Sunday the whole of camp attended church parade, and marched to St. John's Parish Church, headed by the bandsmen. The church was crowded to excess, there not being even standing room. Several of the members of the band accompanied with their instruments in the various hymns selected. The Rev Mr King, the Camp-Chaplain preached the sermon, and took for his text, 2 Timothy II, Verse 3, 'Suffer hardships with me as a good soldier of Christ Jesus'. The preacher said that he valued this church parade as a public recognition of God and of our dependence upon Him and His help at all times. The national characteristic of the British race, viz., choosing hard work and toil either for sport or livelihood, shows the manliness and native hardihood of Englishmen. The discipline of a military life is necessary to teach endurance, efficiency, and thus to ensure peace to the nation. People who laugh at soldiering in peace time are very thankful for the objects of their ridicule when war threatens. The visit of the detachment to England will help the soldiers to realise that they and we are part and parcel of the British Nation with its glorious history. The preacher spoke of true patriotism as being a religious principle and concluded by addressing the members of the detachment, assuring them of the prayers of the congregation that God would bless and keep them in all dangers and bring them home again in health, happiness and honour.

The following officers attended the church service: Major-General French (the guest of Mrs. Macarthur-Onslow), Col. Lassetter, Major Onslow, Captains Antill, AJ Onslow Thompson and Larkins, Lieutenants AJ Onslow, G Onslow, Kelly, Rylie and Sergt. Major Holman. After the service the regiment preceded by the band returned to camp via John and Argyle Streets. Several members of the regiment attended Divine Service at St. Paul's RC Church, John Street; the Reverend Father Kickham preached an impressive sermon.

Camden News
Thursday, June 10, 1897

NSW MOUNTED RIFLES

S. M. Herald **Cables**

London, June 4.

At a military tournament at the Agricultural Hall, Islington, yesterday, a team from the New South Wales Mounted Rifles, defeated a team of New South Wales Lancers at wrestling on horseback.

London, June 8.

The New South Wales representatives achieved considerable success in the competitions at the Military Tournament in the Agricultural Hall, Islington, yesterday. The following were the results in the under-mentioned events:

Heads and Posts - Private V. Tarlington (Mounted Rifles) 1; Private W. Barham (Mounted Rifles), 2
Lemon-cutting - Trooper Harkus (Lancers) 1; Sergeant A. McAllister (Mounted Rifles) 2
Tent-pegging - Sergeant Williams (Lancers) 1; Trooper Robinson (Lancers) 2
Lance Mounted v. Bayonet - Private E. Tarlington (Mounted Rifles) 1; Private H.E. Perry (Mounted Rifles) 2
Sword v. Sword Mounted – Sergeant O'Grady (Lancers) 1; Private J. Finnerty (Mounted Rifles) 2
A team from the Naval Brigade defeated the representatives of the New South Wales Lancers at wrestling.

The displays given by the men of the New South Wales Mounted Rifles and Lancers in the competitions were greatly applauded by the spectators.

Camden and Picton Company

This company of Mounted Rifles will parade in Sydney on Queen's Jubilee on the 22nd instant, the Camden ½ Co will leave by the 7 a.m. tram on the 22nd and entrain at Campbelltown, meeting the Picton ½ Co. The detachment will take part in the military display at the Centennial Park at 11 a.m. After the conclusion of the review the troops will partake of lunch and then march through the Sydney streets returning to their respective headquarters in the evening. Dress: Great coats on saddle, haversack and aiguillettes.[104]

London, June 9.

---

[104] An aiguillette (from French 'aiguillette', *small needle*) is an ornamental braided cord most often worn on uniforms. The New South Wales Mounted Rifles had red aiguillettes

At the Military Tournament at the Agricultural Hall, Islington, yesterday, Lieutenant C Campbell, Captain AJO. Thompson, and Lieutenant AJ Onslow were defeated in the riding and jumping events. They, however, displayed excellent style.

In the event bayonet v. bayonet, the New South Wales representatives defeated a team from the regular army.

In the competition sabre v. sabre, Lance Corporal H Macintosh of the New South Wales Mounted Rifles was first, and Sergeant A McAlister, also of the New South Wales Mounted Rifles was second.

Camden News
Thursday, July 8, 1897

NSW Mounted Rifles
S.M. *Herald* Cable

London, June 30

The horses of the New South Wales Mounted Rifles will be sold by auction by Messrs. Tattersall on the 9th July.

———

The following description of the military tournament, held in London in which the Mounted Rifles took part, will be read with interest.

> *The New South Wales men came upon the scene, with their sketch, which might be entitled 'Bashing the Bold Bad Bushrangers'. The curtain rises (there is no curtain, of course, but that is a small matter) upon a realistic bush hut, the home of five or six bold bad men, addicted to 'bailing up' and cattle-lifting. Two of them only are at home, engaged in domestic operations, the one fooling about with a fire and a billy, and the other keeping a lookout. I am not sure whether a lookout man is entitled to be regarded as being engaged in domestic operations, but that can pass. Suddenly the man with his eye on the horizon declares to his pal that 'They're coming,' and we hear in the distance, with a slight effort of imagination, the thud of many hoofs, and in a few seconds half a dozen horses dash into the arena, closely pursued by the remainder of the gang – a villainous quartet, red-shirted and bearded, armed to the teeth, and cracking stockwhips with infinite gusto. We perceive that in addition to the horses their foray has resulted in the capture of an unhappy station hand. Having corralled their equine spoil, the bushrangers tie up their human captive to a fence, and then proceeded to off-saddle their own horses, prior to taking tea. Whilst they are engaged with their horses the station hand manages to slip his bonds. Losing no time he vaults on to the back of one of the captured horses, slips out of the corral, and makes off. The bushrangers pursue him with bullets, and what the little boy called 'horrid implications', but neither the one nor the other arrest the flight of the fugitive, who makes a bee line for the country that lies beyond the scope of the arena. His disappearance doesn't seem to trouble the bushrangers very much, but almost before the excitement of the escape has died down a faint bugle call is heard, and a moment later a squad of the Mounted Rifles, led by Captain Thompson, are piloted to the bushrangers' reservation by the late captive. Their appearance is the signal for the bad men to bolt into their hut. The troopers having dismounted at a respectful distance from the bushrangers' quarters, rush to the shelter of a couple of*

gorse-trimmed hurdles, and from thence proceed to pepper their quarry. A brisk fusillade results in the swift death of two of the bushrangers and the wounding of a couple more, while they, on their part, only succeed in smashing one trooper's leg and badly wounded the little bugler. Apparently the unharmed robbers prefer the rope to lead, for they make haste to exhibit a white handkerchief in token of their surrender. They are forthwith ordered out of the hut, disarmed with expedition, nicely trussed up, and set astride the stolen steeds. Their captors then attend to their own wounded, who after their injuries have been roughly doctored, are mounted in front of uninjured comrades. The entire party then gallop off, negotiating on their homeward way a couple of low brush hurdles.

The New South Wales Mounted Rifles at Hounslow
L-R: Lieutenant Stanley Stewart Ryrie; Major James William Macarthur-Onslow; Lieutenant Colonel Henry B Lassetter; Captain Astley John Onslow Thompson; Lieutenant Arthur John Macarthur-Onslow; Lieutenant Colin Charles Campbell – photo courtesy Camden Park House collection

Camden News
Thursday, July 22, 1897

NSW Mounted Rifles

Advices received from members of the Mounted Rifles contingent in England, convey the intelligence that the troop expect to leave on the return journey sometime in September; evidently they are going to have a longer stay than was at first contemplated.

It is reported that an offer of £100 ($200) has been made by an English gentleman, for Shoeing-Smith Garlick's well-known brown horse, Brassy. Many, in fact, pretty well everybody, doubted the truthfulness of the report, considering the figure far beyond the value of the horse. We are in a position to say that, according to advices received from a couple of members of the detachment, the report is founded on fact. An offer of £100 for Brassy was received by Colonel Lassetter, and refused. Evidently the Colonel thinks Shoeing-Smith Garlick's mount will bring more, and we hope that events will prove that in refusing the enticing offer he acted in the best interest of the owner.

The 'Short History of The New South Wales Mounted Rifles' includes an excellent description of the event and has been added here for the reader's convenience. As with the history, the shaded sections appeared in the handwritten history but did not appear in the history published in 1914.

Jubilee Contingent

During the year 1896 Lieut.-Colonel Lassetter organised a scheme to raise funds to send a detachment from the regiment to England in 1897, to take part in the Diamond Jubilee celebrations, the necessary funds being raised by units, means of tournaments, entertainments, etc, and private subscriptions.

Representatives were chosen from each half squadron, competitive tests being held, in tournament work, fencing, boxing, horsemanship, and the best men chosen.

On Friday, 15th January 1897 the detachment assembled at Camden for a month's training prior to embarking; a specially selected lot of horses were also taken into camp, which were to accompany the detachment for use in tournament work while in England.

On Friday, 12th February, the detachment proceeded by route march to Sydney, arriving at the Agricultural Grounds, Moore Park, the following afternoon, where they were quartered until the day of embarkation.

On Wednesday 17th February 1897, the Detachment embarked with their horses on board the *SS Gulf of Martaban*, at Cowper Street Wharf, Woolloomooloo Bay.

The following comprised the Detachment:

Rank	Initials	Surname	Role/Unit
Lieutenant-Colonel	H B	Lassetter	in command
Major	J W	Macarthur-Onslow	Second in Command
Captain	A J	Onslow Thompson	
Lieutenant	C	Campbell	
Lieutenant	A J M	Onslow	
Lieutenant	S S	Ryrie	
Warrant Officer	R	Holman	Staff
Staff Sergeant Major	C	Lydiard	No. 1 Bathurst ½ Squadron
Sergeant	A	McAllister	No. 4 Tenterfield ½ Squadron
Corporal	D	Fraser	No. 4 Inverell ½ Squadron
Lance Corporal	H	Munsie	No. 4 Inverell ½ Squadron

Rank	Initials	Surname	Unit		
Lance Corporal	W	Armstrong	No. 1 Bathurst	½	Squadron
Lance Corporal	H	McIntosh	No. 1 Bathurst	½	Squadron
Shoeing Smith	H	Cady	No. 1 Molong	½	Squadron
Private	D	Ball	No. 1 Molong	½	Squadron
Private	P	Bridges	No. 1 Molong	½	Squadron
Private	W	Garlic	No. 1 Molong	½	Squadron
Private	E	Muntz	No. 1 Molong	½	Squadron
Private	R	Barton	No. 1 Molong	½	Squadron
Private	W	Barham	No. 1 Bathurst	½	Squadron
Private	H	Cashman	No. 1 Bathurst	½	Squadron
Private	G	Morgan	No. 1 Bathurst	½	Squadron
Private	A	Thompson	No. 1 Bathurst	½	Squadron
Private	J	Small	No. 2 Camden	½	Squadron
Private	H	Taplin	No. 2 Camden	½	Squadron
Private	A E	Vaughan	No. 2 Camden	½	Squadron
Private	J	Ferris	No. 2 Camden	½	Squadron
Private	J M	Hawkey,	No. 2 Camden	½	Squadron
Private	J	Bollard	No. 2 Picton	½	Squadron
Private	E J	Fairley	No. 2 Picton	½	Squadron
Private	C	Vacchini	No. 2 Picton	½	Squadron
Private	E	Tarlinton	No. 3 Bega	½	Squadron
Private	V	Tarlinton	No. 3 Bega	½	Squadron
Private	W	Handscombe	No. 3 Bega	½	Squadron
Private	H	Perry	No. 3 Bega	½	Squadron
Private	G	Gribble	No. 3 Queanbeyan	½	Squadron
Private	A	Campbell	No. 4 Tenterfield	½	Squadron
Private	P	Kelly	No. 4 Tenterfield	½	Squadron
Private	J	Finnerty	No. 4 Tenterfield	½	Squadron
Private	J	Munsie	No. 4 Inverell	½	Squadron

Captain Scott, Veterinary Surgeon, also accompanied the detachment.

Capt. AJ Onslow Thompson was appointed Adjutant to this detachment, and throughout the English visit did excellent work in that capacity for the well-being and comfort of the troops.

The detachment arrived at the Albert Docks, London, on Thursday 22nd April 1897, after a 64-day voyage. The following day the detachment, with their 30 horses (three having been lost on the voyage), disembarked, and proceeded by rail to Hounslow, where they were quartered with the 2nd Royal Dragoons, 'Scots Greys'.

The following is an extract from a London paper, *The Morning Post*, of 24th April, 1897:

Though the sun was shining brightly, the air was raw and keen yesterday morning when the disembarkation of the detachment of the New South Wales Mounted Rifles commenced at 8 o'clock at No. 8 shed of the Royal Albert Dock, from the steamer Gulf of Martaban, *and a considerable crowd of people were interested spectators of what was taking place. The horses were slung off the ship in boxes, and those who anticipated they would be superlatively frisky on touching earth were disappointed, for the animals seemed thoroughly done up after their long confinement. Some little difficulty was experienced in getting them into the trucks in which they were conveyed to Hounslow, hence the process of disembarkation was slow, and it was nearly 1 o'clock before everything connected with the corps had been landed, and was on board the train. Before leaving the dock, Col. Lassetter received a telegram from Sir Saul Samuel, the*

Agent-General for New South Wales, expressing regret that he was unable to be present. Cheers were raised as the 'special' started at half past one for Hounslow, to reach which a large portion of London was traversed, the route being via Canning Town, Tottenham, Addison Road, and Clapham Junction. A few minutes before 3 o'clock, the train steamed into Hounslow Station. The approaches to the station were crowded with people, who had patiently waited since 11 o'clock, the hour it was stated the troops would arrive. In front of the building was the full band of the Scots Greys, and the composite band of the Middlesex Regiment and the Royal Artillery. The bandsmen had also been in attendance for four hours. The horses, when taken out of the trucks, appeared even weaker than when first landed. This may partly be accounted for by the fact that they were unshod, their shoes having been taken off in Sydney previous to starting. On the platform, awaiting the troops was Captain Miller, the Adjutant of the Royal Scots Greys, who extended a cordial welcome to the visitors.

Outside the station the men formed up, and particularly smart and soldierly they looked in their marching kit. This may be described as consisting of the 'Terai'[105] hat, with the cock-feathers plume, brown tunics, pants, ammunition, boots and gaiters, brown belts, bandolier. They carried Martini-Henry rifles and bayonet. Headed by the bands, a move was made for the barracks, amid the cheers of the assembled people. The horses, with halters, were led by the men of the Scots Greys, who took charge of them at the station. The streets through which the soldiers passed were lined with cheering inhabitants, of the heartiness of whose welcome there could be no question. The following telegram was here received from Lord Carrington, one of the most popular Governors New South Wales has ever had. It was addressed to Col. Lassetter, and was as follows: 'Welcome and congratulations to Mounted Infantry on arrival, hope to see them on return to London', Lord and Lady Carrington, Gwydr Castle, North Wales.

When the barracks were reached, the scene was a stirring one. The Scots Greys and depot troops, as well as several hundred of the recruits of the Militia Battalions of the Middlesex and London Fusilier Regiments, were gathered round the gates, and as the Colonials entered the lively strains of the march the band was playing were lost for the moment in deafening cheers of welcome. The Sergeants of the Scots Greys had prepared an elaborate dinner in their mess, and to this the whole of the NCOs and men. of the troops were invited, while the officers were entertained at luncheon by their colleagues of the Greys; the officers and NCOs of the Mounted Rifles being made members of the officers' and sergeants' messes of the Scots Greys respectively.

The New South Wales troops will be accommodated in the rooms usually occupied by the members of the band of the Scots Greys.

At Retreat last evening three men of the troop mounted stable picket with the-Scots Greys, and this may be taken as an earnest of the thoroughness with which all regimental duties will be shared by the Colonials and the Greys.

On Wednesday 10th May 1897, Corp. Apps (Bathurst) and Bugler Daly (Molong) arrived with a draft of six horses for the detachment, sent over by Mr Danger, to replace those lost on the voyage.

---

[105] The British press referred to the Australian slouch hat as a 'Terai' meaning a wide-brimmed double felt sun hat worn especially in subtropical regions

During the period the detachment was at Hounslow the time was taken up in practising for the Royal Military Tournaments at Islington and Dublin.

From the 27th May to the 10th June, the detachment was quartered at the Royal Agricultural Hall, Islington, where they took part in the Royal Military Tournament, winning almost every competition that they took part in. A Bushranging display was also given by the detachment twice a day during the whole ten days of the tournament, for which the Imperial authorities allowed £500 ($1,000) towards defraying the expenses of the detachment. These displays were repeated at the tournament in Dublin the following week, where they were also successful in securing a fair percentage of the prizes.

On their return from Dublin the detachment took part in the Jubilee Celebrations, the review of the Colonial troops by Lord Wolseley, and witnessed the naval review at Portsmouth.

On June 28th 1897 the detachment proceeded to Aldershot to be attached to the troops under the command of the Duke of Connaught, and were quartered with the 6th Dragoon Guards (Carabineers). They attended all the field days and manoeuvres and left the command on August 6th. Their horses were sold at Tattersall's Bazaar on August 9th for an average of 42 guineas each. A trip was then taken up the River Thames to Oxford, and thence through the neighboring manufacturing districts of the north of England. This trip was organised for them by Colonel Ward and Lord Milton. Mr Joseph Chamberlain took a personal interest in this visit of the troops, and provided the steam launch to take them to Oxford. A stay of two days was made at Windsor, where, by special command of Her Majesty the Queen, the men were shown over the State and private apartments at the Castle, and were entertained at the Cavalry Barracks by Colonel Brocklehurst and the officers and men of the Royal Horse Guards. On arrival at Oxford, the Mounted Rifles were invited to Middleton Park by Lord Jersey and to Blenheim Palace by the Duke of Marlborough, and greatly enjoyed the visit. The cities and towns of Birmingham, Wolverhampton, Stoke-upon-Trent, Manchester, and Sheffield were afterwards visited and at each centre the troops were accorded a hearty welcome.

The Prince of Wales presenting the Queen's Jubilee Medal to members of the NSW Mounted Rifles in front of Buckingham Palace – drawn by W. Small – photo courtesy of Camden Park House collection

The various manufacturing works, including those of Messrs. Cammell and Co, of Sheffield, Walker and Hall, Lloyd and Lloyd, and T and C Clarke were inspected by the men, who were very much impressed with all they saw.

While in the Old Country the detachment competed in the Lloyd-Lindsay competition at Bisley. Speaking of the competition, the *Daily Mail* wrote:

Visitors to Bisley the last day, who watched the Lloyd-Lindsay, could not help admiring the horsemanship displayed by Colonel Lassetter's riflemen from New South Wales, and although they did not succeed in getting any nearer than third, there was absolutely no comparison between them and the Yeomanry. The Australians sat and rode with the knowledge and judgment of born horsemen, and if points had been given them for style equal to their merit they should have been far ahead of other competitors. The opinion of the public was evident when the Colonials came up to take their awards from the Duchess of York, and the hope expressed by the Duke that they would return next year was warmly endorsed by everyone present, for never in the annals of the NRA had a meeting been so full of interest as it had been that year, and thanks were mainly to those Colonial soldiers of the Queen, whose manly bearing and soldier-like qualities have assured the most sceptical that as long as our dependencies produce such men Britain stands in no danger of any foe however powerful.

The New South Wales Mounted Rifles on the Mayflower. *Trip on the Thames to Oxford – photo courtesy of Camden Park collection.*

During this English visit, the whole of the Colonial regiments, of which the Mounted Rifles formed a part, were privately inspected by the late Queen Victoria at a review held in the grounds of Windsor Castle: the only persons present being the Queen, her daughter, and Lord Roberts, who rode on his charger beside the Queen's carriage.

When the Queen inspected the Mounted Rifles, her carriage stopped immediately in front of them, and the Queen was heard to ask Lord Roberts, 'What detachment is this and by what Act are they established?' This was a poser for Lord Roberts, but he was equal to the occasion, and immediately replied, 'By Special Act, Ma'am'.

*Lord Roberts reviewing the NSW Mounted Rifles in front of St. Paul's Cathedral London
– drawn by W. Small – photo courtesy of Camden Park House collection*

St. George's Barracks witnessed the last scene in the stirring drama of the Jubilee Celebrations. There the detachment, under Colonel Lassetter, paraded for the last time on the morning of the 3rd September. Thirty-five officers and men answered the roll under arms, and underwent a thorough inspection by the Commanding Officer. The drum and fife bands of the Grenadier Guards and the band of the Artist Corps of Volunteers attended to do honor to the departing guests. After the inspection, the men were marched to Charing Cross Station, en route for Fenchurch Street, where they entrained for Tilbury. Later in the day, they embarked on the Orient liner *Oruba* for Sydney.

All the men were enthusiastic in praise of the reception they had received in the Mother Country.

Members of NSW Mounted Rifles at Hounslow. Lieutenant-Colonel Lassetter centre – photo courtesy of Camden Park House collection

NSW Mounted Rifles participating in the Royal Military Tournament at Islington – photo courtesy of Camden Park House collection

The Camden and Picton men who attended the Jubilee Celebrations were:

BOLLARD, Albert John: *Rank:* Private. *Born:* 2 September 1875 Stilton, Picton, NSW. *Parents:* Thomas William Bollard and Annie Connellan. *Occupation:* farmer. *Died:* 1953 Perth, WA. *Married:* Ethel Rosina Stewart.

Bollard also served during the Boer War.

DWYER, Thomas John: *Rank:* Private. *Born:* 1876 Camden Park, Menangle. NSW. *Parents:* Michael Dwyer and Margaret O'Neil. *Occupation:* groom. *Died:* 8 July 1899 St. Vincent's Hospital, Darlinghurst, NSW.

Dwyer was not on the official list but was, according to his obituary, part of the contingent. It is possible he attended as James William Macarthur-Onslow's servant.

Camden News
Thursday, July 20, 1899

MR. T. J. DWYER
ÆAT[106] 23
A MILITARY FUNERAL,

We regret to report the death of Mr Thomas John Dwyer, a native of Camden, in Sydney, on Saturday last the 8th instant, from a fall from a horse. Dwyer was born on the Camden Park Estate, and was the trusted personal servant of Lieut. Colonel Macarthur-Onslow. It will be remembered that the young man—a member of the Camden ½ Co. of NSW Mounted Rifles—accompanied the contingent that visited England during the Queen's Jubilee. The deceased was of a happy disposition and a faithful servant and his loss will be greatly missed by his large circle of friends and by his companions-in-arms. The remains were to have been brought to Camden but owing to the flooded state of the Nepean River were conveyed to Menangle, where the undertaker, Mr J D Rankin was in waiting. Many members of the Camden Mounted Rifles met the cortege on the route, under the command of Captain Onslow Thompson with his Lieutenant AJM Onslow. After arrival in Camden at the time appointed a short service was held at St Paul's RC Church, the Rev Father Comaskey conducting the service. The casket, which was of polished cedar with massive silver handles, was then borne to the hearse by four members of the rifles then to the RC Cemetery, on the right of the Main Southern Road, the members of the Mounted Rifles proceeding the immediate relations of the deceased. At the grave a firing company was formed under command of Corporal Veness and at the conclusion of the impressive ceremony honours were accorded the deceased by the firing of three volleys over the grave. Rev CJ King MA, Chaplain of the regiment was also present. This was the first military funeral held in Camden.

FAIRLEY, Edward James: *Rank:* Private. *Born:* 1876 Picton, NSW. *Parents:* William Fairley and Letitia Mulholland. *Died:* 5 April 1953 Camden Hospital, Camden, NSW. *Buried:* St. Mark's Church of England, Picton, NSW. *Spouse:* Margaret Agnes Bollard.

---

[106] At age

Picton Post
Wednesday 8 April 1953

DEATH OF MR. EDWARD FAIRLEY
One of Picton's Oldest Identities

The death occurred at Camden District Hospital on Sunday, April 5th of Mr Edward James Fairley, after a prolonged illness. The late Mr Fairley, who died in his 76th year, was born at Picton and his death marks the passing of one of the district's oldest identities. In early life Mr Fairley was a member of the Australian Militia Light Horse and attained the rank of Sergeant Major. He was one of three selected from this district to represent New South Wales at Queen Victoria's Golden Jubilee celebrations held in London. He later married Margaret Agnes Bollard and resided at Abbotsford, a well-known property in Picton, where he conducted a dairy farm. He retired from dairy farming about 15 years ago and continued on the farm holding with cattle grazing. Both ventures proved successful. Widely known throughout Picton and district, the late Mr Fairley was a likeable personality. He was ostensibly a home-loving man and possessed a quiet disposition. He earned the respect of all who knew him. He is survived by his wife, one daughter (Mrs Stan Woods, Coull Street, Picton) one son (Edward, Abbotsford, Picton), two sisters (Miss C Fairley, Campbell Street, Picton and Mrs R Hydes, of Batlow) and six grandchildren. Burial took place in the grounds of St Mark's, Picton, on Monday afternoon, after a brief service conducted by the Rev DA Langford. Many beautiful floral tributes from relatives and friends draped the casket. Sincere sympathy is extended to his wife and family in their sorrow.

FERRIS, John Dabinett: *Rank:* Private. *Born:* 3 December 1877 Razorback, NSW. *Parents:* Alexander Samuel Ferris and Emma Dabinett. *Occupation:* police officer. *Died:* 30 July 1960 Lidcombe, NSW. *Spouse:* Helen Maud Mary Neely. *Married:* 1901 Ryde, NSW.

Ferris was accused of assaulting James Cameron at Fairfield, NSW on 17 February 1906. Cameron was at the local hotel and quite drunk. As a joke some of the other drinkers, William James McNamara, Robert Henry Hempson, Edward Stanley Bourke, James Ivors Bourke and Ferris tied Cameron up in a sack with holes for his head and legs but the arms were inside. Ferris said he had only kicked him in the backside and told him to go home. Cameron subsequently set himself on fire and died as a result.

The Coroner found:

> *Cameron was in a state of intoxication when being placed in the bag, and, further, I find that while Cameron was in the bag in efforts to extricate himself he ignited some matches that were in his pocket, and set fire to his clothes, by reason of which his body was so badly burned that he died; and I further find that the above-mentioned accused did feloniously and wilfully kill and slay the said James Cameron.*[107]

Ferris lost his job in the police force and was fined £150 ($300); the others were fined £100 ($200) each.

HAWKEY, John Martin: *Rank:* Private. *Born:* 12 October 1877 Camden Park, Menangle, NSW. *Parents:* Richard Hawkey and Mary Ann Burton. *Occupation:* farmer. *Died:* 16 June 1958 Minto, NSW. *Spouse:* Annie Louisa Krinks. *Married:* 27 September 1905 Sydney, NSW.

---
[107] *Australian Town and Country Journal* (New South Wales: 1870–1907) Wednesday 20 June 1906

At the Jubilee Hawkey gave a stock whip display in the Queen's presence. He also served during the Boer War and WWI and was later an instructor for the Australian Army Ordnance Corps.

Camden News
Thursday, July 15, 1897

NSW Mounted Rifles
(S.M. Herald Cables)

London, July 8

The New South Wales Mounted Rifles, who have been attached to the 6th Dragoon Guards (the Carabineers), attended a field day at Aldershot to-day, forming part of the Imperial Force. The detachment was complimented by the Duke of Connaught, commanding at Aldershot.

During the reconnoitring Private J Hawkey, of Camden, fell with his horse into a canal, but both he and the horse swam to the bank.

London, July 10.

The various detachments of the colonial troops who took part in the record reign celebrations have disbanded.

The men are visiting the provinces, and will reassemble in London prior to embarkation for their return home.

Second Lieutenant William Edward O'Brien is transferred from the New South Wales Lancers to the Mounted Rifles, to have seniority from date of first appointment, viz. 22nd May, 1893.

HOLMAN, Richard Charles Frederick: *Rank:* Warrant Officer. *Born:* 26 September 1861 Broadway, Dorsetshire, England. *Parents:* Frederick Holman and Louisa Puckett. *Occupation:* army officer. *Died:* 13 December 1933 Ingleburn, NSW. *Buried:* Denham Court - Anglican, Ingleburn. *Spouse:* Harriette Blanche Mills. *Married:* 10 December 1890 St. Mary's Church of England, Balmain, NSW. *Note:* also served during Second Boer War and WWI.

LASSETTER, Henry Beauchamp: *Rank*: Lieutenant-Colonel. *Born:* 19 March 1860 Darling Point, NSW. *Parents:* Frederick Lassetter and Charlotte Hannah Iredale. *Died:* 17 February 1926 Sydney, NSW. *Buried:* South Head Cemetery. *Spouse:* Elizabeth Anne Antill. *Married:* 19 August 1891 St. Mark's Church of England, Picton, NSW.

Colonel Henry (Harry) Beauchamp Lassetter was a remarkable yet not well-known soldier of the late colonial era in Australia and is considered as the founder of the Australian Mounted Rifle Brigades. He reluctantly resigned his commission and position as Commanding Officer of the 2nd Australian Light Horse Brigade in 1906 to attend to the family's successful mercantile business.

He commanded the Colonial Escort in Queen Victoria's 60th Jubilee Regiment and saw active service under Lord Wolseley with the Nile Expedition. This expedition crossed the desert to Metemmeh (Ethiopia) to relieve the siege of Khartoum. Lassetter re-joined the British Army shortly after World War I began and by January 1915 had been promoted to Brigadier General in command of a British Territorial unit.

Lassetter served with the British Army in the Sudan and Territorials Brigade (the Terriers) during WWI.

MACARTHUR-ONSLOW, Arthur John (Jack): *Rank:* Lieutenant. *Born:* 29 April 1873 Camden Park, Menangle, NSW. *Parents:* Arthur Alexander Walton Onslow and Elizabeth Macarthur. *Died:* 20 April 1953 Gosford, NSW. *Spouse:* Christian Leslie Bell. *Married:* 1902 England.

Arthur John Macarthur-Onslow also served during the Boer War.

MACARTHUR-ONSLOW, James William: *Rank:* Major. *Born:* 7 November 1867 Camden Park, Menangle, NSW. *Parents:* Arthur Alexander Walton Onslow and Elizabeth Macarthur. *Occupation:* Professional soldier. *Died:* 17 November 1946 Camden Park, Menangle. *Buried:* Camden Park Private. *Spouse:* Enid Emma Macarthur. *Married:* 15 December 1897 St. John's Church of England, Darlinghurst, NSW.

James William Macarthur-Onslow served in the British Army during the Chitral Expedition – India; and also during the Boer War and WWI.

SMALL, James: *Rank:* Private. *Born:* 16 September 1858 Cawdor, NSW. *Parents:* James Small and Mary Ann Haddon. *Died:* 14 August 1906 Camden Hospital, Camden, NSW. *Buried:* St. John's Church of England, Camden, NSW.

On Tuesday, 14 August 1906[108] Small was bringing a wagon load of hay from Camden to Theresa Park and whilst going down an incline attempted to apply the brakes on the wagon. He lost his foothold and fell and the wheels of the laden wagon passed over the lower portion of his body. Severely injured he was taken to Camden Hospital for surgery but died at 8:00 pm the same day. Small was accorded a military funeral.

TAPLIN, Henry Edwin: *Rank:* Private. *Born:* 1873 Wagga Wagga, NSW. *Parents:* Edwin Taplin and Mary Lysaght. *Died:* 3 April 1919 Wellington, NSW. *Spouse:* Arabella Schneider. *Married*: 18 July 1894 St Paul's Church of England, Cobbitty, NSW.

Camden News
Thursday, March 24, 1897

NSW Mounted Rifles
THE ENGLISH DETACHMENT

Private H. Taplin writes to his brother William as follows:

On board *SS Gulf of Martaban*

I was rather upset in leaving you all, as this is the first time I ever went away and taking such a journey as this, and having heard so much about the horrors of travel on a troop ship, well, no doubt it is rough, it was rough enough in the way we used to get our meals served in Camden but this is simply awful, the stench from the horses down below used to make us almost ill, this combined with sea sickness and an officer rousing us up to feed our horses and keeping us moving about it was terrible. I am pleased to say I am now alright, some of our men have been sick nearly all the way. We had good weather from Sydney until near Melbourne where we stayed three days. We have no drill on board as there is not enough room. After leaving Melbourne we experienced a rough passage to Portland, the seas breaking over the ship. One man, the boatswain, would have been washed overboard if one of the sailors and myself had not caught him. From 7.30 to

---

[108] *Camden News* 16 August 1906

1.30 it was something terrible. We had to cut the horses loose because the battens used by the horses as a foot hold gave way and they slipped up on their backs, then it was terrible, all the horses loose, slipping and falling over one another, and back from one side of the boat to the other the horses got a terrible knocking up about. Of them Vacchini's and the buckskin has since died. We have the horses as well as possible, although if it gets worse we will lose all on dock. Portland is a quiet little place with a dangerous harbour.

THOMPSON, Astley John Onslow: *Rank:* Captain. *Born:* 3 January 1865 Wales, England. *Parents:* Astley John Thompson and Udea Marianne Moriarty Onslow. *Occupation:* General Manager Camden Park. *Died*: 26 April 1925 Johnson's Gully, Gallipoli, Turkey (KIA).

Astley John Onslow Thompson had served with the NSW Mounted Rifles from 1892. In private life, Onslow Thompson was a well-known company director who for some years had managed the Camden Park Estate.

VACCHINI, Caleb Francis: *Rank:* Private. *Born:* 9 May 1870 Sydney, NSW. *Parents:* Tiberio Vacchini and Ann Elizabeth Whitfield. *Occupation:* farm labourer. *Died:* 29 October 1947 Western Suburbs Hospital, Concord, NSW. *Spouse:* Louisa Swann. *Married:* 1900 Paddington, NSW.

Astley John Onslow Thompson

Vacchini also saw service during the Boer War. He died after falling from a building.[109]

VAUGHAN, Alfred Edward: *Rank:* Private. *Born:* 1867 Sydney, NSW. *Parents:* Henry Edward Vaughan and Mary Anne Brown. *Died:* 22 August 1939 Booker Bay, NSW. *Buried:* Rookwood, NSW. *Spouse:* Amy Maude Matthews. *Married:* 1898 Port Macquarie, NSW.

Camden News
Thursday, 4 March 1897

During the voyage from Sydney to Portland, Victoria, of the NSW Mounted Rifles Detachment, Private Vaughan, of Campbelltown, met with a serious accident whilst attending to one of the horses in the stalls; the horse pawed him seriously with the result that he sustained a fracture of the ribs.

---

[109] *Sydney Morning Herald* 31 October 1947 p.18

BOER WARS

The term Boer is of Dutch origin and means husbandman or farmer and was used to refer to a South African of Dutch, German, or French Huguenot descent, especially the early settlers of the Transvaal and the Orange Free State. Today the descendants of the Boers are commonly referred to as Afrikaners.

In 1648 one of the ships of the Dutch East India Company was shipwrecked in Table Bay (i.e. now Cape Town) and the stranded crew were forced to forage, for several months, on shore. When the crew were finally able to return to the Dutch Republic (Holland) they provided a favourable report on the Cape to the Directors of the Dutch East India Company. Recognising the advantages, by 1652 the Company had established a fort and vegetable gardens at Table Bay. The Dutch colony was strengthened in 1685 when King Louis XIV of France revoked the Treaty of Nantes which had previously protected the Calvinist (Huguenot) population of France from the Catholic majority. The Huguenots were given the option of converting to Catholicism or leaving France. At least 300 of the refugees sought safety in the new Cape Colony.

When Holland came under the control of the revolutionary French government in 1795 a British force was sent to Cape Town to secure the colony for the exiled Prince of Orange. The First and subsequent Fleets travelling to the new colony of New South Wales stopped at Cape Town to obtain stock and supplies. In February 1803 following the peace of Amiens the Cape Colony was handed over to the Batavian Republic.

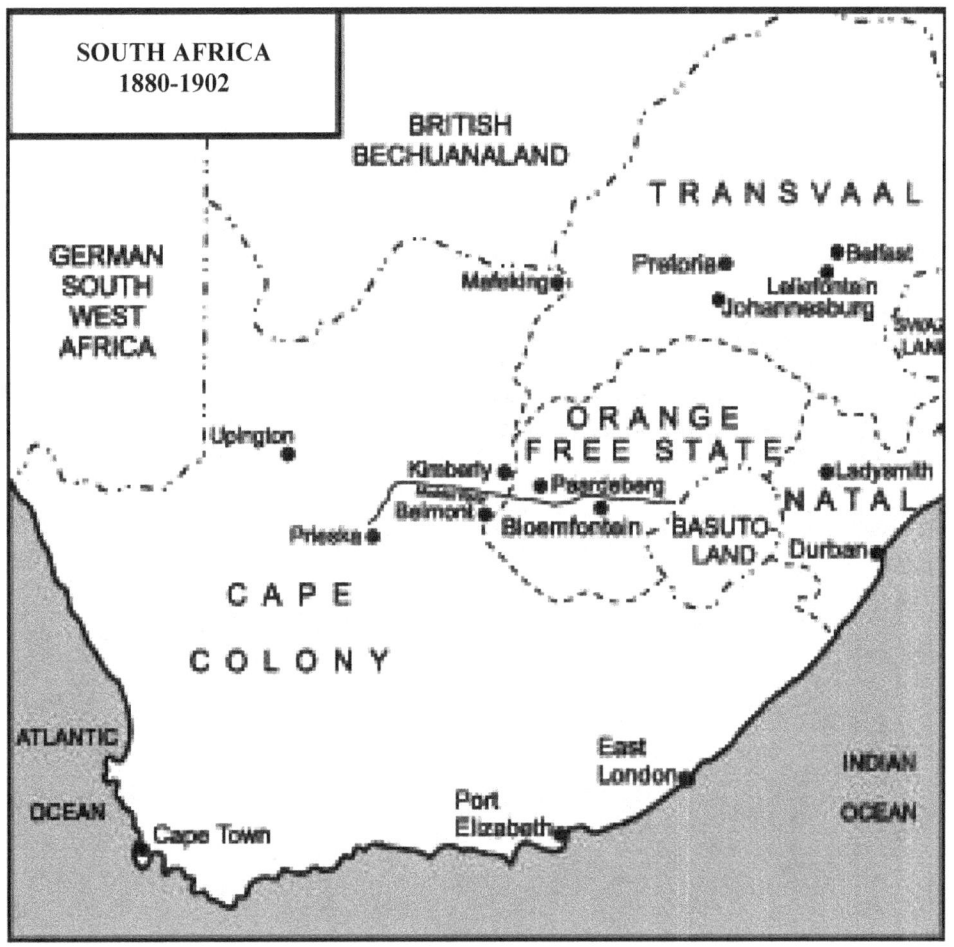

When the Cape Colony had come under British control the Boers had declared the Transvaal and the Orange Free State as independent republics, but as the Boers were aggressive and hostile to the indigenous African people it is little wonder that the indigenous Africans gave their allegiance to Britain. The Boer Wars were two wars fought during 1880–1881 and 1899–1902 by the British Empire against the settlers of the two independent Boer republics.

The cause of the Boer Wars was British aggression based on commercial and strategic motivation. To put it simply, Britain wanted the gold mines located in the Transvaal Republic – the gold was of lower grade than other recent discoveries in America and Australia but what it lost in quality it made up for in quantity.

First Boer War (1880–1881)

The First Anglo-Boer War was a fight to keep sovereignty by the South African Republics against British invasion. In 1867 diamonds had been discovered near the Vaal River quickly turning the small village of Kimberley into a town of 50,000 and attracting British imperial interest. However, there were more pressing concerns for the two Boer Republics squeezed between the British Cape Colony and Zululand, Matabeleland and Bechuanaland. In 1877 Britain annexed West Griqualand, the site of the Kimberley diamonds in the Transvaal, and tried to bring them by force into a union. This angered the Boers who were also facing aggression from the Zulus.

Britain was reluctant to be involved in a war with the Zulus but believed that British military superiority would intimidate the Zulus despite Transvaal locals stressing the need for caution. Britain failed to heed the warning and the Zulu War eventuated and Britain lost 1600 soldiers on 22 January 1879 when a Zulu attack caught them in the open. On 4 July 1879 reinforcements arrived and the British were victorious over the Zulus and then annexed Zululand (Natal) and consolidated its control over Transvaal and Natal.

After the defeat of the Zulus the Boers gave voice to their increasing resentment of Britain's annexation of the Transvaal and on 16 December 1880 revolted and successfully attacked the 94th Regiment of Foot, and declared independence. The war was relatively short-lived but British losses were heavy and the South African Republics were victorious with Britain signing a Peace Treaty on 23 March 1881.

There is no record of any Camden men being involved in the First Boer War.

Bechuanaland Expedition 1884–1885

Camden did, however, have some involvement in the Bechuanaland Expedition (also known as the Warren Expedition). In December 1884 Major-General Charles Warren was sent as Her Majesty's Special Commissioner to command a military expedition to Bechuanaland. Warren's orders were to assert British sovereignty in the face of encroachments from German South West Africa and the Transvaal and to suppress the Boer states of Stellaland and Goshen. The latter two states, backed by the Transvaal, were stealing land and cattle from the local tribes.

Warren's expedition was successful and its goals were achieved without bloodshed. He dissolved the Republics of Stellaland and Goshen, and Bechuanaland became a British protectorate.

HOLMAN, Richard Charles Frederick: *Rank:* unknown. *Unit:* Northern Border Expedition. *Born:* 26 September 1861 Broadway, Dorsetshire, England.

Parents: Frederick Holman and Louisa Puckett. *Died:* 13 December 1933 Ingleburn, NSW. *Buried:* Denham Court - Anglican, Ingleburn. *Spouse:* Harriette Blanche Mills. *Married:* 10 December 1890 St. Mary's Church of England, Balmain, NSW.

Holman also served during the Second Boer War and in WWI.

Second Boer War 1899–1902

In contrast to the First Boer War, the Second Boer War was a lengthy and bitter one. It involved large numbers of troops from the British Empire and resulted in the Boer Republics becoming British colonies. Unlike the First Boer War, the Empire forces defeated the Boer armies in open warfare after a long and bitter guerilla campaign.

The colonial forces according to a commentator[110] of the time were far superior to the British (Tommy) in their horsemanship and bushcraft. It was said: –

> *The horse is a noble animal, and the friend of man. That is very true; but Tommy is certainly not a friend of the horse. That is exactly where the Australian scores, or where (to use racing phrase) 'he romps in', he understands his horse to perfection, and knows how to save its energies; above all, he knows how to feed his best-loved companion. It is no unusual thing to see an Australian digging in the apparently fruitless veldt with a penknife. 'Just look at that fellow!' shouts Tommy, scornfully. 'What does he think he's doing?' Of course it is obvious that the man is searching for little roots and herbs which ease and help his horse.*[111]

However, it was not only in horsemanship the Australians proved their superiority. According to the same commentator –

> *For example, cooking, which strikes one as being rather a needful accomplishment, Tommy doesn't understand. He can't light a fire or make a cup of tea for himself; he has not learnt how to adapt nature to his uses. Whenever we rested for a while on the march, you would see the Australians drinking cups of tea, wither perhaps a little cake they had baked to eat with it, while poor Tommy would be looking round aimlessly for a bit of wood.*[112]

Camden men who were members of the New South Wales Mounted Rifles were among the first to enlist. Their familiarity with the Australian bush would prove invaluable on the South African veldt.

---

[110] Menpes, Mortimer Luddington – born in Port Adelaide, S.A. was a war artist for the British weekly illustrated magazine *Black and White.*
[111] Menpes, M., *War Impressions: Being a Record in Colour* (London, 1903)
[112] ibid

L-R Front: Unknown; Sergeant John Martin Hawkey; Unknown
L-R Back: Unknown; Private Richard Sharpe; Private Henry Sharpe
Photo courtesy Camden Historical Society

Camden News

Thursday July 6, 1899

The NSW Mounted Rifles

We understand that in the event of hostilities breaking out in the Transvaal the bulk of the Mounted Rifles would be willing to give their services, should the Government decide to make the offer of a contingent to the Imperial Authorities. Camden is the Headquarters of this regiment. The training of the 'Rifles' being on similar lines to that adopted by the Boers would appear to make them peculiarly fitted to African service. The regiment is well horsed and for the last four years has headed the list in musketry. The local range has been closed for several months and its loss is much felt.[113]

Camden News
Thursday October 26, 1899

Camden Mounted Rifles

Yesterday (Wednesday) morning was particularly lively by the members of the Camden Company assembling in Camden to undergo the necessary examination

---

[113] The Rifle Range was closed for maintenance due to it being deemed unsafe. The military authorities then decided they would not do the work because of the costs involved.

of their kit prior to their leaving the district for the seat of war at the Transvaal. We append the list of the members of the Mounted Rifles, who have so far presented themselves.

The examination was most satisfactory, and only in a few instances was the equipment replenished. The men assembled at the Mounted Rifles Drill Hall. We understand that the accepted mounted men will leave Menangle to-day (Thursday) for Sydney under command of Capt. JM Antill (Adjutant Mounted Rifles), with Lieut. AJ Onslow. The men chosen are of fine physique, and well trained practical horsemen. The examination of the kits was held under the supervision of Sergt. Major Holman, Staff Sergt. Richards, Lieut. GMM Onslow and other officers, several local civilians being present. Amongst the many soldiers present we noticed:—

Camden

Sergt.	Hawkey	Corp.	Nethery
Pte.	Butler	Pte.	Sharpe
	Rex Smith		Burke
	Axam		Potts
	Mills[114]		Learmonth[115]
	Parsons[116]		

Picton

Corpl.	Wardrobe	Corpl.	Bateup
	Osborne	Pte.	Maxwell
Pte.	Reilly		Cleary
	Field		Smith Geo[117]
	Seymour[118]		Longhurst[119]
	Sharpe		

Private Parsons,[120] of Camden, has been chosen to act as farrier, or shoeing smith to the regiment. The wish of the Camden residents is, that honour may attend the efforts of the local contingent, and may they reach our shores after the faithful and honourable discharge of their duties.

Camden News
Thursday November 16, 1899
NSW Mounted Rifles
LAST DESPATCH OF THE MEN

From our shores the balance of the Rifles contingent left Newcastle yesterday (Wednesday) by the steamer Langton Grange, for South Africa. The men were accorded an enthusiastic send off. The steamer conveys near 700 horses, which our local men will have charge of. The following are the names of the officers and men leaving by the Langton Grange: 1st Lieut AJM Onslow, Sergt. J Wasson, Sergt. Farrier J Hawkey, Corpls. A Bateup, E Osborne, J Wardrobe, Ptes. F Axam, J Blackwood, AJ Bollard, M Burke, A Butler, E Cleary, J Hughes, WG Lloyd,

---

[114] Mills, James Ebeneezer - Name does not appear on Nominal Roll or in Murray Index
[115] Learmonth, Joseph Stuart - Name does not appear on Nominal Roll or in Murray Index
[116] Parsons, Archibald - Name does not appear on Nominal Roll or in Murray Index
[117] Smith, George - Name does not appear on Nominal Roll or in Murray Index
[118] Seymour, Arthur Allan - Name does not appear on Nominal Roll or in Murray Index
[119] Longhurst, James Patrick - Name does not appear on Nominal Roll or in Murray Index
[120] No reference to Private Parsons of Camden can be found in the Australian War Memorial records for the Boer War

J Maxwell, PT Moore, R Nethery, H Pearce, P Reilly, G Clifford, H Sharp, R Sharp, B Spearing, W Tweedie, W Wintle, J Field.

Camden News
Thursday December 21, 1899

The officer commanding the New South Wales Mounted Rifles (Lieutenant Colonel Macarthur-Onslow) of Camden has offered his services to go to the front. The regiment is already represented there by 100 men, which is 25 percent of the strength, but it seems another 50 will be readily available. We are in receipt of information that it is the intention of the Mounted Rifles, of which Camden is the head centre, to obtain men from each squadron, viz., Camden, Picton, Bega, Inverell, Molong, Tenterfield, Bathurst and Forbes. The regiment is 400 strong, made up of half squadrons of 50 men in each centre. Much local enthusiasm prevails at each of the townships named, the men being typical Australians are anxious that their services might be accepted. The barracks, or head centre in Camden, is daily in receipt of telegrams, letters etc. from members of the regiment and others offering their services. We are unable to obtain the names of those volunteering for active service, as the officers in charge are naturally and discreetly most reticent. Much activity prevails locally by the regimental officers and absorbing interest is daily manifested as the latest war news is posted up on the Camden News *large war board.*

Major Astley John Onslow Thompson of the Camden Mounted Rifles, also Manager of the Camden Park Estate, did not participate in the war. However, he was tasked by the Government to purchase suitable remounts to be sent to South Africa. He travelled to areas such as Carcoar, Blayney and Parkes in search of suitable mounts.

The Carcoar Chronicle
Friday, 5 January 1900, page 3

Last Thursday 42 horses were purchased here for the Imperial Government by Major Thompson. The horses averaged £13 per head. Major Thompson complimented Mr T Gordon upon the number and condition of the horses he bought from that gentleman. Major Thompson will probably be back about the 26th January to make further purchases.

However, to the disappointment of many, Onslow Thompson had a keen eye for horseflesh and could not be tricked into purchasing unsound horses.

Western Champion (Parkes)
Friday, 9 February 1900, page 6

Much disappointment was expressed in town on Friday at the studied care with which Major Thompson purchased horses for South Africa. The Major could not be 'got at', and sent most of the horses inspected to the right about. Out of 750 inspected, only 75 were selected. This shows how carefully the Major made his choice. Some horses were sold at £20 ($40), but the average price was £11 1s ($22.10).

Not all the men who volunteered were accepted for service overseas. One who was rejected, and/or was denied the rank he believed his due, was Captain Willie Larkin of the New South Wales Mounted Rifles, Picton Half Company, who had been placed on the reserve list in January 1899.

LARKIN, Willie: *Born* 2 February 1870 Picton, NSW. *Parents:* Edward Gerald Larkin and Ann Bollard. *Occupation:* auctioneer, Mayor Camden. *Died*: 8 October 1963 Camden, NSW. *Buried:* St Paul's Church of England, Cobbitty, NSW. *Spouse:* Doris Vicary. *Married:* 27 February 1918 Camden, NSW.

Camden News
Thursday February 1, 1900

We are in a position to state that, unless extreme circumstances arise Capt. Larkin, (Reserve) NSW Mounted Rifles, will not be leaving for the seat of war. Capt. Larkin resigned his position as the council clerk of Picton, simply owing to pressing business and his many future engagements as an auctioneer and amanuensis[121] to Mr RH Inglis of Camden and Picton.

Camden News
Thursday February 8, 1900

On Tuesday at the Camden Sale Yards, we interviewed Capt. Larkin and asked *him if it was his intention to leave for the seat of war. The reply was, 'Yes certainly, I think I have been a soldier for peace long enough and now I go as a soldier for war.' Capt. Larkin takes with him his noted horse Butcher Boy, 15.2, which has been at work, and won prizes in Camden.*

Lieutenant-Colonel J Macarthur-Onslow to rank as Major proceeds with Bushmen's Contingent to the Transvaal with Captain W Larkin as Adjutant. Captain Larkin left on Wednesday morning to take up his duties in camp prior to leaving Australia. To Major Onslow and Captain Larkin the wish of all is a speedy return to their native country. Major Onslow has already experienced active service in India, a capable soldier and devoted to soldier work and deeply in touch and sympathy with his subalterns. We wish both local men God Speed.

Despite Captain Larkin's willingness to go to South Africa he was again rejected and Camden was indignant.

Camden News
Thursday February 22, 1900

The Bushmen's Contingent
INDIGNATION MEETING IN CAMDEN
WHY WAS NOT CAPTAIN LARKIN
ACCEPTED!

Tuesday evening at the Camden School of Arts showed by attendance the eagerness in which the importance of the occasion demanded. Those who attended the sale were agreeably surprised, nay, expected to find a requisition to the Government why Capt. Larkin (Reserve) was not included amongst the officers appointed to take up a prominent position in the contingent. Within an hour the attendance at the Camden sale signed the requisition which had been roughly drawn up, asking the mayor to call a public meeting to offer their indignation as to why and wherefore Capt. Larkin had been excluded. The rough

---

[121] A person employed to write or type what another dictates or to copy what has been written by another, and also refers to a person who signs a document on behalf of another under the latter's authority

benches of the sale yards were accorded the honour of an 'office'. In less than an hour 200 names were placed on the written requisition to the mayor.

The public meeting was held at the Camden School of Arts. The mayor was unanimously appointed to the chair. The attendance was even greater than could be expected at the limited notice given.

The mayor, being absent from Camden during the day, read the various papers submitted to him, declared the meeting open.

(We regret that owing to the telegraphic communication being cut off at 8.45 p.m. from Camden to Campbelltown no report of the meeting appeared in the Sydney newspapers of Wednesday.)

[THE OBJECT IN BRIEF]

On or about the 30th January Captain Larkin was asked if he would accept the position of Adjutant of the Bushmen's Contingent. He replied to the effect that he would if allowed to go into camp on Wednesday the 7th February, as he required a week to settle his private affairs. He received a wire the following day, telling him that Wednesday the 7th February would do, and to come into camp that day. He at once made all preparations to go, dissolved his partnership, sold his horses and cattle for whatever he could get for them, resigned various positions that he held, and insured his life at a heavy cost. He heard nothing further from the military authorities, and on Wednesday the 7th February presented himself at the camp at Kensington, in uniform with his horse and all camp necessaries, ready for immediate duty. On reporting himself to the senior officer on the ground he was curtly informed that he would not have the adjutancy as it was to be given to Lieut. Ryrie[122] of the Artillery. No apology was offered him nor an explanation why he had been brought down under false pretences. Captain Larkin left camp and returned to his residence by the next train. On the following day he was asked by telegram if he would now accept the position of Adjutant, he replied, 'Yes if it would not injure Ryrie,' or words to that effect. He next day received a further telegram asking him if he wished to throw up his commission in the Bushmen's Contingent. He replied, 'No,' that he was ready to take up the duties of adjutant any minute. To this he received a reply stating that that position had been filled and offering him a position as Squadron Officer, which he declined.

Mr. Whiteman, an alderman of Camden, then moved the following resolution:

> 'That this meeting having been informed, on reliable authority, that the particulars of the offer of Captain Larkin to proceed to South Africa on active service with the Bushmen's Contingent are true, desires to express the sympathy of the inhabitants of Camden and the surrounding district, with that gentleman in the trying and false position in which we believe he has been placed by the military authorities.'

Ald. Whiteman considered that an enquiry was due to Capt. Larkin and the townships which that gentleman represented, and if an injustice had been done full enquiry should be made and the parties, whoever they may be, are brought to account, he felt an enquiry should be held. He doubted not that a gross injustice had been done to Capt. Larkin, and that the authorities should be made to explain their action. Ald. Rankin seconded the resolution.

---

[122] Ryrie, Stanley Stewart – born 1874 Cooma, NSW youngest son of the Hon. A. Ryrie, M.L.C., Micalago, NSW

The following resolutions were then put to the meeting, and each were unanimously carried, not a single hand being held up to the contrary;

> 'That this meeting for the sake of the well-being of the Contingent, and the good name of our military forces, and in justice to Captain Larkin, respectfully and confidently prays the Hon. the Minister for Defence to order an immediate enquiry to be held on the matter and an explanation furnished to the numerous subscribers to the Bushmen's Fund in NSW as to why an officer, described as one of the finest and most able mounted officers in the colony by General Hutton,[123] late GCO of the NSW Forces, and by the late and existing commanding officers of the Mounted Rifles, is passed over in favour of an artillery subaltern, and that with marked and unseemly discourtesy and disregard to his personal feelings.
>
> That a copy of these resolutions be forwarded to the Member for the district, Mr John Kidd, this afternoon, and that he be requested to forward it to the Minister for Defence immediately as the Contingent may sail any day and the necessary evidence be unavailable.'

The meeting then terminated.

No reply to the meeting's resolutions appears in the *Camden News*.

The following men enlisted from the Camden/Picton district but only a few wrote home and their letters were published or they were interviewed by their local newspapers.

AKERS, Stanley Ernest: *Rank:* (1) Trooper #555 (2) Trooper #4. *Unit*: (1) New South Wales Lancers (2) 5th Battalion, Australian Commonwealth Horse. *Departed: (1)* 3 March 1899 *SS Nineveh* (to UK), 30 November 1899 (to South Africa). *Returned: (1)* invalided to Australia 30 July 1900. *Departed: (2)* 22 May 1902 *SS Columbian.*
Returned: (2) 1 August 1902 *HMT Manchester Marshal*. *Born:* 1877 Burrawang, NSW. *Parents*: Henry Akers and Elizabeth Quenall. *Spouse:* Elizabeth Firman. *Died:* 14 March 1973 Dorrigo, NSW. *Buried:* Dorrigo Cemetery. *Honours:* Queen's South Africa Medal.

Akers was one of a squadron of 100, under Captain Charles Frederick Cox, who had gone to England in 1899. The squadron arrived in London on 28 May 1899 to take part in the annual military tournament at Islington, and undertook training with the 6th Dragoon Guards at Aldershot; the expense for the trip was defrayed by the regiment. When the 2nd Boer War broke out Cox cabled Sydney for permission for volunteers to participate as part of an Australian contingent; this was agreed to. The squadron, with their horses, then proceeded to Cape Town, where they were equipped with service uniforms.

Akers returned to Australia in January 1901 but enlisted for the second time in 1902. His second unit, the 5th Battalion Australian Commonwealth Horse, was still at sea when the Boer War ended. The unit stayed for only a few weeks before returning to Sydney.

---

[123] Hutton, Sir Edward Thomas Henry – was a British regular soldier and first organiser of the Australian Army,

Bowral Free Press and *Berrima District Intelligence*
Wednesday, 8 August 1900

Letter from Trooper Akers

Trooper Stanley Akers, of East Kangaloon, has forwarded us the following further particulars of his experience while engaged in the campaign against South Africa: -

We left New South Wales, under Captain Cox, for Aldershot, where we received six months' sound training. After the expiration of that time we went to the Cape, and from there to Stellenbosch, where I was engaged a few months in breaking-in horses; from there we journeyed to de Aar, where we separated, twenty-eight of us going to Naauwpoort and the remainder to the Orange River. At Naauwpoort we stopped a month, principally patrolling. The next move was to Arundel, where we had a skirmish with the enemy. From Arundel to Rensburg we proceeded next, and had several skirmishes, at which several of our men were killed. From Rensburg we returned to Arundel; another fortnight's patrolling; then to Belmont; camped and changed horses and started for Keats River, where we had a sharp encounter; next, to Modder River, at which place we captured a large Boer camp; from Modder River went to the relief of Kimberley, on which route water was very scanty, after which we engaged in very heavy fighting – many casualties on both sides.

From here we went to Paardeberg, where we were engaged in more severe fighting and had a very rough time; provisions being very scanty on account of the river being flooded. At Paardeberg we assisted in the capture of Cronje,[124] and from there we fought our way to Abram's Cross; here I had a very narrow escape, a bullet passing through my haversack. From thence to Bloemfontein where we had more heavy fighting. I was taken ill here with enteric fever, and walked twenty miles to hospital, where I was laid up for seven weeks and four days. I had a very severe attack, and the doctors gave no hope of my recovery; it affected my head principally, and I was most of the time delirious, being six weeks unconscious, as were nearly all the other sufferers. Many succumbed to this fatal disease, and few days passed without someone being carried out dead before my eyes; however, I was fortunate enough to pull through, and at the end of the aforesaid time was sufficiently recovered to be removed to Wynberg hospital, and so make room at Bloemfontein hospital for those coming from the front. At Wynberg I was laid up for seven weeks and two days. As regards the treatment in these hospitals, I have much pleasure in saying that I was treated with every consideration and kindness, and excepting that they were worked a little short-handed, I fail to see on what grounds anyone could reasonably find room for complaint.

ANDERSON, William Samuel: *Rank:* Trooper #162. *Unit:* 2nd New South Wales Mounted Rifles. *Departed:* 15 March 1901 *SS Maplemore* or *SS Custodian*. *Returned:* 4 June 1902 *HMT Aurania*. *Occupation:* labourer, Picton. *Born:* 1882 Sydney, NSW. *Parents:* Archibald Anderson and Ann Jane Taylor. *Died:* 13 June 1953 East Sydney, NSW. *Buried:* Rookwood General. *Honours:* Queen's South Africa Medal with 2 clasps.

---

[124] Cronje, General Pieter

ANTILL, Edward Augustus: *Rank:* (1) Lieutenant (Acting Captain) (2) Major. *Unit:* 'A' Battery Royal Australian Artillery. *Departed:* 4 November 1899 *SS Aberdeen*. *Returned:* 15 September 1901 *SS Harlech Castle*. *Occupation:* Professional soldier. *Born:* 4 December 1867 Jarvisfield, Picton, NSW. *Parents:* John Macquarie Antill and Jessie Hassall Campbell. *Died:* 19 March 1905 Franklin Fort, Vic. *Buried:* Vault Hill, Picton, NSW. *Spouse:* Lilian Mary Christian. *Married:* 19 June 1902 Sydney, NSW. *Honours:* Companion of the Order of Bath, Queen's South Africa Medal with 3 clasps.

Edward Augustus Antill

Darling Downs Gazette
Wednesday, 22 March 1905

DEATH OF MAJOR ANTILL

Major EA Antill RAA died from Bright's Disease[125] at Point Franklin Fort, near Queenscliff (Vic), on Saturday morning. Deceased, who was 38 years of age, had been a member of the New South Wales Military Forces for several years, and served with the 'A' Battery in South Africa. He was transferred to Victoria 12 months ago, and received command of No. 5 Company of the RAA.

The late Major Antill came of a well-known Picton family, and was born in 1867. He joined the Permanent Artillery Forces here in 1891. When the 'A' Battery left Sydney for the Boer War on December 30, 1899, he held the rank of Lieutenant, and was second in command to Colonel Smith.[126] He served in Cape Colony, the Orange Free State, and the Transvaal, and received the Queen's medal with three clasps. Soon after returning to New South Wales, in 1901, he was sent to Queensland on military duty, and after another short term of service here, was transferred to Victoria. He obtained the rank of Captain in 1903 and in the same year that of Brevet-Major also. For about two years past he has been stationed with the garrison at Queenscliff. The deceased officer was a brother of Lieutenant-Colonel JM Antill, of the Australian Light Horse, and brother-in-law to Colonel Lassetter.[127]

---

[125] kidney disease that would be described in modern medicine as acute or chronic nephritis.
[126] Smith, Sydenham Campbell Urquhart
[127] *Australian Town and Country Journal*, 22 March 1905, p 24

ANTILL, John Macquarie: *Rank:* (1) Captain (2) Major. *Unit:* (1) 'A' Squadron New South Wales Mounted Rifles (2) 2nd New South Wales Mounted Rifles. *Departed: (1)* 4 November 1899 *SS Aberdeen. Returned: (1)* January 1901 *HMAT Orient. Departed: (2)* 15 March 1901 *SS Maplemore or SS Custodian. Returned: (2)* 4 June 1902 *HMT Aurania. Occupation:* Professional soldier. *Born:* 26 January 1866 Jarvisfield, Picton, NSW. *Parents:* John Macquarie Antill and Jessie Hassall Campbell. *Died:* 1 March 1937 Royal Prince Alfred Hospital, Sydney. *Buried:* Vault Hill, Picton, NSW. *Spouse:* Marion Agnes Wills-Allen. *Married:* 24 October 1901 St James' Church of England, Sydney, NSW. *Honours:* Companion of the Order of Bath. Queen's South Africa Medal with 7 clasps, twice Mentioned in Despatches.

John Macquarie Antill

Antill, known as Bullant, did a tour of duty with the British Army in India in 1893, where he served with the 1st Battalion, Devonshire Regiment and the 2nd Dragoon Guards (The Queen's Bays). This period of service with the British Army in India had been arranged by Major-General Edward Hutton, the commander of the New South Wales Military Forces. On his return to Australia in 1894, Antill was commissioned into the state's regular forces as a Captain. Antill saw only limited action during the war, but he was present during the Battle of Paardeberg on 18 February 1900. Antill returned to Australia in January 1901, but returned to South Africa in March as second in command of the 2nd New South Wales Mounted Rifles, taking part in the capture of Potgieter's convoy on the River Vaal.

He also served WWI #5002 firstly as a Staff Sergeant and later as a Brevet Lieutenant-Colonel with the 3rd Light Horse Brigade.

Camden News
Thursday, 16 November 1899

SOUTH AFRICA CONTINGENT

From Capt. JM Antill, as follows in reply to the telegram sent by the Mayor.

> *SS Aberdeen, Sunday, 6th November,*
> *From the Officer Commanding Troops,*
> *To His Worship the Mayor of Camden.*
>
> *Sir, —*
> *On behalf of myself and this portion of the NSW Contingent I have to thank you for your kind wishes and beg that you will convey to your fellow aldermen our appreciation of their thoughtful act in sending the telegram received by me on Friday. I sincerely hope that the same warm welcome may await the troops on their return from South Africa. Yours etc.,*
>
> *JM Antill, Capt. Commanding troops per SS Aberdeen*

Camden News
Thursday, 4 January 1900, page 2

LETTER FROM CAPTAIN ANTILL THE
ABERDEEN TROOPSHIP IN A STORM

Mr JM Antill, of Jarvisfield, has received a letter from his son, Capt. Antill, who went in the Aberdeen *in command of the Mounted Rifles and Infantry detachments to South Africa. In the course of it he says, in a letter written on board, just before he reached Port Elizabeth: —*

> We had very rough weather since we left Albany, and I thought, more than once, we would lose a lot of the horses. It was a frightful storm, and one could only stand and hope the fixings would not give way, huge seas breaking over the ship. It seemed impossible for the horses to stand, but they got very cunning, and swayed backwards and forward like old salts. Some of them got down, and then came the job of landing them on their feet again. It was no light work, as, having been standing for a month and being very weary, they preferred stopping as they were. But this could not be chanced, owing to the danger of them kicking the next horses and breaking their legs. Many of my men were also laid up at the very time their services were most required. They had been vaccinated a week before, and as the lymph was bad I had 35 men down with what seemed a sort of blood poisoning, the temperature of 12 of them being over 103.5. But at the time I am writing they are all doing better, and I hope to land them well, although weak. All the NCOs and men behaved splendidly all through. A gust carried away part of the roofing of the stables, and it sailed across the ship, just missing a dozen men, but fortunately hurting none of them. The ship officers are a capital lot of fellows, and they, with our officers, constitute a very happy family. All our officers, NCOs, and men are very impatient to get at the Boers.

Near the end of his letter, Captain Antill says: —

> We have reached Port Elizabeth without any casualty. Got orders at once to go on to Cape Town. Latest news promises to give us a good fight. I make everybody carry out the duties just as in camp in every detail. It is funny sometimes, when going through drill, to see a whole rank suddenly break away with a lurch of the ship and see them flounder about like a mob of sheep.

On the outside of the envelope Captain Antill writes: —

> Cape Town: Arrived this morning (6th). Changing to khaki and magazine rifles. Go straight to De Aar. No losses to men or horses. I think it will prove a record voyage.

Camden News
Thursday, 11 January 1900, page 2

LETTER FROM CAPTAIN ANTILL

Mr JM Antill has received the following letter from his son, Captain Antill, who commands the Mounted Rifles detachment which went to South Africa by the Aberdeen:

> Cape Town, December 8

We got here all right, without loss or casualty, and moved out to Green Point, to await the arrival of the Langton Grange, *expected in a few days. They are taking over our transport and transport horses and giving us mules and vehicles as more adaptable to the country. It is going to be a big thing, and will last three months at least. There are a lot of Boer prisoners here, decent enough looking fellows, and more arriving every day. The Boers are using explosive bullets in the north, and some of the wounds are terrible. An arm hit is shattered to pieces, and some of the hits are extraordinary. One of our chaps got a bullet through the temple and went out at the other and is all right. Another through the temple and out at the lip, and is doing first rate.*

The Imperial staff here is splendid. No red tape, gives you all you want in five minutes. It is refreshing having to deal with them. No bother, fuss or anything of the kind.

They are taking all our colours off, black stripes, puttees, etc. and in fact everything which shows and substituting brown, and even painting the buttons. And officers have to leave their swords behind and take carbines. Bayley went on last night in charge of about 100 men (infantry), but the other specials are here with the AMC. My men are a fine lot and I would not wish for better. Holman (Sergeant-Major) is all that could be desired, also the NCOs, McLean idem.[128] *The feathers in our hats are a great draw, going to take them out before we go and probably take helmets.*

Camden News
Thursday, 22 February 1900, page 2

THE WAR
New South Wales Mounted Rifles.
THEIR BAPTISM OF FIRE
NEWS FROM CAPTAIN ANTILL

Writing from Honwater, near Britstown, Orange River, on the 17th January, to a friend at Waratah, Captain JM Antill, of the New South Wales Mounted Rifles, says: —

We stayed at Cape Town for 10 days, awaiting the second draft of horses by the Langton Grange, *and then entrained to De Aar, where, after a week in the dirtiest horriblest hole it has been my lot to strike, we were sent by forced march of 135 miles to Prieska, a pretty town on the Orange River (which is practically the boundary between the Cape Colony and Griqualand); there to rout out a force of rebels who had taken possession of the north side of the river and threatened to take the town. Got there at 8 a.m., 3rd instant, and, under cover of the last hour of dark, lined the river, and got the 'cards' on the hop at 4.30. Wounded a few of them, sending them sheltering over the kopjes as if the devil were after them. Only got two wounded, one of whom had four bullets through him, but annexed a quantity of arms, ammunition, and stores. Two days after made a sally into the enemy's country with a troop just after midnight, and 16 miles out surprised and took eight Boers, together with their arms, ammunition, 10 horses, two real nice carts and harness, and 1000 sheep. After waiting four days, a force of 1000 came down, in a devil of a rage, and having only 80 men I was directed to retire on Britstown, there being a great danger of our*

---

[128] 'the same'

being cut off. Got clear away with my prisoners, sheep, etc. at 3 o'clock a.m., and three hours after, the enemy, on occupying the town, was much disgusted to find we had slipped them.

Here I am to stay keeping watch over Britstown and De Aar until further orders; expect to be recalled, though, in a few days. The Boers are having the best end of the stick so far owing to the tremendous extent of country we have to watch, with an inadequate force. The Boers are first-rate shots, good artillerymen, and are well entrenched in every position they take up. As soon as our guns find the range of one of theirs, they stop firing, leave the gun, which our people fondly imagine they have destroyed or silenced, go away and smoke for an hour or two, then start again. So you never know exactly when you have them. They won't, however, attack at night, or expose themselves, leaving all the attack to us, while they ensconce their men behind good cover and wait until our men expose themselves in open country at short ranges to their accurate fire, and then they pour a hail of lead upon the poor Tommy, who is entirely without cover or protection. It will be a long and bloody fight, and I expect it to last six months longer anyway, but it should be a good go, and promises lots of fun for those who can keep a clean skin.

At the present time we are resting on one of Cecil Rhodes' farms, and I am the guest of the manager.

Camden News
Thursday, 5 April 1900, page 8

THE WAR
New South Wales Mounted Rifles
LETTERS FROM THE FRONT

Captain Antill, commanding the New South Wales Mounted Rifles in South Africa has written to his father the following interesting letter, dated Bank's Drift, Modder River, 21-2-1900

A bitter battle has been raging here the last five days, and we have a few hours off so I will send a few lines along.

The last nine days have been very eventful, and it is wonderful how our fellows have got through so far without any of us being killed. We have been under hot fire five days out of the eight. A few horses have been killed and five men wounded, one dangerously - flint through the chest. The others — T. Ball[129], Chesher[130], Corporals Owens[131] and Nethery[132] — not seriously.

We had our first hot fight at Ramah on the 8th – eight hours under fire without seeing a Boer although there were 1000 of them on a line of kopjes 700 yards off with two guns. We were protecting our convoy with about 800 men; our total casualties being about 100. I joined General French,[133] who left us at Reit River next day, and marched into Kimberley. We started next day to follow him under Kitchener at 3 a.m., and before we got four miles

---

[129] Ball, Thomas #70 – invalided to Australia 14 July 1900
[130] Chesher, George # 23 – wounded Paardeberg, invalided to Australia arrived 30 August 1900
[131] Owens, Frank Patrick #12 – wounded Paardeberg, invalided to Australia arrived 28 May 1900
[132] Nethery, Robert John #94
[133] French, General John

we struck the tail of Cronje's[134] *army from Magersfontein and had a hard fight with him. He was off to Bloemfontein, and we were just in time to turn him. Had the honour to lead the attack to take two kopjes occupied by his rear-guard, and the men marched up to and took them just as steadily as if on parade, to the admiration of all the other troops. We drove them off without loss, only having poor Flint*[135] *knocked down. The bullets and shrapnel like a hailstorm all round. This brought on a general engagement in which we knocked him about a good deal, forcing him to retreat during the night 16th eastward. Camped out on the veldt that night, and were sent on by General Kelly-Kenny*[136] *early next morning to hang on to Cronje's tail. Followed him all day with only my squadron, with the Imperial MI, for supports. At 3 we bumped against him in force, and were met with heavy rifle fire and the Unrighteous pom-pom, the only gun which disconcerts our troops. One man was wounded, although it was a miracle that half of us were not killed. The CO was very much pleased with our work and reports, which enabled Lord Kitchener to locate the enemy exactly.*

Next day the big battle raged all day. We were kept ready on the river with other mounted troops, it being supposed that he would try to get out. In the meantime General French returned from Kimberley round his left and got round his front, and here we have him cornered since. Have utterly destroyed his laager and ammunition, but as yet he has not struck. The day before yesterday he offered to surrender on condition that he should be allowed to march out, men and all, but Lord Roberts would not listen to it and we have been at him ever since. Yesterday Lord Kitchener sent me to move round his right front and capture a long range of kopjes he (the enemy) had taken during the night, it being supposed that he had only 200 men there. We struck a snag — there were several hundreds and being five miles out were nearly cut off. The Boers gave us pom-pom again (pound shelling at 100 per minute) but we got off with one wounded (Corporal Owens).[137]

The men had tried several times to storm their trench but could not get in. They are magnificent fighters and their courage is quite equal to the best traditions of the British Army. Never a Boer has been seen to leave his position. They have the river heavily sheltered for about 100 yards as well, and with their smokeless powder it is impossible to find them. Our side has lost heavily, and among them poor Grieve,[138] *who was killed the 18th while storming the trenches with the second battalion of the Black Watch (the old 73rd grandfather's*[139] *regiment). He was hit in the stomach while assisting a wounded man and afterwards through the chest and head. It was in time to put the poor fellow (who had won golden opinions everywhere and especially with the Highlanders) into his last resting place, together with 26 of his regiment who had fallen the same day. The old 73rd have so far, out of 27 officers, only three untouched. The Seaforths have lost heavily, too — in fact, all the infantry. They always give us the scouting and advance guard work.*

---

[134] Cronje, General Pieter Arnoldus
[135] Flint, Private Clive died at Wynberg, South Africa 24 June 1900
[136] Kelly-Kenny, General Sir Thomas
[137] Owens, Corporal Frank Patrick #12 – wounded at Paardeberg 19 February 1900 and invalided home
[138] Grieve, Lieutenant Gordon James, Special Service Officers, attached to 2nd The Black Watch; killed Paardeberg Drift, South Africa 18 February 1900
[139] Antill, Major Henry Colden of the 73rd (Perthshire) Regiment of Foot (formerly the Black Watch) who arrived as aide-de-camp to the Governor.

We are on one-third ration – two large supply columns having been surprised at Jacobsdal and taken. The horses are on 6 lb per day. I have not seen Ted [his brother with A Battery]. He must be at Modder. Will write if I get through this after it is settled but one can't say who will be the next to go. But we are all doing our best, so are satisfied with whatever may happen. After the surrender of General Cronje a staff officer galloped up and asked, 'Is this the NSW Mounted Rifles?' 'Yes sir.' 'Then Lord Roberts wishes you to report yourself at headquarters at once.' This was done, when Lord Roberts paid our squadron the high compliment of deputing it to be the first of all the troops present to enter the laager of the enemy and take possession of it.

Captain Antill's New South Wales Mounted Rifles commandeering the enemy's milk en route to Prieska; (Illustrated London News, reprinted Camden News April 5, 1900)

Camden News
Thursday, 3 May 1900, page 2

THE WAR
Official Letter from the Front
CAPTAIN ANTILL AND THE MOUNTED RIFLES
CONSPICUOUSLY STEADY UNDER FIRE

Major-General French has received from Bloemfontein an official letter from Captain J Antill, officer commanding the New South Wales Mounted Rifles, dated March 22, from which the following extracts are made :–

My last advice was from Ramah, which we left on February 10, joining Colonel Hannay's brigade en route to Modder River. There has been continuous marching and fighting up to March 12 when we were at Abraham's Kraal. The hours are long, generally 16 daily. The squadron acted in the advance guard right up to the present, and has taken part in almost every action. The men have been conspicuously steady under fire, and have been fortunate to earn warm praise from Colonel Hannay[140] (who was killed at Paardeberg). Our casualties to date are 6 wounded and one killed — Private W. Abrahams,[141] who was shot through the heart on the 10th. Abrahams came from Bega, was an excellent steady, and first-rate young soldier.

Rations and forage have been very scarce, and for the last month have been reduced to half issue. We lost several horses under fire, but made them up by commandeering ponies from the enemy. The following men have gone to hospital suffering, it is feared, from enteric fever: — Privates Spearing,[142] H Sharpe,[143] W Pearce,[144] Miller[145] and Kirkland.[146] There dropped out on the road, sick, Privates M Symonds,[147] Bateup,[148] Gosper,[149] Trevitt,[150] and Potts,[151] and they have not yet returned, so am unable to say if yet discharged. The six wounded are also on the line of communication, but all doing well. The discipline of all ranks is excellent, and their work everything which can be desired.

General Edwin Alderson who commanded the mounted infantry described Antill as '*a dashing and capable leader in action and remarkably* cool *under fire'.*[152]

AXAM, Francis William: *Rank:* Private #85. *Unit:* 'A' Squadron New South Wales Mounted Rifles. *Departed:* 16 November 1899 *SS Langton Grange. Returned:* 8 January 1901 *HMT Orient. Born:* 1879 Wollongong, NSW. *Parents:* Charles Axam and Sarah Blow. *Died:* 9 February 1953 Bundaberg, Qld. *Buried:* Bundaberg General. *Spouse:* Gertrude Mary Robinson. *Honours:* Queen's South Africa Medal with 6 clasps.

Francis' brother Charles Edward Axam, and Uncle, Joseph Axam, were working at Camden Park, Menangle at the time he enlisted; he also attended King George V Coronation in 1911.

---

[140] Hannay, Colonel Ormelie Campbell – Argyll & Sutherland Highlanders Killed in action near Paardeberg. 18th Feb. 1900 aged 51
[141] Abrahams, William John #15 killed in action 10 March 1900 Abraham's Kraal
[142] Spearing, Benjamin Charles #98
[143] Sharpe, Henry #96
[144] Pearce, Wellington Henry #101
[145] Miller, Christian #47
[146] Kirkland, Wilfred John #35
[147] Symonds, Michael James #62
[148] Bateup, Amos Albert #82
[149] Gosper, Charles #31
[150] Trevitt, George Spurway #63
[151] Potts, Pembroke #53
[152] Records of Australian Contingents to the War in South Africa 1899–1902; compiled and edited for the Department of Defence by Lieut-Colonel P.L. Murray, RAA (Ret)

The Campbelltown Herald
Wednesday, 7 February 1900, page 2

LETTER FROM PRIVATE F. AXAM

Private F Axam, a Campbelltown representative at the seat of war, writes to a friend under date de Aar, Dec. 29 1899, as follows: —

According to promise I am writing you this letter. I have very little chance of writing – sometimes have to make two or three starts. My writing table is a bag spread on the ground, with a piece of paper under my writing materials, so you can guess our trouble in scribbling a few lines; but that doesn't matter, as we are having pretty fair times, plenty of work in the saddle, just what we came for.

Francis William (Frank) Axam

I will tell you a little about our voyage across to Cape Town and then the train journey of 700 miles to here. We left Newcastle amidst great excitement, thousands of people crowding the wharves to give a last cheer. The pilot and ferry boats followed out through the Heads, and kept with us till long after dark. We saw the Australian coast now and then for five or six days, and then for twenty-eight days we only sighted two sailing vessels. Our first call was Port Natal, where we unloaded 350 horses. We had the chance of landing for about half an hour, spending most of the time watching the niggers [sic.], who line the shores in hundreds. The scenery about this place is grand. The hills in the distance look very green, with orchards and farms scattered about. After a short delay we started our voyage to Port Elizabeth, about two days sail; stayed there about four hours. This is a very pretty place —a very nice town, and everything lively. There are plenty of niggers [sic.] here, and they seem to do a good deal of road work. They are in lots of about fifty, with an Englishman over them. He carries a whip, and drives them about like a mob of calves, not forgetting to make use of the whip.

We again started off for Cape Town, and anchored in Table Bay after thirty-five days at sea. In the evening we got alongside the wharf, unloaded our horses, and then proceeded to camp. I enjoyed the trip very much, not getting the least seasick. Most of the others were sick for a week. We had a few days' rough weather, which shook the boat a good deal. I did not mind the rough weather in the least. Sometimes one would think the boat was *going to turn over, and then she would make a dive in the next wave and the spray would break over the bow and someone would get well drenched, and then you would hear some murmurs. My mare looks real well after the long voyage, considering that she had to stand in the same place the whole time; she was a bit lively when I first got on her.*

After spending a day and a night in the camp at Cape Town, we had our horses put on the train and started our journey. We were 40 hours in the train, travelling through rough, mountainous country. All bridges and passes were guarded by soldiers. The railway runs through the most desolate country imaginable, nothing but bare and rocky hills and flats. I asked how long it was since it rained, and they said three years. No rain has fallen for nine months where we are camped, so we are living in dust. No one could believe what it is like unless they saw it. The rivers we have crossed are dry, not a drop of water in any of them. We have plenty of water to drink and also for the horses, obtained from bores. After two or three days' spell we started patrolling the country. Yesterday we came across a party of niggers [sic.] and Germans, and searched them and found something that belonged to the British, so made the Germans prisoners of war.

We leave here for the front in about nine days, about 200 miles from here; we are going to escort the Royal Artillery, so expect a good time. I spent a good Christmas (plenty of cake and wine), and hope to hear that you and your people did the same. How are they getting on at home? We have had no colonial mails yet. Have no time to write any more; just ordered to be in the saddle in ten minutes to go somewhere, so conclude by wishing you a happy New Year.

The Campbelltown Herald
Wednesday, 7 March 1900, page 2

Letter from the Front

Writing to his parents at Mount Gilead, Campbelltown, under date Orange River, February 2nd, Private Frank Axam says: —

I received your letter, and was glad to hear all was well. I am getting the best of health. This is the first day's spell we have had for a fortnight, having been on the road almost all the time, day and night. We start again at 3 a.m. tomorrow. I feel much better than when I started. I have not slept in a tent for over a month, but I like sleeping out; it does not hurt anyone. We are going to Modder River, 75 miles from here, and by the end of next week there will be 70,000 troops stationed there. I scarcely know how the war is going on, as we have had no news since we started on the march. We crossed the Orange River yesterday, into Griqualand West – the first Boer land we have been stationed on, although we crossed the river before and captured some of the enemy who have been sent to Cape Town. The Orange River is large and muddy. It runs with a strong current. The water is the same as that in a dirty waterhole – not too good to drink. While on the road we passed a number of farmhouses, where we obtained a good supply of water, which is got by sinking about 35ft; it is pumped by a wind-mill. We came across a few English people and loyal Dutch, who are always pleased to see us marching through the villages. A great many of the Dutch show a black face, but say nothing. Some of the towns are very pretty. I saw Shaw last night. He is all right, and is going with us to the river. No time to write more.

The Campbelltown Herald
Wednesday, 18 April 1900, page 2

The War
Letter from Private F Axam

Writing to his parents from Modder River under date March 3rd Private Frank Axam says: —

We have just got a few minutes to write, as four men are going down to a station on the river where mails are sent to and posted. We have not received a mail for about six weeks. One has been following us very closely for some days, and an officer is going to try and find it today, so I expect to hear some news.

We have got to the front at last, and have had a hot time, being under fire about a dozen times scouting, and in three fights. In one we were under fire for five hours, not one of us receiving a scratch, but one horse was wounded with a shell. In the second we were with General French's column. We were in the rear and galloped to the front, and advanced in a perfect hail of bullets, shell, and what we call the 'pom-pom'. The English had a good start on us, but we soon passed them and were on the top of the kopje, almost half-an-hour before them, with one man wounded. They lost several. In other fights several men have been wounded; a couple of useless fellows accidentally wounding themselves. We have taken a very active part in the Battle of Paardeberg which was started on the 18th February and lasted till the 27th. In the beginning there was very heavy rifle firing, until the Boers – who were chiefly Transvaalers – were driven to their laagers and fortifications in the river, and then the artillery commenced their work. It was grand to hear the cannonade from the respective batteries and naval guns, which carry a 115 lb shell. The noise this shell makes whilst travelling through the air can be heard for two or three miles like a train rumbling along. You will know a great deal more about the battle than what I do, as we know little more than we see. Since the battle we have been attached to the headquarters staff, and have been in camp. The only change is that we have shifted four miles above the laager.

I have heard that the second contingent has arrived, also that Lieutenant Newman and Sergt. Lacey are with it. Lord Roberts says that all the colonials will be on their way home in seven weeks, so that will not be long in passing. Our horses are low in condition. They have had great hardships being without water and food almost 2 days at a time. Fall in now – not time to finish. You may not hear from me for some time. It is only a chance that we can write. I am getting on well, nothing being wrong with me since leaving de Aar.

The Campbelltown Herald
Wednesday, 6 June 1900, page 4

Letter from the Front
PRIVATE F AXAM

Writing from the seat of war under date Springfontein,[153] *April 4th, to his parents at Mount Gilead, Private Frank Axam says: —*

By the above address you will see we are getting near the Transvaal border. We have just joined General French's column. When on the march it is magnificent to see the large army (40,000 men) and its convoy. As far as can be seen – either in front flank or rear – is one moving mass of khaki. The convoy is about ten miles in length some of it being towed by mules, ten in a team, and others by oxen, from 16 to 32 in a wagon.

We arrived at Jacobsdal[154] *in time to see the finish of a fight. From this place we marched day and night, reaching Modder River three days later. On arrival there we found a battle raging. It was the third day, and it lasted two days longer. After a day's rest we started for Kimberley at 2 a.m., and on crossing the river some two hours later we heard the command given, 'New South Wales Mounted Rifles to the front'. Away we went at a gallop and soon found ourselves amongst the bullets. After riding through them for a while we dismounted and were ordered to take the kopje from which the enemy were firing. After advancing a short distance, the shells came flying over our heads, which told us that the artillery were supporting us. It did not do much to steady the fall of bullets, as a crossfire was being poured in on us, also a shell fire, some of them exploding and sending pieces a great distance. Luckily for us, they fell either short or behind.*

We gained the kopje thoroughly exhausted, as we had to double most of the way, the distance being quite a mile from where we left our horses. The hail of bullets was terrific, and for a part of the time the ground was cut almost from under our feet. I have been in a much heavier storm since, so have had the pleasure of a good experience. After chasing the Boers from this kopje, they fired upon us from another position, when I got hit on the arm with a piece of an explosive bullet, but was not hurt. The next day we were sent out as scouts to locate the enemy, when a small party fired on us. Shortly after daybreak they disappeared, and we did not get sight of them again till late in the afternoon, when we got a view of their convoy. Here we put in a few rounds at long range, which quickly drove them to cover. Our captain, being anxious to find out more about their movements, moved forward again, sending an advance party of five about half a mile in front of the main body (myself one of the number). We got within 150 yards of the Boers' laager, when we were met with a very heavy fire. Our only chance was to retire as fast as our horses would carry us. This we did in good style till we gained our party.

This was our most marvellous escape, and if the Boers can shoot, they should have proved it at 200 yards. It is a chance we cannot get I believe we were specially mentioned for this, as it proved to be General Cronje's laager. We had the pleasure of finding and the privilege of being the first to enter it on his surrender ten days later. I heard a staff officer directing an artillery officer as to operations to be carried out. He finished with the words, 'The Australians have done their work; you go and do yours'. Wheeling his horse round, he soon disappeared.

Early next morning the Battle of Paardeberg commenced, and lasted for nine days. It proved a grand, though an awful, sight. After the battle we had a week's rest. Leaving Paardeberg, we joined General Tucker's division of

---

[153] Springfontein is a small mixed farming town in the Free State province of South Africa
[154] A hamlet in the North West province

General French's column, but had only been in camp half-an-hour (10 p.m.) when an order came that ten good men and horses were wanted to do some ticklish work at 3 o'clock next morning. Lieutenant Onslow was the officer selected and I was one of the men. At 8 o'clock we were in the saddles and a start was made. In half an hour we gained the river, and then for the next half hour we witnessed the grandest sight I have yet seen – between 30,000 and 40,000 men (artillery, cavalry, MI, etc.), all ready to take their positions on the battlefield. Through these we made our way, following along the river till sunrise, when we came in view of the Boers about 1000 yards ahead. We passed without molestation. About half a mile on we could see them in hundreds on the kopjes, evidently waiting for some movement on our side. They did not attempt to trouble us, so keeping on our advance we gained a low hill and obtained a view of their trenches and position on the hill. (This is what we were sent out for.) I suppose they thought we had advanced far enough and had seen a little too much. They opened a sharp fire from the full length of their trenches, and as we had found out all we wanted, we started to retire. Not a bit too soon, for they began to send some shells about us, but as they did not explode they did no harm. We then returned to headquarters, and having made a report, we were sent back in advance of the artillery, which silenced the enemy's guns (later on captured), after an hour's practice. They eventually retired, leaving everything behind. Our next engagement was at Abraham's Kraal, where we had one man killed. On March 12th Lord Roberts entered the Orange Free State capital without resistance. Our camp was pitched about four miles from the town for a few days. On visiting the town I found it nicely laid out and to be possessed of some very nice buildings. Later on we continued our march in a northerly direction till we joined the main column.

When on outpost duty or mounted patrol, which falls to our lot every second night, we experience rather a rough time. The night we are off duty we have to sleep in our breast-works and then go out on patrol at 4 a.m. Yesterday morning we got within 100 yards of a party that was ambushed in the grass, and as it was dark we were unable to see them till they stood up. They opened a severe fire, and our party retired a short distance, dismounted, and returned a sharp fire. One of our men was wounded, and a horse shot. Later in the day four wounded Boers were found in a house close by, and I believe several others were also wounded, but they managed to get away. They said it was the Australians who did it, so you see they know us.

It is impossible for you to imagine the ups and downs we have been through, marching day and night to gain certain positions. It is quite a common thing to have the saddles on our horses for two and three days without removing them, riding the whole time, and being unable to sit down to a meal, merely eating our biscuits and bully beef when we feel inclined. We carry four days' rations and horse feed – a nice load for our horses. We have got quite used to this kind of thing, and do not mind it. We have had a front position since leaving the Reit River. The best sights we have seen during the campaign is the artillery galloping into and out of action. We have escorted the Royal Artillery during part of the advance. The Second Contingent of Mounted Infantry were attached to us about a month ago. The Campbelltown representatives were quick to find us out. I was pleased to see them and hear all the news they had to tell, as I had not received either a letter or a paper for six weeks. The Bushmen are at Bloemfontein, very eager to 'get a slap' as they say.

I saw my picture in a paper which Lieut. Onslow brought to the camp. It was a surprise to me, and was in great demand amongst the men. Lieut. Onslow is a great favourite. He is so steady and cool, whether in or out of action. Soon after entering this State I lost my mare, and I do not expect to see her again. However, I have got another good horse now. I am in the best of health, and have no fear of anything happening to me after what I have gone through.

The Campbelltown Herald
Wednesday, 4 July 1900, page 4

The Boer War
Letter from the Front

Trooper Frank Axam writes as follows to his brother, under date Welgelegen May 8th:

At about 8.30 on May 1st we got orders to move out from this place at 4 o'clock next morning with Major-General Hutton. We had no idea where we were going. We were out at 3.30 a.m., marched about five miles, and then camped for the day. Next morning we were in the saddle at 4 o'clock and made an advance towards a small town called Brandfort. At about 11 o'clock the enemy opened fire on us. A battery of artillery was brought up and soon got into action. It is wonderful how these guns are worked. They had not been operating more than an hour when they had the Boers going helter-skelter all over the veldt, with shells falling well among them. We were escorting the guns, so had a perfect view of the performance. As soon as the fight was over, we received orders to capture the town. This meant a gallop of three miles, which nearly knocked our horses out. Here we sighted the Boer convoy and followed it up, but could do no good, as the guns were unable to get up before dark. Next morning we got out among the kopjes, which were rather rough, and in the evening we had a lively time, but the enemy would not make a stand. Making a further advance next day, we found they were making a stand at a small river (I can't think of the name at present), but the guns shelled the vicinity of the drift and we soon captured it.

We had to advance for about two miles under fire of their 'Long Tom', which put shells right in our lines. One shell passed with a whizz between me and the man on my left, but a miss is as good as a mile. When we got close to the river we got a good supply of bullets and Martini-Maxims. After gaining the river we had to wade through it, and by successive rushes we captured the kopjes and a Maxim gun, a lot of horses and saddles, and ammunition. I believe the Boers had 83 casualties, and our side only two slightly wounded. This was a very hard day's work, as, after leaving our horses we had to double about half a mile to the river (which is called the Vet) and then the same distance again before gaining the kopjes. It was a fine sight to see the shells breaking amongst the Boers when they were retiring. Prior to starting out the next morning, the General paid us a visit and complimented us upon the gallant work we had done, finishing up by saying, in old style, 'It was good business, lads, and I wouldn't be afraid to send you anywhere'.

Our next move was to a small village on the railway, where we camped for the night, and yesterday morning we started for the Zand River, about ten miles distant. When we had got about half way, we could see great floods of smoke rising and hear loud explosions. It was the Boers blowing up the bridge over the river. (I have seen four bridges they have destroyed; they make great wrecks of them.) We rushed ahead, under Captain Antill to see what they were doing, and on gaining a view we could see them with a great number of wagons and cattle. There were also three trains loading and unloading a big army. It was reported that there were 10,000 holding the river. We advanced to within a mile of the river, when they opened fire upon us with their 'Long Tom', which plumped the shells in quite thick enough to check an army. I think they had about five guns on us at a range of a mile and as we had to retire behind the hill they had a clear range of about two miles to play on us with rifle and 'Long Tom' fire. The enemy's guns outranged ours, so we were without any support, and had a lively time – two horses blown up and six men slightly wounded. It was dark when we got to camp, and I was awfully tired. After we had our supper of bully beef and biscuits, we had to march about two miles for outpost duty, as the majority of our horses were done up. Today we are waiting for the big guns to come up as we are a couple of days ahead of them. I dare say it will be sometime before I will be able to send another letter as we are forcing the way to Pretoria.

BATEUP, Amos Albert: *Rank:* Corporal #82. *Unit*: 'A' Squadron New South Wales Mounted Rifles. *Departed:* 14 November 1899 *SS Langton Grange. Returned:* invalided to Australia 3 July 1900. *Born:* 1876 Abbotsford, Picton, NSW. *Parents:* Amos Bateup and Jane Brookes. *Occupation*: farmer. *Died:* 23 May 1943 Kiama, NSW. *Buried:* St. Mark's Church of England, Picton. *Honours:* Queen's South Africa Medal with 1 clasp. *Memorial:* Wollondilly Heritage Centre, The Oaks.

Bateup was a member of the Picton Half Squadron New South Wales Mounted Rifles before enlisting. He was struck down by enteric fever and invalided to Australia.

Picton Post
Thursday, 27 May 1943, page 2

MR. AMOS ALBERT BATEUP

It is with regret that we record the death of a very old and respected resident of the district in the person of Mr Amos Albert Bateup, who passed to regions beyond at his home, Stilton Farm, on Sunday last, 23rd May. From what we have learned, he was in his usual health up to a few days before his death, and what exactly overcame him does not appear to be known. He lived alone on his farm at Upper Picton and was found in a bad state shortly before death took place.

The deceased was a native of Picton, having been born at Abbotsford 68 years ago, and spent all his life here, following farming pursuits, as did his parents who, it is said, were also natives of the district.

In his younger days, the late Mr Bateup was actively associated with almost all organisations in the district, and in one capacity and another did much useful work. He was a past master of the Rose of Picton Masonic Lodge and at the time of his death a keen member of the local bush fire brigade.

The funeral took place on Monday afternoon and the esteem entertained for the deceased during his life was indicated by the large attendance, which included a number of members of the Masonic Lodge. The interment took place in St Mark's

Cemetery, the Rev. FAS officiating in the church and at the graveside, where Wor. Bro. E Oakman read the impressive masonic service for such occasions.

The late Mr Bateup was a bachelor, and is survived by a brother (Samuel), who resides at Guildford, and two sisters (Mrs Turner, Lismore, and Mrs Murray, Lidcombe).

BECKHAUS, Frederick: *Rank:* Sergeant #494. *Unit:* 4th New South Wales Imperial Bushmen. *Departed:* 23 April 1900 *SS Armenian. Returned:* invalided to Australia 17 August 1901. *Born:* 28 November 1874 Camden, NSW. *Parents:* Louis Aloysius Beckhaus and Maria Rigney. *Occupation:* NSW Mounted Police Sergeant. *Died:* 17 June 1935 Annandale, NSW. *Buried:* Rookwood Roman Catholic Church. *Spouse:* Adelaide Maud Cook. *Married:* 24 August 1904 Enfield, NSW. *Honours:* Queen's South Africa Medal with 5 clasps.

Frederick Beckhaus

Beckhaus served from May 1900 in Rhodesia, West Transvaal including the capture of Jacobus Herculaas de la Rey's convoy and guns at Wildfontein (24 March 1901) and Orange Free State. It is believed he worked within Headquarters and with the Commanding Officers (Lieutenant-Colonels James Alexander Kenneth Mackay and Haviland le Mesurier) on administrative matters. In 1930 he was awarded the Police Imperial Service Medal New South Wales.

BELL, George Lawluck: *Rank:* Lieutenant Medical Officer. *Unit:* 5th Battalion Australian Commonwealth Horse. *Departed:* 22 May 1902 *SS Columbian. Returned:* 1 August 1902 *HMT Manchester Marshal. Born:* 1864 Leigh, Vic. *Parents:* Robert Lewis Bell and Robina Carstairs. *Occupation:* doctor, surgeon. *Died:* 20 July 1951 Rose Bay, NSW.

Bell was a doctor in Hill Street, Camden when he joined the Camden Mounted Rifles in 1892 as a 2nd Lieutenant. He continued with his practice in Camden until at least 1908. He was a brother-in-law of Arthur John Macarthur-Onslow.

Camden News
Thursday, 24 April 1902, page 4

It is announced that Dr GL Bell, of Camden, is proceeding to the war, with the Commonwealth Horse Contingent, as Medical Officer.

BILLETT, John Ernest Edward (Ted): *Rank:* Farrier-Sergeant #1744. *Unit:* 3rd New South Wales Mounted Rifles. *Departed:* 15 March 1901 *SS Maplemore* or *SS Columbian. Returned:* 3 June 1902 *HMT Aurania. Born:* 3 March 1874 Mt Hunter, NSW. *Parents:* Thomas Billett and Sarah Jane Jenkins. *Occupation:* blacksmith. *Died:* 9 March 1942 Bathurst, NSW. *Honours:* Queen's South Africa Medal. *Note:* Boer War records spell surname as Billet.

BLACKWOOD, James: *Rank:* Private #86. *Unit:* 'A' Squadron New South Wales Mounted Rifles. *Departed:* 14 November 1899 *SS Langton Grange. Returned:* 8 January 1901 *HMT Orient. Born:* 24 April 1870 Condell Park, Wilton, NSW. *Parents:* William John Blackwood and Ellen Jeffery. *Occupation:* farm labourer. *Died:* 30 June 1950 Bulli, NSW. *Buried:* Bulli General Cemetery. *Spouse: (1)* Rebecca Ellen Wonson.

Married: (1) 1902 Campbelltown, NSW. *Spouse: (2)* Margaret Mary Cruise. *Married: (2)* 1935 Bulli, NSW. *Honours:* Queen's South Africa Medal with 4 clasps. *Memorial:* Wollondilly Heritage Centre, The Oaks.

Blackwood had joined the Picton Half Squadron New South Wales Mounted Rifles in 1895.

BLENCOWE, Arthur William: *Rank:* Trooper #145, Trooper #2635. *Unit:* (1) New South Wales Lancers (2) 3rd New South Wales Imperial Bushmen. *Departed*: (1) 3 March 1899 *SS Nineveh* (to UK) (2) 30 November 1899 (to South Africa). *Returned:* 11 August 1902 *SS Drayton Grange. Born:* 1875 Berrima, NSW. *Parents:* Thomas Blencowe and Eliza. *Occupation*: farmer. *Died:* 17 January 1916 Wollongbar, NSW. *Buried:* Lismore General Cemetery. *Spouse:* Bertha Winifred Smith. *Married:* 1901 Sydney, NSW. *Honours:* Queen's South Africa Medal with 4 clasps.

Blencowe was a member of the West Camden Half Squadron of the New South Wales Lancers who went to England in March 1899 as part of the Lancer squadron to train with British Regular Cavalry at Aldershot. He was one of about 90 fellow Lancers who paid their own passage to England (£20) to train with the Imperial cavalry.

When war was declared in South Africa he was one of 28 Lancers from the *SS Nineveh* under Lieutenant Septimus Osborne, who volunteered and were quickly equipped and attached to the 9th Lancers, as part of Lord (Baron) Paul Methuen's Force. This troop of Lancers was referred to as The Fighting 29.

On 22 November 1899, they had their first contact with the Boers at Thomas' Farm near Belmont Station some 160 km north west of Colesberg.

On 4 May 1901 he transferred to the 3rd New South Wales Imperial Bushmen which had been raised at Klerksdorp, Transvaal.

BOLLARD, Albert John: *Rank:* Private/Lance Corporal #87. *Unit:* 'A' Squadron New South Wales Mounted Rifles. *Departed:* 14 November 1899 *SS Langton Grange. Returned:* 8 January 1901 *HMT Orient. Born:* 2 September 1875 Stilton, Picton, NSW. *Parents*: Thomas William Bollard and Annie Connellan. *Occupation*: farmer. *Died:* 1953 Perth, WA. *Buried:* Karrakatta General – Presbyterian, WA. *Spouse:* Ethel Rosina Stewart. *Married:* Perth, WA. *Honours:* Queen's South Africa Medal with 6 clasps. *Memorial:* Wollondilly Heritage Centre, The Oaks; Perth, WA.

Albert John Bollard

Albert John Bollard joined the Picton Half Squadron New South Wales Mounted Rifles in 1896 and in 1897 was chosen, along with three other men from Picton to participate in Queen Victoria's Diamond Jubilee. He was a first class shot and an outstanding horseman. Albert returned to Australia with the Squadron on 8 January 1901. He then went back farming the family property at Wilton but found time to serve with the Mounted Rifles and was promoted to Farrier Sergeant.

BRESNAHAN, Patrick: *Rank:* #450 Trooper. *Unit:* New South Wales Lancers. *Departed:* 3 March 1899 *SS Nineveh* (to UK). 30 November 1899 (to South Africa). *Returned:* 6 December 1901 *HMT Harlech Castle. Born*: 1868 Victoria. *Parents:* Daniel Bresnahan and Ann Duggan. *Died:* 17 October 1946 Bowral, NSW. Late of Wildes Meadow, NSW.

Bresnahan was a member of the West Camden Half Squadron of the New South Wales Lancers who went to England in March 1899 as part of the Lancer squadron to train with British Regular Cavalry at Aldershot. He was one of about 90 fellow Lancers who paid their own passage to England (£20) to train with the Imperial cavalry. He was one of 28 Lancers from the *SS Nineveh* under Lieutenant Septimus Osborne, which were quickly equipped and attached to the 9th Lancers, as part of Lord Methuen's Force. This troop of Lancers was referred to as The Fighting 29. On 22 November 1899, they had their first contact with the Boers at Thomas' Farm near Belmont Station some 160 km north west of Colesberg.

He returned from South Africa on 6 December 1901 and was one of those accorded a welcome home reception at Moss Vale. His father had arrived in Port Phillip from Ireland in 1849. The Bresnahan family farmed at Wildes Meadow near Bowral.

Patrick Bresnahan was mentioned in a letter from a Trooper Wilkes to his brother in Maitland in *The Maitland Weekly Mercury* of 30 December 1899.

> '...I had to laugh, in the midst of the skirmish, at one of our chaps, named Patrick Bresnahan – a 'hard case'. His hat blew off, and he fairly flew through the mountains. He was chaffed about it afterwards. The names of our men under fire were — Tom Morris, Sergeant Gould, Jack Houston, Bert Barclay, Singleton; J Wilks, Maitland; SM Reid, Sydney; Sergt. Houston, Parramatta; Captain Vaughan, Pat Bresnahan, Berry; Corporal Williams and Trooper H Allen, Cape Mounted Police; and two civilians ...'

BREW, Phillip Carvell: *Rank:* Trooper #629. *Unit:* New South Wales Lancers. *Departed:* 30 May 1899 *SS Nineveh* (to UK). 30 November 1899 (to South Africa). *Returned:* 6 December 1901 *HMT Harlech Castle*. *Born:* 1874 Wellingrove, NSW. *Parents:* Robert Brew and Annie Penron Carvell. *Occupation:* blacksmith. *Died:* 1952 New Zealand. *Buried:* Katikati, New Zealand. *Spouse:* Lily Lindsay. *Married:* 1901 Robertson, NSW. *Memorial:* New South Wales Lancers Memorial Museum, Parramatta.

Brew was a member of the West Camden Half Squadron of the New South Wales Lancers who went to England in March 1899 as part of the Lancer squadron to train with British Regular Cavalry at Aldershot. He was one of about 90 fellow Lancers who paid their own passage to England (£20) to train with the Imperial cavalry.

He was one of 28 Lancers from the *SS Nineveh* under Lieutenant Septimus Osborne, which were quickly equipped and attached to the 9th Lancers, as part of Lord Methuen's Force. This troop of Lancers was referred to as The Fighting 29. On 22 November 1899, they had their first contact with the Boers at Thomas' Farm near Belmont Station some 160 km north west of Colesberg.

BRIDGES, William Frederick: *Rank:* Trooper #1619. *Unit*: (1) 2nd New South Wales Mounted Rifles (2) 3rd New South Wales Imperial Bushmen. *Departed*: 15 March 1901 *SS Maplemore* or *SS Custodian*. *Returned:* 3 June 1902 *HMT Aurania*. *Born:* 1888 Newtown, NSW. *Parents:* John Gordon Bridges and Annie McLaughlin. *Died:* 11 April 1970 Lismore, NSW. *Spouse:* Rose Elizabeth Byrnes. *Married:* 1910 Molong, NSW. *Honours:* Queen's South Africa Medal with 2 clasps. *Memorial:* Wollondilly Heritage Centre, The Oaks.

Bridge's unit, the 2nd New South Wales Mounted Rifles, became the 3rd New South Wales Imperial Bushmen on 4 May 1901.

BULL, Edward Canute: *Rank:* Private #21. *Unit:* 'A' Squadron New South Wales Mounted Rifles. *Departed*: 3 November 1899 *SS Aberdeen*. *Returned:* 8 January 1901 *HMT Orient*. *Occupation:* saddler. *Born:* 23 July 1878 Sydney, NSW. *Parents:* Edward

Knud Bull and Elizabeth Steward. *Died:* 14 June 1930 St. Peters, NSW. *Spouse:* Florence Adelaide Scott. *Married:* 1905 Marrickville, NSW. *Honours:* Queen's South Africa Medal with 6 clasps.

Boer War records show him as Edward Counde Bull but he was born, married and died as Edward Canute Bull.

BURKE, Michael Joseph: *Rank:* (1) Private #88 (2) Sergeant #1732. *Unit:* (1) 'A' Squadron New South Wales Mounted Rifles (2) 3rd Battalion Australian Commonwealth Horse. *Departed:* (1) 14 November 1899 *SS Langton Grange. Returned:* (1) invalided to Australia 12 July 1900. *Departed:* (2) 1 April 1902 *SS Manhattan. Born:* 4 May 1861 Penrith, NSW. *Parents:* Richard Burke and Margaret Anderson. *Occupation:* farmer. *Died:* 25 April 1943 South Africa. *Buried:* Benoni, Gauteng, South Africa. *Spouse:* Elia Marie van Musschenbroek. *Honours:* Queen's South Africa Medal with 7 clasps.

Michael J Burke

Burke served from December 1899 with 1st New South Wales Mounted Rifles in North-West Cape Colony, Free State, and Transvaal. He was repatriated on 12 July 1900 with enteric fever before he signed up again in 1902. He arrived in Durban on 30 April and moved to camp at Kitchener's Kop near Newcastle, Natal. The 3rd Australian Commonwealth Horse unit was involved in escorting Boer delegates to the peace conference location south of Johannesburg.

He saw service in the Cape Colony, Orange Free State, Transvaal, Paardeberg, and Johannesburg and at Diamond Hill.

Burke had been a member of the Camden Half Squadron New South Wales Mounted Rifles but remained in South Africa following the war and became a farmer at Benoni, near Johannesburg. Name also spelt Bourke.

BUTLER, Arthur Albert: *Rank:* Private #89. *Unit:* 'A' Squadron New South Wales Mounted Rifles. *Departed:* 14 November 1899 *SS Langton Grange. Returned:* 8 January 1901 *HMT Orient. Born:* 12 July 1879 Brownlow Hill, Camden, NSW. *Parents:* Charles Butler and Lucy McLennon. *Occupation:* farmer. *Died:* 3 May 1961 Narrabeen, NSW. *Spouse:* Elizabeth Kirkpatrick. *Married:* 1907 Sydney, NSW. *Honours:* Queen's South Africa Medal with 6 clasps.

He also served as a 2nd Lieutenant with the 1st Light Horse Regiment during WWI.

Camden News
Thursday, 25 October 1900

The War
LETTER FROM PRIVATE BUTLER OF CAMDEN
AT THE FRONT

The Kopje, South Africa,
Sept 20th. 1900

Dear Parents — we are in the Orange River Colony again, and are going after de Witt. We marched in to Pretoria and packed our wagons, horses, luggage, etc. on the train and travelled down about 35 miles north of Kroonstad. The trip down took us 2½ hours. We rode on top of the loaded trucks and had to hang on; we halted at Johannesburg as it was not safe to run trains at night. This was our first railway journey since nine months ago; it gave us an opportunity of witnessing how matters are carried on with lines of communication. Every culvert and bridge is guarded by companies of infantry, and some of the important places have big guns. At places there are tons of oats and hay, and provisions with ammunition.

Talk about the way the Boers make trenches and fortifications, they should look at the way 'Tommy Atkins'[155] gets to work. The Tommies make holes and live in them along the railway cuttings, and everything is kept clean. Outside the trenches barbed wire entanglements are put, and outside this again a circle of empty tins and bottles and anything that will rattle, to give the alarm at night, biscuit tins are placed showing the range every one hundred yards. Gangs of kaffirs are employed to keep the line in repair, and some of the destroyed bridges are being built. Soldiers on the line have a very monotonous life.

Major Antill came back from Cape Town and looks well, his orderly, Private Rex Smith, came up in a complete MR uniform, he looked quite swellish beside our dingy khaki. Some of our men are up at Belfast under Major Lenehan. We have our Corps Colonel (de Lisle) back again: he was wounded about a month ago; he volunteered to come after de Witt if they would give some Australians: he prefers the NSW MR and West Australians.

I was out on patrol yesterday and we fetched in ten Dutchmen living on their farms; they are to be sent away. All we are allowed to carry is one shirt and socks, and three blankets to two men; this country is all mountains. This place is called The Kopjes, but the only kopje is a clump of rocks in the middle of the rolling veldt; a good large paddock could be got here without grubbing trees or stumps.

This letter has taken me two days to write, when off duty much of my time is occupied in patrols, fatigues and guards.— Yours, etc.

CLEARY, Edward Thomas: *Rank:* Lance Corporal #90. *Unit:* 'A' Squadron New South Wales Mounted Rifles. *Departed*: 14 November 1899 *SS Langton Grange*. *Returned*: invalided to Australia 13 August 1900. *Born*: 11 January 1876 Sydney, NSW. *Occupation:* railway shunter. *Parents:* John Cleary and Alice Burns nee Sheehan. *Occupation*: labourer in Bargo. *Died:* 19 August 1968 Nelson, NSW. *Buried:* Rookwood Roman Catholic Cemetery. *Spouse:* Elizabeth Pearl Briggs. *Married:* 1919 Bathurst, NSW. *Honours:* Queen's South Africa Medal with 3 clasps.

---

[155] Tommy Atkins (often just Tommy) is slang for a common soldier in the British Army. It is known to have been in use since 1743. It was well established in the 19th Century, but is particularly associated with World War I.

Cleary had been a member of the Picton Half Squadron New South Wales Mounted Rifles prior to enlisting for the Boer War. He was invalided home with enteric fever in August 1900. He also served as a private in the 12th Light Horse during WWI.

CLIFFORD, George: *Rank:* Private #91. *Unit:* 'A' Squadron New South Wales Mounted Rifles. *Departed*: 14 November 1899 *SS Langton Grange*. *Returned:* 8 January 1901 *HMT Orient*. *Born:* 1861 Chippendale, NSW. *Parents:* James Clifford and Mary Lawler. *Occupation*: mail driver. *Died:* 24 April 1953 Arncliffe, NSW. *Buried:* Woronora General Cemetery. *Spouse:* Vera Muriel Hooker. *Married:* 1915 Lismore, NSW. *Honours*: Queen's South Africa Medal with 1 clasp.

CULSHAW, Richard Matthew Wyoming: *Rank:* Trooper #1942. *Unit:* 3rd New South Wales Mounted Rifles - E Squadron. *Departed:* 21 March 1901 *SS British Princes*. *Returned:* 3 June 1902 *HMT Aurania*. *Born:* 8 October 1883 Gosford, NSW. *Parents:* Richard Culshaw and Elizabeth Mitchell. *Occupation:* commercial painter. *Died:* 12 February 1967 Liverpool, NSW. *Buried:* Camden Catholic Cemetery. *Spouse:* Emily Phillips. *Married:* 1911 Bombala, NSW. *Honours:* Queen's South Africa Medal with 4 clasps.

Culshaw saw service from April 1901 to April 1902 in the Free State and East Transvaal under Sir Michael Frederic Rimington including the Boer breakthrough at Langverwagt (24 February 1902) under the command of Lieutenant-Colonel Charles Cox.

It would appear Richard lied about his age in order to join. On 12 August 1908 he joined the New South Wales Police Force. He was promoted to Constable 1st class on 1 January 1922 and posted to Bombala, Araluen, Queanbeyan, Braidwood and Goulburn; he retired in 1941.

DAVEY, Walter George: *Rank:* Trooper #449. *Unit:* New South Wales Lancers. *Departed*: 28 October 1899 *SS Kent*. *Returned:* 8 January 1901 *HMT Orient*. *Born:* 1865 Bristol, Gloucestershire, England. *Parents:* Thomas Davey and Ann. *Occupation:* blacksmith. *Died:* 17 March 1949 Archerfield, Singleton, NSW. *Buried:* Whittingham Anglican, Singleton. *Spouse:* Rebecca Bartlett. *Married:* 1886 Robertson, NSW. *Honours:* Queen's South Africa Medal. *Notes:* late of the Buffs Regiment British Army, England. Name also spelt as Davy.

The Buffs (Royal East Kent Regiment), of which Davey had been a member was formerly the 3rd Regiment of Foot. The Buffs were an infantry regiment of the British Army until 1961 and have a history dating back to 1572. The Buffs were one of the oldest regiments in the British Army being third in order of precedence (ranked as the 3rd Regiment of the line). It provided distinguished service over a period of almost 400 years accumulating 116 battle honours. British records indicate Davey served in the 2nd East Kent Regiment S/798 as a private. Davey saw service with this regiment in the Anglo-Egyptian Conflict (the Sudan).

Walter George Davey

DIVALL, William: *Rank:* Private #475. *Unit:* 1st New South Wales Mounted Rifles - C Squadron. *Departed:* 17 January 1900 *Southern Cross*. *Returned:* 29 April 1901 *SS Morayshire*. *Born:* 1865 Goulburn, NSW. *Parents:* William Divall and Elizabeth White. *Died:* 24 August 1935 Newcastle, NSW. *Buried:* Sandgate Cemetery, Newcastle, NSW. *Spouse: (1)* Kate Maxwell. *Married:* 1885 Goulburn, NSW. *(2)* Jane Neill. *Married:*

1897 Newtown, NSW. *Honours:* Khedive's Star 1882–1891 (Sudan), 1914–1915 Star, British War Medal, Victory Medal.

Divall had been a railway guard in Campbelltown prior to enlisting for the Boer War. He had served in E Company, NSW Volunteer Infantry (Goulburn) prior to serving in C Company of the Sudan Contingent in 1885. He also served as a Corporal #63 in the 6th Light Horse Regiment during WWI and saw service at Gallipoli.

The Campbelltown Herald
Wednesday, 2 May 1900, page 2

TROOPER DIVALL

Trooper W. Divall writes to his wife from Modder River, March 6th as follows:—

Just a few lines to let you know that I am quite well and I hope all at home are the same. I hope to see you all again someday and I think I will after what I went through yesterday. I was under fire for three hours, and could not move; the bullets were flying all around me. There were only 25 of us, and we went to take 425 men. We got within 700 yards of them and they fired on our horses before we could get them undercover. Only one horse got shot and two wounded; one man killed and eight wounded. I fired 60 shots in about ten minutes.

I have not had my clothes off for three weeks, and I cannot tell you when I had a wash last. We joined Mr. Holman this morning. He looks all right. We opened fire on the Boers this morning with the big guns. There were 500 of them, and they were on a hill three miles distant. When the shells burst you should have seen them run off across the plain to the next hill, but before they could reach it our big gun played on them, and I don't think that one got over. You could see the shells burst right in amongst them and scatter them all over the place. We are going on to Mageresfontein, where I think it will finish and I won't be sorry.

You thought we were badly treated at Randwick, but I don't know what you would say if you knew that we only got two hard biscuits for one day and no tea or coffee. I was for two days without anything to eat; only bad water, and very little of that.

Later: I have had a rough time these two days. We went out to take some Boers on a hill. It was said there were only about 60 of them, but when we got there we found 115 of them. They opened fire on us and we fought for 36 hours before we could take the hill. There were 400 British killed. I came out all right, but very tired, being 36 hours without any food. My horse was shot, so I have been walking this past two days.

We took a lot of farms the other day, all pretty well stocked. One farm had 200 head of stock and no end of poultry. We took them all, and left them without anything – I have one of the Boer's rifles, but I don't think I can keep it. I get hardly a minute to myself, and only about two hours' sleep out of the 24. I was under fire the other day, and was so tired that I went to sleep behind a rock. I had to lie very still for if I had lifted my head I would have been shot. I was for three hours lying down, the bullets flying about like hailstones.

DUNBAR, Frederick

Camden News

Thursday, 14 October 1943, page 1

OBITUARY.

MR. FREDERICK DUNBAR.

The death occurred on Saturday week at the Dubbo District Hospital, at the age of 67 years, of Mr Frederick Dunbar. The deceased gentle man was born at Camden, and lived most of his life in the districts between Camden and Dubbo, where he was very well known. He dealt largely in stock, and held properties at Camden, Penrith and other parts of the County of Cumberland, Orange, Wellington and Wongarbon. Mr Dunbar was married 37 years ago in the Dubbo Methodist Church to Miss Annie Harford, of Dubbo, who survives him. The burial service was conducted by the Rev. HN Whiteman, who was a personal friend of the Dunbar family, near whom he was reared at Camden. Mr Dunbar enlisted at Camden with the First Bushmen's Contingent that went to South Africa, to participate in the Boer War. He had always been regarded as one with a special knowledge of various classes of livestock. He had always kept a stud of pure Illawarras, and these are at the present day on the property of his son, Mr. Harford Dunbar, Wongarbon. Besides his wife, who resides at Orange, he is survived by the following family: Rosely (Dubbo), Mrs Roman (Auckland, New Zealand), and Harford (Wongarbon). The following brothers and sisters are still living: Jack and Joe (Camden), Harry (Orange), Thomas (Wellington), Mrs Harrison (Orange), Mrs Trevillin (Camden), Mrs Dallas (Lithgow), Mrs Provan (Manly), Mrs Shaw (Manly), and Mrs Robert Lynn (Orange). At the graveside Rev. HN Whiteman remarked that it was pleasing to see that four families, who were associated with the Dunbars at Camden, were represented at his funeral, viz., himself, Mr Herbert Wheatley, Mr 'Dick' Dennis, and Mr Harry Dunbar (Orange), who is 85 years of age.

FARRELL, Edward Nicholas: *Rank:* Trooper #645. *Unit:* 2nd New South Wales Mounted Rifles. *Departed:* 17 March 1901 *SS Custodian*. *Returned*: 22 May 1902 *SS Aurania*. *Born:* August 1880 Picton, NSW. *Parents:* Patrick Farrell and Mary Ann Jeffery. *Occupation:* labourer. *Died:* 1967 Queensland. *Spouse:* Florence Mabel Dillon. *Married:* 1919 Junee, NSW. *Honours:* Queen's South Africa Medal with clasps, King's South African Medal with clasps, Mentioned in Despatches. *Memorial:* Wollondilly Heritage Centre, The Oaks.

After the Boer War Farrell continued to serve in the New South Wales Mounted Rifles and lived in Wilton, NSW before moving to Queensland. He also served during WWI as a Sergeant #467 in the 1st Light Horse Regiment and was twice Mentioned in Despatches and awarded the Military Medal.

FENWICK, George Thomas: *Rank:* Trooper #317. *Unit:* New South Wales Lancers. *Departed:* 28

Edward Nicholas Farrell

October 1899 *SS Kent*. *Returned*: Invalided to Australia 13 November 1900. *Born:* 21 November 1873 Kiama, NSW. *Parents:* Robert Fenwick and Helen Rankin. *Died:* 24 June 1950 Cooroy, Qld. *Buried:* Cooroy General Cemetery, Qld. *Spouse:* Mary Walsh. *Married:* 1904 Sydney, NSW. *Honours:* Queen's South Africa Medal with 8 clasps.

George Fenwick was one of those from Lismore who put up £20 ($20,000 in 2011 terms) to go to England in April 1899 and train with the British cavalry. One of the Lancers' Fighting 29, he was one of those who at Belmont on 23 November 1899 were the first Australian soldiers to take part in a combat engagement. He served with the squadron until it reached Pretoria. Major Lee, commanding Lancer squadron wrote of George Fenwick when he was to be invalided to Australia: 'I think Fenwick goes home at once; he is a good young fellow and any man may be proud of such a lad as a son.'[156]

Fenwick took part in the following engagements - Belmont, Modder River, Relief of Kimberley, Paardeberg, Orange Free State, Transvaal, Johannesburg and Diamond Hill.

George Thomas Fenwick

Camden News
Thursday, 15 February 1900, page 8

From Trooper Fenwick of the Lancers

Arundel, South Africa December 27, 1899

Dear R –

Just a few lines to let you know I am still alive. Well, since last I wrote I have been through four heavy battles; at Belmont, at Enslin, at Modder River, and one at Magersfontein. The latter lasted nearly two days and the firing and cannonading was something terrific, bullets and shells falling like rain and all the harm they done was to kill one horse and if the horse had not got it I would have been hit fair in the hip, as the horses were under cover and I was laying down in front of him and the bullet struck him in the side so I had a narrow escape. Twenty-nine of us were ordered to go to the Orange River so we had to part with comrades whom we might never see again. We left the Orange River at 2 o'clock in the morning of the 21st November, (my birthday) and marched to a place called Wittipure where we camped for the night. Next morning at 2 we were up and away to take up a position for the main body. Next day we reached there safely and stopped till dinner time when the Boers who were camped about a mile and a half away started to shell us and they kept it up till 4 o'clock when our artillery arrived with 8 guns and gave the Boers as lively an hour as ever they had. They would not let us go near the water. But when the Artillery came

---

[156] *The Northern Star* 5 September 1900

we got water and we went to bed amongst rocks to get ready for the fight next day.

Now for our first fight. At 4 o'clock on the 23rd we moved out of camp and at daybreak it started. The rifle fire was terrific, the bullets began. One of our boys got a scar on the elbow and one had his horse shot, but no other casualties. After three hours fighting the Boers were in full retreat. We were firing at them from a small hill and I think I got one horse for my shots. At 12 all was over and we went back to camp, thoroughly tired out, and so ended the first fight that the NSW Lancers had taken part in. The next three fights were something similar, only we lost a few more men each time, not of the Lancers but of the English. You would hardly know any of us now as all have a long beard and terrible sunburn.

I had a letter from home and they are anxious about me but they would sooner me see fire here than go home to be scorned and called a coward, and I would sooner be dead than that take place. Well, no more at present, so with all good wishes to all.

FIDDEN, Charles William: *Rank:* Lance Sergeant #336. *Unit:* Army Medical Corps. *Departed:* 28 October 1899 *SS Kent. Returned:* 8 January 1901 *HMT Orient. Born:* 6 September 1864 Elderslie, NSW. *Parents:* James Joseph Fidden and Mary Hilder. *Occupation:* printer. *Died:* 3 December 1911 Coast Hospital, Malabar, NSW. *Buried:* Eastern Suburbs Memorial Park – Presbyterian. *Spouse:* Olive Matilda Thompson. *Married:* 1905 Newtown, NSW. *Honours:* Queen's South Africa Medal with 5 clasps.

Fidden also served in the Sudan in 1885 as Private #330.

FIELD, John: *Rank:* Private #102. *Unit:* 'A' Squadron New South Wales Mounted Rifles. *Departed:* 14 November 1899 *SS Langton Grange. Returned:* invalided to Australia 3 July 1900. *Born:* 1872 Yass, NSW. *Parents:* William Field and Mary A Burke. *Occupation:* railway employee in Picton. *Died:* 1942 Liverpool, NSW. *Honours:* Queen's South Africa Medal with 3 clasps. *Memorial:* Wollondilly Heritage Centre, The Oaks.

Field was invalided home with enteric fever in July 1900.

FORSTER, George Brooke: *Rank:* Lieutenant. *Unit:* 2nd New South Wales Mounted Rifles. *Departed:* 17 March 1901 *SS Custodian. Born:* 12 May 1859 Richmond, Vic. *Parents:* Christopher Brooke Forster and Catherine Marzetti. *Occupation:* Bank Manager, Commercial Bank, Picton. *Died:* Killed in action, 10 December 1901 Grootvlei, Transvaal, South Africa. *Buried:* Military Cemetery Bethel, reinterred 1964 Primrose Garden of Remembrance, Germiston, South Africa. *Honours:* Queen's South Africa Medal with 3 clasps, King's South Africa Medal. *Memorials:* Wollondilly Heritage Centre, The Oaks; Parramatta Light Horse Memorial; St. James Anglican, Sydney, NSW.

George Brooke Forster

GEARY, Edmund: *Rank:* Private #344. *Unit:* 4th Victorian Imperial Bushmen. *Departed:* 1 May 1900 *SS Victorian. Discharged:* South Africa 2 August 1900 and made his own way home. *Born:* 21 June 1878 Camden, NSW. *Parents:* David Geary and Bridget Woods. *Occupation:* driver.

Died: Killed in action, 7–14 August 1915 Gallipoli. *Buried:* Lone Pine Cemetery, Gallipoli, Turkey. *Honours:* Queen's South Africa Medal.

Geary served May 1900 to June 1901 in Rhodesia, West Transvaal and Cape Colony including relief of Philipstown (11 February 1901), capture of Boer guns at Read's Drift (23 February 1901), and capture of a Boer patrol near Doornkloof (1 March 1901). The 4th Victorian Imperial Bushmen contingent separated mid 1900 with the C, D, and E squadrons on garrison duty in Rhodesia. It is not known what squadron Private Geary served in. He took his discharge in South Africa on 2 August 1901 and made his own way back to Australia.

He also served during WWI as Private #739 with the 2nd Infantry Battalion but was killed in action at Gallipoli.

GRAHAM, Alfred Adolphus Doran: *Rank:* Private #139. *Unit:* 'A' Squadron New South Wales Imperial Bushmen. *Departed:* 4 November 1899 *SS Aberdeen. Returned:* 8 January 1901 *HMT Orient. Born:* 5 January 1875 Picton, NSW. *Parents:* Alfred Adolphus Doran Graham and Julia Derriman. *Occupation:* auctioneer's assistant. *Died:* Killed in an MV accident, 29 September 1956 Sydney, NSW. *Buried:* Upper Picton – Roman Catholic Cemetery. *Spouse:* Teresa May Devitt. *Married:* 1909 Redfern, NSW. *Honours:* Queen's South Africa Medal with 5 clasps. *Memorial:* Wollondilly Heritage Centre, The Oaks.

HAWKEY, John Martin: *Rank:* Farrier Sergeant #81. *Unit:* 'A' Squadron New South Wales Mounted Rifles. *Departed:* 14 November 1899 *SS Langton Grange. Returned:* 8 January 1901 *HMT Orient. Born:* 12 October 1877 Camden Park, Menangle, NSW. *Parents:* Richard Hawkey and Mary Ann Burton. *Occupation:* farmer. *Died:* 16 June 1958 Minto, NSW. *Spouse:* Annie Louisa Krinks. *Married:* 27 September 1905 Sydney, NSW. *Honours:* Queen's South Africa Medal with 5 clasps.

Hawkey saw service during the Boer War, December 1899 to December 1900, in the north-west Cape Colony, Free State, and Transvaal.

John Hawkey also served as a Major during WWI and was awarded the Military Cross. He was promoted to Honorary Major in the Permanent Military Forces 1 May 1920 and transferred to the Australian Instructional Corps 14 April 1921, Area Officer 1 May 1920 to 15 February 1921, Adjutant 21st Light Horse 1 May 1921 to 30 September 1929, Adjutant and Quartermaster 53rd Infantry Battalion 1 October 1929 to 30 June 1930, Instructor, Australian Army Ordnance Corps, 2nd District Base, 15 October 1930 until retirement. He retired as Honorary Lieutenant Colonel, according to the Retired List, 28 November 1936.

John Martin Hawkey

HAYES, Frederick St. Leger: *Rank:* Private 100. *Unit:* 'A' Squadron New South Wales Mounted Rifles. *Departed:* 3 November 1899 *SS Aberdeen. Returned:* invalided to Australia 3 November 1900. *Born:* 17 August 1871 Burwood, NSW. *Parents:* William George Hayes and Lydia Elizabeth Howell. *Died:* 7 July 1949 Beaudesert, Qld. *Buried:* Woodhill Cemetery. *Spouse:* Isabel Windeyer Phillips. *Married:* 1901 Waverley, NSW. *Honours:* Queen's South Africa Medal with 1 Clasp. *Memorial:* Wollondilly Heritage Centre, The Oaks.

Hayes had previously been a member of the Camden Half Company New South Wales Mounted Rifles. He was invalided home in November 1900 with enteric fever.

HILL, William: *Rank:* Trooper #2133. *Unit:* 3rd New South Wales Mounted Rifles. *Departed:* 15 March 1901 *SS Maplemore. Returned:* 3 June 1902 *HMT Aurania. Born:*

Frederick St. Leger Hayes

1866 Crookwell, NSW. *Parents:* Thomas Hill and Mary Ann Barnes. *Occupation:* school teacher. *Died:* 1948 Granville, NSW. *Spouse:* Elizabeth Phillips. *Married:* 1903 Picton, NSW. *Honours:* Queen's South Africa Medal. *Memorial:* Wollondilly Heritage Centre, The Oaks.

HOLMAN, Richard Charles Frederick: *Rank:* (1) Regimental Sergeant Major (2) Lieutenant. *Unit:* (1) 1st New South Wales Mounted Rifles (2) 2nd New South Wales Mounted Rifles. *Departed: (1)* 17 January 1900 *SS Southern Cross. Returned:* 8 January 1901 *HMT Orient. Departed: (2)* 15 March 1901 *SS Maplemore or SS Custodian. Returned:* 3 June 1902 *HMT Aurania. Born:* 26 September 1861 Broadway, Dorsetshire, England. *Parents:* Frederick Holman and Louisa Thomson nee Puckett. *Occupation:* army officer. *Died:* 13 December 1933 Ingleburn, NSW. *Buried:* St. Mary the Virgin Church of England, Denham Court, NSW. *Spouse:* Harriette Blanche Mills. *Married:* 10 December 1890 St. Mary's Church of England, Balmain, NSW. *Honours:* Twice Mentioned in Despatches, Distinguished Conduct Medal and Companion of the Distinguished Service Order, Queen's South Africa Medal with 6 clasps. *Memorial:* Wollondilly Heritage Centre, The Oaks.

Holman first enlisted in the ranks of the British Army and served with the 1st Mounted Rifles in the Bechuanaland Expedition of 1884–1885. He came to Australia soon afterwards and served with the New South Wales Police Force from 1886 to 1888. In 1897 he spent several months in England on attachment to the 4th Dragoon Guards and the 1st Battalion Scots Guards. He also attended Queen Victoria's Diamond Jubilee celebrations as a member of the New South Wales military detachment.

He was promoted Captain on 26 September 1906 and Major on 1 October 1911. He visited Canada as an exchange officer in 1912–1913. Holman was Brigade Major with the 3rd Light Horse Brigade from December 1913 to September 1916 when he relinquished the post to take command of the Liverpool Concentration Camp, NSW, with the rank of Lieutenant-

Richard Charles Frederick Holman in NSW Mounted Rifles uniform

Colonel. Liverpool was the main internment centre in Australia for enemy aliens, and internees numbered over 5000 when Holman assumed a command which he carried out with competence and compassion until his retirement on 4 February 1920 with the honorary rank of Colonel.

Holman was the only Australian to receive two awards during the Boer War.

Camden News
Thursday, 13 November 1902

Captain R. C. Holman DSO

Captain RC Holman, New South Wales Mounted Rifles, has been made a Companion of the Distinguished Service Order. His first South African service was in 1884, when he formed one of Lord Methuen's Corps of 800 picked volunteers from the Imperial Army which took part in the Bechuanaland Expedition.[157] He joined as a Private and left as a Sergeant. Coming to New South Wales he entered the police force and resigned after 2½ years' service at The Rocks. He was the first man to join the Mounted Rifles in 1888, starting as a Private and working his way up until in June 1900, he was promoted to Warrant Officer. Captain Holman went to England with the Mounted Rifles detachment in 1897— the Jubilee year. In 1899 he left for South Africa as Warrant Officer in the first contingent of Mounted Rifles and served with them throughout the campaign, including the relief of Kimberley, the engagements at Paardeberg and Bloemfontein, the general advance with Lord Roberts to Kroonstad, Johannesburg, and Pretoria. He was Mentioned in Despatches and for persistent good work, especially at Diamond Hill on June 12 1900, when he behaved in a very gallant manner. He was, on Colonel de Lisle's recommendation, awarded the Distinguished Conduct Medal. Returning to Sydney in January 1901, he was immediately offered and accepted the Adjutancy of the Second Mounted Rifles under Lieutenant-Colonel Lassetter with the rank of Lieutenant. In 1901, for good services in the field he was promoted to Captain by Lord Kitchener. With his chief he was again Mentioned in Despatches by the Commander-in-Chief on June 23rd last. Capt. Holman is well known in Camden and the honour of his promotion is indeed, well and worthily merited by his companions in arms.

HUCKSTEPP, George Edwin: *Rank:* (1) Private #366 (2) Corporal #146. *Unit:* (1) 1st NSW Imperial Bushmen (2) 3rd Australian Commonwealth Horse. *Departed:* (1) 23 April 1900 *SS Armenian. Returned*: 17 June 1901 *SS Drayton Grange. Departed: (2)* 1 April 1902 *SS Manhattan. Returned:* 11 August 1902 *SS Drayton Grange. Born:* 26 July 1879 Campbelltown, NSW. *Parents:* Charles Huckstepp and Rachel Lees. *Occupation:* labourer and blacksmith. *Died:* 11 June 1945 Granville, NSW. *Buried:* ashes scattered Rookwood Rose Garden. *Spouse:* Rose Anna Agnes Castles. *Married:* 1907 St. Peter's Church of England, Campbelltown, NSW. *Honours:* Queen's South Africa Medal with 3 clasps, King's South Africa Medal with 1 clasp. *Memorial:* Honour Roll of St Peter's Church of England, Campbelltown, NSW.

Huckstepp saw two periods of service in South Africa but arrived for the second time in Cape Town just after the end of the war. The *SS Manhattan*'s departure from Sydney was not without incident; 23 men had drawn their pay after embarkation but had then deserted before the ship left port. As a result Colonel Ernest Townshend Wallack was relieved of his command by Major-General Sir Edward Thomas Henry

---

[157] The Bechuanaland Expedition or Warren Expedition, of late 1884/1885, was a British military expedition to Bechuanaland, to assert British sovereignty in the face of encroachments from Germany, the Transvaal and to suppress the Boer freebooter states of Stellaland and Goshen.

Hutton. His return voyage was not without incident either as he returned on the ill-fated *SS Drayton Grange*. An outbreak of measles on board the ship resulted in seventeen deaths.

An enquiry found that the ship was overcrowded, hygiene poor, clothing was inadequate and the blankets (two per man) had quickly become vermin infected. The sleeping quarters also were used as living quarters and hammocks had been slung over mess tables. Moreover, the hammocks were stored during the day in communal bins. Disease control was non-existent.

The West Australian
Thursday, 9 October 1902 page 5

TROOPSHIP SCANDALS
THE DRAYTON GRANGE INQUIRY FORECAST
OF THE COMMISSION'S REPORT BLAME
CAST UPON SEVERAL AUTHORITIES

Melbourne, October 8. The Drayton Grange *Royal Commission completed its report at a meeting that it held to-day. The members will meet again at noon to-morrow, to append their signatures, so that it may be presented to Parliament later in the afternoon.*

The members, it has been said, find that the troopship Drayton Grange *was unduly overcrowded, and that, while the cubic space available for the troops might have been sufficient to comply with the army transport regulations, it was not sufficient in the case of a troopship entering upon such a long voyage and with some of the 1900 officers and men suffering from measles. By diligent inquiry, the members of the Commission have, it has been said, discovered that the germs of the measles epidemic were actually taken out to South Africa by some of those who came back in the* Drayton Grange, *and, consequently, it was not surprising that cases began to develop after the vessel had been only a few hours at sea. In view of the number of troops aboard, the Commission will state that the medical stores that were provided were quite inadequate. In this and other respects they will probably assert that the chief blame for the unfortunate occurrences of the voyage from South Africa rests with the Durban authorities. Colonel Lyster[158] the general officer in command on board the troopship protested, it has been found, against so many men being shipped by the vessel, but his objection was disregarded. As he did protest in some measure, the Commission will absolve him from the primary responsibility, but, at the same time, it will declare that the discipline on board was lax, and that, to some extent he was at fault for the occurrences on the voyage.*

The Commission may also assert that in its opinion Colonel Lyster was not sufficiently insistent on the off landing of sick troops at Albany. Captain Shields[159] the principal medical officer on board, will also, probably, be charged with not having fully realised the responsibilities of his position, and with not having displayed sufficient resource in the circumstances. This, the Commission appears inclined to attribute to inexperience. The Commission will, it is believed, announce that in its opinion the West Australian health authorities acted wrongly in practically refusing to allow the sick soldiers to be landed at Albany, in spite of Captain Shields's representations, and accordingly they will be condemned for

---

[158] Lyster, James Sanderson, Lieutenant-Colonel
[159] Shields, Douglas A. Captain (Chief Medical Officer from Victoria)

the attitude that they adopted towards both the medical and military officers on the Drayton Grange.

Following the war Huckstepp was a gardener and nurseryman at the Government Nursery, Campbelltown until its closure in 1930 and then transferred to the Royal Botanical Gardens, Sydney.

HUER, Edward Theodore George: *Rank:* Trooper #567. *Unit:* 2nd New South Wales Mounted Rifles. *Departed:* 15 March 1901 *SS Maplemore. Returned:* 3 June 1902 *HMT Aurania. Born:* 1872 Sydney, NSW. *Parents:* Johann (John) Theodore Huer and Mary. *Died:* 7 August 1966 Camden, NSW. *Buried:* St Paul's Catholic Church, Camden. *Spouse:* Margaret Matilda Gunn. *Married:* 1902 Burwood, NSW. *Honours:* Queen's South Africa Medal with 5 clasps. *Note:* Edward's medal is on display in the Camden Museum.

Edward Theodore George Huer

HUGHES, John Samuel: *Rank:* Private #103. *Unit:* 'A' Squadron NSW Mounted Rifles; *departed:* 14 November 1899 *SS Langton Grange. Returned:* Invalided to Australia 17 August 1900. *Born:* 1850 Sydney, NSW. *Parents:* Samuel Terry Hughes and Charlotte Mary Keck. *Died:* 4 November 1914 Douglas Park, NSW. *Buried:* Waverley General – Roman Catholic. *Spouse:* Josephine Taylor. *Married:* 1878 Sydney, NSW. *Honours:* Queen's South Africa Medal with 3 clasps. *Notes:* Listed amongst Camden men departing for South Africa.

HUMPHRIES, Frederick James (Frank): *Rank:* Sergeant #170. *Unit:* New South Wales Imperial Bushmen. *Departed*: 23 April 1900 *HMT Armenian. Returned:* 17 July 1901 *HMT Orient. Born:* 1 May 1869 Eldorado, Ballarat, Vic. *Parents:* George Humphries and Jane. *Died:* 2 April 1938 Bondi, NSW. *Buried:* Rookwood Crematorium. *Spouse: (1)* Pauline Elizabeth Maria Alcock Robins. *Married:* 6 June 1902 Paddington, NSW. *(2)* Florence May Potts. *Married:* 1913 Newtown, NSW. *Honours:* Queen's South Africa Medal with 6 clasps.

Frederick James Humphries

Humphries was born Walter Edward Frederick James Humphries. He enlisted as Frederick James Humphries. He had been secretary of the National Rifle Association of New South Wales in 1897 and was recruited at the rank of Sergeant in the 1st New South Wales Mounted Rifles. He was living in Camden in 1914 when a son was born.

Humphries served at Wittebergen, Diamond Hill, Johannesburg, Driefontein and the Cape Colony.

JESSOP, Joseph: *Rank:* Trooper #2860. *Unit:* 2nd New South Wales Mounted Rifles. *Departed:* 15 March 1901 *SS Maplemore. Returned:* 3 June 1902 *HMT Aurania. Born:* 1877 Burragorang Valley, NSW. *Parents:* Jonas Jessop and Susannah Collins. *Died:* 14 December 1949, Nerrigundah, NSW. *Spouse:* Catherine Callaghan. *Married:* 1915 Moruya, NSW. *Honours:* Queen's South Africa Medal with 2 clasps.

Jessop had been a member of the Picton Half Squadron New South Wales Mounted Rifles.

JONES, Walter: *Rank:* Private #3190. *Unit:* 48th (Northamptonshire) Regiment of Foot. *Born:* 1873 Bonnington, Kent, England. *Died:* 21 October 1940 Paddington, NSW. *Buried:* Camden General – Anglican.

Jones served with the Northamptonshire Regiment of Foot during the North Indian Frontier campaign before serving with that unit during the Boer War. Burial records for St. John's Church of England Camden note him as 'an Imperial Soldier – old age pensioner'.

KING, William Henry: *Rank:* Trooper #663. *Unit:* 2nd New South Wales Mounted Rifles. *Departed:* 15 March 1901 *SS Maplemore*. *Returned:* 3 June 1902 *HMT Aurania*. *Born:* 1877 Cox's River, Burragorang, NSW. *Parents:* John King and Julia O'Brien. *Occupation:* miner at Yerranderie, NSW. *Died:* 21 April 1937 Camden, NSW. *Buried:* Camden Catholic Church. *Spouse:* Hannah Moriah Hunt. *Married:* 1902 Katoomba, NSW. *Honours:* Queen's South Africa Medal. *Memorial:* Wollondilly Heritage Centre, The Oaks.

LASSETTER, Henry Beauchamp (Harry): *Rank:* Lieutenant-Colonel. *Unit:* 2nd New South Wales Mounted Rifles. *Born:* 19 March 1860 Darling Point, NSW. *Parents:* Frederic Lassetter and Charlotte Hannah Iredale. *Occupation:* Professional soldier. *Died:* 17 February 1926 Sydney, NSW. *Buried:* South Head Cemetery. *Spouse:* Elizabeth Anne Antill. *Married:* 19 August 1891 Picton, NSW. *Honours:* Queen's South Africa Medal with 5 clasps.

Lassetter was a businessman and career soldier. In 1880 he enlisted in the 38th Regiment, British Army as a 2nd Lieutenant. In 1881 he was a Lieutenant in the 80th (South Staffordshire) Regiment of Foot and served with that regiment during the Sudan Expedition, 1884–1885 where he was awarded the Nile Medal with clasp and the Khedive's Star. He was promoted to Captain in 1887 and in 1888 returned to New South Wales where he helped establish and train the New South Wales Mounted Rifles. In 1895 Lassetter was promoted to Lieutenant Colonel and in 1897 he led the Mounted Rifles Contingent which attended Queen Victoria's Diamond Jubilee Celebrations in London. During the Boer War he participated in operations in the Transvaal and Orange River Colony.

He became Managing Director of his father's firm in 1911.[160] When WWI commenced hetravelled to England and was appointed Brigadier General British Army Territorials Brigade (the Terriers).

Among the other honours he received were the Order of St. Michael and St. George (CMG), he was Mentioned in Despatches (twice) and also received the Order of Bath (CB).

Camden News
Thursday, 6 March 1902

A private cablegram has been received from Colonel Lassetter, South Africa, in charge of the 3rd Mounted Rifles, as follows: —

---

[160] Nairn, B., 'Lassetter, Henry Beauchamp (1860–1926)', *Australian Dictionary of Biography*, National Centre of Biography, Australian National University, http://adb.anu.edu.au/biography/lassetter-henry-beauchamp-4429/text6323

'We are all well. We captured Trichardt's[161] *laager,*[162] *168 prisoners. Many captures made since then. Report surrenders daily at Middleburgh.'*

Colonel Lassetter was the instigator of the Mounted Rifles in this State.

Camden News
Thursday, 24 April 1902

Mr. Frederic Lassetter has received the following private cablegram from Colonel Lassetter: —

'Received orders regiment embark. Just finished drive from Middleburgh to Standerton line, lasting three days and nights. 143 Boers captured. A good wind-up to our service. Arrived Standerton, all well.'

LEES, Thomas James: *Rank:* (1) Lance-Corporal #159 (2) Corporal #484. *Unit:* (1) 1st New South Wales Mounted Rifles C Squadron (2) 3rd New South Wales Mounted Rifles D Squadron. *Departed:* (1) 17 January 1900 *HMT* Southern Cross. *Returned*: Invalided to Australia 30 July 1900. (2): 15 March 1901 *HMT Maplemore*. *Returned*: 3 June 1902 *HMT Aurania*. *Born:* 1871 Campbelltown, NSW. *Parents:* William Wilson Lees and Rachel Barter. *Occupation:* fettler. *Died:* 22 January 1955 Bondi, NSW. *Spouse:* Mary Jane Martin. *Married:* 1897 Sydney, NSW.

Lees also served during WWI as a Trooper #1328 with the 2nd Australian Remount Unit.

The Campbelltown Herald
Wednesday, 9 May 1900, page 4

Letters from the Front
LANCE-CORPORAL T. J. LEES

Bloemfontein, Mar. 20, 1900

We are now up near the front, 24 miles from Kimberley. Some of our fellows saw Cronje. He was brought to our camp, but was taken on to Cape Town the next day. We have also 4000 Boer prisoners here.

Things are very bad here for water and food. We did not see a bit of anything for a week unless we bought it and my word they do charge. We left Cape Town on Sunday afternoon at 4 o'clock by train, and did not arrive here, till Wednesday morning at 10 o'clock — all the time in the train. You never saw such a country as this, and would not stay at any price. Fancy travelling day after day without seeing a tree of any kind. No wood to make a fire with, having to break down the fences; then they are only posts and barbed wire. We are having a very bad time as regards food. We have a job to get any at all, not even bully beef and biscuits. Everybody is dissatisfied. Even the horses have been days without a bite of any kind. It means go hungry or pay terrible prices. We send into town and buy jam at 2s per tin, butter 3s, milk 2s, bread 1s 6d a loaf and bad at that, and so on. We are camped about six miles from the town. Our horses are nearly all sick with colds and sore backs. I will be going into town tomorrow with Sergeant

---

[161] Lieutenant Colonel Stephanus Petrus Erasmus Trichardt was Commander of the Staats Artillerie and was responsible for the re-equipping of the force
[162] A defensive encampment encircled by armoured vehicles or wagons

Vacchini,[163] *who is a really nice fellow. The Boers are about the worst rifle shots I ever saw. Our fellows are not a bit afraid of them. I have had a couple of funny experiences. The first engagement we had I was sent up to the top of a hill with my officer. While there, we were about to partake of a little refreshment when our fellows, who were then nearly a mile from us, got the word to gallop towards the enemy, who had fired on scouts. They went in the opposite direction to which we were. By the time we got started they were out of sight, so we did not know where our troops were. We galloped in pursuit, my horse falling with fatigue, giving me a nasty buster. I told the officer to go on, that I would be alright, little dreaming the experience that would follow. My horse would not budge an inch, and there I was, on my own, with bullets whizzing all over the place. It makes one feel funny, I can assure you, especially when by yourself. I got my horse to go after about an hour's spell, when I ran nearly into a party of Boers, which had come around the right flank of our troops. I turned at once, making for the camping place of the night before, three or four Boers after me. I got to the top of a kopje, when I dismounted and allowed them to get about 700 or 800 yards off and then I fired, and had the pleasure, if it may be so called, of seeing one fall. They pulled up, and I did a gallop and arrived safe and sound at the camping place of the night before, but here I was in a dilemma again. Instead of my regiment coming back they went on, and there was a distance of about twenty miles between us. The next day they marched on again, and it was after a very hard day's riding on a bad horse, that I caught up to them safe and sound. We had about twelve casualties.*

March 22nd. — I got leave and went to Bloemfontein. I was a little disappointed, as my mate, Sergeant Vacchini, could not get away. I went in with another young fellow named Fred Porter,[164] *from Balmain. We were told it was four miles, but when we came to walk it was nearer six. It is not a very large town considering it is the capital of the Free State. There are some very nice buildings. The president's residence is a lovely mansion. The post office is another lovely building, and some of the business places are splendid buildings, as well as the hotels, but it is nothing near the place I imagined it to be. We had a walk round the town, which is packed with soldiers from all parts of the world, all looking for victuals, chiefly jam, golden syrup, and tinned milk, which can scarcely be procured. Bread is also scarce, and you have to wait for hours outside the bakers' while they bake it – not half cooked and heavy as lead when you do get it. You have to pay from 1s to 2s a loaf. We returned to camp next day.*

Everyone here is bad with dysentery. Spooner and Divall are both very bad. Divall is on light duties, and Spooner I have sent away out of the road so that he will not be called upon to do anything. We are all very anxious to move from the place, but we have no idea when that will be. Our horses are dying wholesale. The sergeant says it is a poison which has got into their blood and he thinks not one will get over it. We do not hear much news over here. We heard Buller was within forty miles of Pretoria; if so, I don't think we will do much more fighting. We are under Lord Roberts; he gave us all great praise. All his column is situated here around Bloemfontein, which is about 300 miles from Pretoria, so something must be on or we would not all be waiting here. The only thing I saw to remind me of Australia since I left was a roadway with Australian gum trees growing on each side, which looks very nice. Divall, Spooner, and myself went the other day and we came across a place where the Boers had camped, and we were lucky enough to find two Boer rugs. There is a great rush here for Boer money; all the

---

[163] Vacchini, Sergeant Caleb Francis – C Squadron 1st Mounted Rifles
[164] Porter, Private Frederick Stanley

officers are buying it up. I don't know whether I told you we had joined Captain Antill, so we are together now.

March 27. — Well. I have just enjoyed a good dinner. We had a little boiled mutton – not too well boiled nor too clean, but with a little sauce, which is 2s 6d [$0.25] a bottle, I made a fair meal. Divall made some coffee and we had bread, butter, and jam. You would not imagine we were the same fellows now. I can drink tea and coffee without milk or sugar, and think nothing of it.

We will manage very well for food now, as we have a supply in, but it becomes very expensive. We had a concert the other night (St Patrick's Night) got up by our captain, and it went alright. He sang himself, and the Rev. Father Fegan also sang an Irish comic. We have some very good talent.

Bill Divall made the porridge this morning for our four, and it went OK. It is frightfully hot here in the daytime and very cold at night. We have had no shelter since we landed here. The saddles that we had were a very bad lot and have all given the horses sore backs. They are going to give us Imperial saddles and new helmets. There is going to be a grand march of the colonial forces through Bloemfontein, and we all have to be up to it. I suppose there is nothing new I could tell you about the war, as you will get it more fully than I can tell you. I get on tip top with all the fellows. We have not heard anything about the Bushmen yet, whether they are landed or not and who is with them. I am sending you a paper. You will see the prices articles are supposed to be charged at, but that is all rot. They charge you what they like – it is take it or leave it, and rather than go hungry we buy at fabulous prices. Three of our fellows have gone into Bloemfontein Hospital today with fever, and there are others walking about with it. The doctors say we are too weak to do anything with until we are better fed.

I have often had a yarn with the Boers. They say the Australians are the only people they are really frightened of, as they are too quick with their horses, and if an Australian were taken prisoner he would have a very rough time of it. We saw all the prisoners that were taken at the time of Cronje's surrender. We had to stand around them all night; they waved their hands to us next day as we walked past. I don't think I will write any more this time. Remember me to all the people in Campbelltown.

The Campbelltown Herald
Wednesday, 21 August 1901, page 2

LETTER FROM SOUTH AFRICA
FROM SERGT. TOM LEES

Writing to his mother from camp near Standerton in the Transvaal on July 5th, Sergt, T. J. Lees formerly of Campbelltown says:

We are having a pretty rough time here. We have been travelling ever since we came over, and have been nearly all through the Transvaal, destroying farms, burning the grass, driving the cattle away, and doing general destruction. We take the women and children and hand them over to the refugee camps. We are now marching back to Standerton for a few days' rest and then I believe we are to be split up and sent with other generals.

We are now with General Rimington,[165] who is very hard on man and beast. He is very fond of night travelling, and we have these marches two or three

---

[165] Rimington, Sir Michael Frederick – British Army officer

times a week. We have been 22 hours out of the 24 in the saddle with no food for ourselves or beasts. It is a very mountainous part of the country where we are; it is very rough and steep, and we have plenty of climbing to do. I was very fortunate in getting a good horse, but someone the other night ran a bayonet into the poor animal's leg, and it will not be fit to work again for months. I have got another good one now. Our Sergeant-Major was shot through the head, and he is away from us; the Captain gave me his horse. W Chapman,[166] a relation of Mrs Graham, sen., is our Sergeant-Major, and we camp together. We sewed two blankets together and made a tent to hold the two of us, and we are quite comfortable. I have been promoted to sergeant, and am getting along splendidly. I feel proud to think that I have received my promotion without any influence at all. I now receive 7s a day, so that is not too bad. We had a big fight yesterday, and captured 2000 head of beautiful cattle. There is a lot of fighting going on yet, and it is just as dangerous, if not worse, than what it was before. The Boers are all in small bodies. They hide between the mountains, and when you get in the pass they let bang from all parts, and you cannot get a shot at them, as the pass is very narrow and long, with steep banks on each side. I hear we are to go next towards Pretoria. No more news this time.

Lees, who lived in Campbelltown, was a member of the Camden Half Squadron New South Wales Mounted Rifles and saw two periods of service during the Boer War.

LEWIS, George: *Rank:* Private #160. *Unit:* 48th (Northamptonshire) Regiment of Foot. *Departed:* England October 1899. *Born:* 1875 Kingsthorpe, Northampton, England. *Parents:* Edward Lloyd Lewis and Mary Wall. *Died:* 27 June 1930 Camden Hospital, Camden, NSW. *Buried:* Camden General – Church of England. *Spouse:* Emily Kate Wilson. *Notes:* Also saw active service on the Indian Frontier. Arrived Australia 1921.

The Northamptonshire Regiment were at Belmont on 23 November 1899 and at Enslin on 25 November 1899, and on 8 December they were at Graspan. Early in 1901 the battalion was taken to the Central Transvaal and along with the Wiltshire Regiment occupied posts on the line between Warm Baths and Pietersburg.

Camden News
Thursday, 3 July 1930, page 1
Obituary
GEORGE LEWIS

The death occurred at the Camden District Hospital on Friday last, of George Lewis, of Moreton Park, Menangle. The deceased, who was 55 years of age, was born at Kingsthorpe, Northampton, England, and came to Australia early in 1921, coming to this district in March of the same year, where together with his brother James he took up dairying on the farm now owned by Mr. Pat Maher, near Spaniards Hill School, subsequently the brothers purchased the eastern half of the same holding between the railway and the river and continued dairying. In his earlier years Mr. Lewis, as a member of the Northamptonshire Regiment, saw active service on the Indian frontier and afterwards in the Boer War. The funeral took place on Saturday afternoon at the Camden General Cemetery, the Rev. T. G. Paul performing the last sad rites. A wife and one daughter are left to mourn the loss of a loving husband and father.

---

[166] Chapman, William Sergeant

LLOYD, William George: *Rank:* Private #104. *Unit:* 'A' Squadron NSW Mounted Rifles. *Departed:* 14 November 1899 *SS Langton Grange*. *Returned:* Invalided to Australia 13 August 1900. *Born:* 1874 Sydney, NSW. *Parents:* William Logan Lloyd and Susan O'Meara. *Died:* 7 December 1948 Marrickville, NSW. *Spouse:* Mary Lavinia James. *Married:* 1901 Orange, NSW. *Honours:* Queen's South Africa Medal with 3 clasps.

LOADER, Charles Arthur Clarendon: *Rank:* Trooper #1627. *Unit:* 3rd New South Wales Mounted Rifles. *Departed:* 15 March 1901 *HMT Maplemore*. *Returned:* 3 June 1902 *HMT Aurania*. *Born:* 24 August 1879 Parkes, NSW. *Parents:* Charles Thomas Loader and Janet Smart. *Died:* 17 October 1956 Brisbane, Qld. *Buried:* Evans Head, NSW. *Spouse:* Mary Elizabeth Sackley. *Married:* 1907 Sydney, NSW. *Note:* Listed in Australian War Memorial data as Arthur Charles Loader.

MACARTHUR-ONSLOW, Arthur John (Jack): *Rank:* Lieutenant. *Unit:* 'A' Squadron NSW Mounted Rifles. *Departed:* 14 November 1899 *SS Langton Grange*. *Returned:* invalided to Australia 30 August 1900. *Born:* 29 April 1873 Camden Park, Menangle, NSW. *Parents:* Arthur Alexander Walton Onslow and Elizabeth Macarthur. *Died:* 20 April 1953 Terrigal, NSW. *Spouse:* Christian Leslie Bell. *Married:* 1902 England. *Honours:* Queen's South Africa Medal with 4 clasps.

Arthur John Macarthur-Onslow

The *Short History of the New South Wales Mounted Rifles* indicates that Arthur John Macarthur-Onslow was in 'the vanguard of the troops that captured General Cronje' and had 'received the white flag from Cronje'. Cronje's column had been intercepted by Major General Sir John French at Paardeberg, and the General eventually surrendered after a prolonged siege, and an attempted assault by Lieutenant General Horatio Kitchener. Cronje eventually surrendered at 6 a.m. 27 February 1900. British historians make no reference to the part played by the Australian troops in the offensive but do mention the bravery of the Canadian contingent. However, the *Sydney Morning Herald*'s correspondent, Andrew Barton (Banjo) Paterson indicates that the Canadians were supported by the New South Wales Mounted Rifles ('A' Squadron). John Macquarie Antill, Francis William Axam and Robert Nethery and other members of 'A' Squadron indicated their contingent was the first to enter Cronje's laager with Antill stating the honour was given to them by Lord Roberts.

The surrender of General Cronje – copyright exempt

Arthur John was afterwards wounded at Grootveld near Heilbron which had for a short time been proclaimed the Boer capital of the Orange Free State, following the British victory at Bloemfontein, until it too was captured. The *Short History* indicates he was shot on 21 May 1900 and was then 'a prisoner in the hands of the Boers at Heilbron where he was placed in hospital and well treated, his orderly was able to secure the Town Hall Boer flag, which he brought to Australia'. He was subsequently invalided home on 30 August 1900.

Britain exiled General Cronje to St. Helena (in the Atlantic Ocean east of Rio de Janeiro) as it believed no South African prison was strong enough to hold him. Many saw this as equivalent to Bonaparte's exile to Elba. Cronje never returned to South Africa.

Camden News
Thursday, 7 June 1900

To date no farther cable has been received by Mrs Onslow as to her wounded son Lieutenant Onslow; the latest cable from South Africa is that he is seriously wounded in the knee.

Camden News
Thursday, 14 June 1900

Lieutenant Onslow

Mrs Onslow, of Camden Park, Menangle, has received a cable stating that her son Lieutenant AJ Macarthur-Onslow, who was reported as severely wounded on May 21, is doing well.

MACARTHUR-ONSLOW, Arthur William: *Rank:* 2nd Lieutenant, Captain. *Unit:* 16th (The Queen's) Lancers. *Born:* 25 May 1877 Camden Park, Menangle, NSW. *Parents:* Arthur Alexander Walton Onslow and Elizabeth Macarthur. *Died:* 5 November 1914 Ypres, Belgium. *Buried:* Ypres Cemetery, Belgium. *Spouse:* Christabel Emily Sarah Beech. *Married:* 1911 Warwickshire, England. *Honours:* Queen's South Africa Medal. *Memorials:* St. John's Church of England, Camden, NSW, St. James' Church of England, Menangle, NSW.

Arthur William Macarthur-Onslow

Arthur William 'was slightly wounded in action when a bullet pierced his ear. After the declaration of peace he remained with his regiment in South Africa on garrison duty, and on returning to England was appointed an instruction officer in connection with the Territorial Army scheme, Cambridge being his headquarters for several years. In this capacity his service was lent to the New Zealand Government when compulsory training came into force in the Dominion, and he was at Christchurch for three years, his appointment terminating in June 1913.'[167] He also served with the 16th (The Queen's) Lancers during WWI and was killed in action near Ypres.

MACARTHUR-ONSLOW, Francis Arthur: *Rank:* Lieutenant. *Unit:* 7th (The Princess Royal's) Dragoon Guards. *Departed:* March 1900 SS Medic. *Born:* 7 June 1879 Camden Park, Menangle, NSW. *Parents:* Arthur Alexander Walton Onslow and Elizabeth Macarthur. *Died:* 3 March 1938 Sydney, NSW. *Buried:* Camden Park Private. *Spouse:* Sylvia Seton Raymond Chisholm. *Married:* 16 May 1903 Goulburn, NSW. *Honours:* Queen's South Africa Medal with 5 clasps.

Francis Arthur saw action in Johannesburg, Diamond Hill, and Bergendal. He then contracted rheumatic fever and was invalided to London. He returned to Australia in January 1902. He also served with the British Army during WWI.

Francis Arthur Macarthur-Onslow

---

[167] *Sydney Morning Herald*, Wednesday 11 November 1914 – Killed in Action. Captain A.W. Macarthur-Onslow

MACARTHUR-ONSLOW, James William: *Rank:* Lieutenant-Colonel. *Unit:* (1) 60th (King's Royal Rifles) Regiment (2) 5th Australian Commonwealth Horse. *Departed:* 7 March 1900 *SS Salamis* at own expense. *Returned:* 21 March 1901 *SS Australia.* Born: 7 November 1867 Camden Park, Menangle, NSW. *Parents:* Arthur Alexander Walton Onslow and Elizabeth Macarthur. *Died:* 17 November 1946 Camden Park, Menangle. *Buried:* Camden Park Private. *Spouse:* Enid Emma Macarthur. *Married:* 15 December 1897 St. John's Church of England, Darlinghurst, NSW. *Honours:* Queen's South Africa Medal with 4 clasps, Mentioned in Despatches. *Memorials:* St. John's Church of England, Camden; St. James' Church of England, Menangle, NSW.

James William Macarthur-Onslow – photo courtesy Camden Park House collection

James William served in the 60th (King's Royal Rifles) Regiment as a Special Services Officer and Aide-de-Camp to Major-General Hutton until 10 October 1900. The King's Royal Rifles were a mounted light infantry regiment. He participated in operations in the Orange Free State from February to May 1900, including the actions at Vet River and Zand River, and operations in the Transvaal from May to November 1900. For this service, he was Mentioned in Despatches by Field Marshal Lord Roberts. He then went on to serve with the 5th Australian Commonwealth Horse. During WWI he served as a Colonel with the Sea Transport Service of the First Australian Imperial Force, commanding troop ships travelling between Australia, the Middle East and Britain between 1915 and 1917. He was Aide-de-Camp to the Governor-General of Australia in 1902 and for a second time from 1917 to 1920. He retired with the rank of Major General in 1924.

MAXWELL, Alfred Ernest: *Rank:* Private #119. *Unit:* 'A' Squadron NSW Mounted Rifles. *Departed:* 14 November 1899 *SS Langton Grange. Returned:* invalided to England 27 November 1900. *Born:* 1875 Liverpool, England. *Parents:* Alfred Maxwell and Annie Helena. *Died:* 10 May 1965 Wahroonga, NSW. *Spouse:* Elizabeth Rispen. *Married:* 1909 Chatswood, NSW. *Honours:* Queen's South Africa Medal with 4 clasps. *Memorial:* Wollondilly Heritage Centre, The Oaks.

Alfred was wounded on 30 April 1900 at Thaba N'Chu, South Africa. He also served during WWI as a Private #2449 with the 55th Infantry Battalion.

MAXWELL, John Cornelius: *Rank:* Private #92. *Unit:* 'A' Squadron NSW Mounted Rifles. *Departed:* 14 November 1899 *SS Langton Grange. Returned:* 8 January 1901 *HMT Orient. Born:* 1875 Bimlow, Burragorang Valley, NSW. *Parents:* John Joseph Maxwell and Theresa Seckold. *Died:* 1955 Wentworthville, NSW. *Spouse:* Grace A Thomas. *Married:* 1913 Waverley, NSW. *Honours:* Queen's South Africa Medal with 1 clasp. *Memorial:* Wollondilly Heritage Centre, The Oaks.

McBARON, Matthew Montgomery (Monty): *Rank:* Trooper #788. *Unit:* New South Wales Lancers. *Departed:* 16 February 1900 *SS Australian. Returned:* 6 December 1901 *HMT Harlech Castle. Born:* 1 April 1881 Robertson, NSW. *Parents:* James McBaron and Margaret Montgomery. *Occupation:* farmer. *Died:* 1 February 1972 Raleigh, NSW. *Buried:* Bellingen General Cemetery. *Spouse:* Florence Emily Rutledge. *Married:* 15 March 1904 Kiama, NSW. *Honours:* Queen's South Africa Medal with 4 clasps. *Memorial:* Memorial Museum Parramatta, NSW.

McBaron was a member of the West Camden Half Squadron and served under Captain Charles Edward Nicholson.

McEWEN, James Fraser: *Rank:* (1) Private #346 (2) Staff Sergeant #1264. *Unit:* (1) Army Medical Corps (New South Wales) (2) 1st Battalion Australian Commonwealth Horse (NSW). *Departed: (1)* 17 January 1900 *SS Moravian. Returned: (1)* 8 January 1901 *HMT Orient. Departed: (2)* 18 February 1902 *SS Custodian. Born:* 14 June 1877 Goulburn, NSW. *Parents:* John McEwen and Kezia Victoria Seear. *Died:* 1 November 1911 Kingston, Jamaica. *Spouse:* Frederika Caroline Melville.

Matthew Montgomery McBaron – photo courtesy Australian War Memorial

James McEwen was a Sunday School Superintendent at St. David's Presbyterian Church, Campbelltown. A memorial plaque is held in the church. He spent his early years in Campbelltown and joined the New South Wales Army Medical Corps as a private in 1900 and sailed for South Africa. In 1902 he returned to South Africa with the Commonwealth Army Medical Corps as a Staff Sergeant. He acquired his degree as a Doctor of Dental Surgery after service in the Boer War.

Following the end of the war McEwen sailed for England to watch the coronation of King Edward VII.

The Campbelltown Herald
Wednesday, 27 June 1900, page 2

The Boer War
LETTER FROM THE FRONT

Lance-Corporal J McEwen with the New South Wales Army Medical Corps in South Africa writes as follows to his parents at Campbelltown, letter dated Winburg, May 6th 1900:

> *I should have written from Bloemfontein only that we were rushed away to advance with the Mounted Infantry Brigade, under Colonel Hutton, at a few minutes' notice, at 3 a.m. We were at Bloemfontein only two days, and were jolly glad to get away. It is a pretty fair little town, about the size of Goulburn, but owing to the crowd of troops and dead animals lying around, it is very, very smellful. At Bloemfontein I met Will[168] and Joe Newman,[169] G Spooner,[170] Tom Lees,[171] W Divall,[172] F Axam and J Hawkey,[173] also RC*

---

[168] Newman, Lieutenant William Arthur 1st New South Wales Mounted Rifles
[169] Newman, Captain Joseph 2nd New South Wales Mounted Rifles
[170] Spooner, Charles Greenwood 1st New South Wales Mounted Rifles
[171] Lees, Thomas James
[172] Divall, William 1st New South Wales Mounted Rifles
[173] Hawkey, John Martin 'A' Squadron New South Wales Mounted Rifles

Holman.[174] *All were in splendid health and spirits. I had a fine yarn with Will and Joe, and found them enjoying themselves well. The other boys and I also had a long 'chin', and Spooner passed with his troop a few minutes ago. They are all forward with us now. Part of the camp is a regular Campbelltown street.*

Well, we've had our baptism of fire at last. We left the railway at Bethany and cut across towards Basutoland. At a little place called Dewetsdorp we came up with a commando in a splendid position and exchanged shell compliments for five days. Whew! It was merry. They pitched our camp too close, and the shells dropped round quick and sudden. It was very fascinating listening to the shells going whiz-z-z-s-s-slap and seeing the more nervous customers doing 'a duck' behind the wagons when they dropped too close. We shifted and got it a bit worse, as parties crossed the skyline and drew the fire of the Boers; but though a couple of pieces fell in the lines and some over the hospital, no damage resulted, to our corps. One poor nigger [sic.]*, however, got hit and we had to amputate his leg. Altogether in the 'scrap' we had about fifty wounded, only one nigger* [sic.] *of those we treated dying. We have been very successful, only losing two patients (and those Kaffirs) out of about 500. The Boers were left in retreat, with French after them, and we came on to Bloemfontein, where, as I have said, we joined the mounted division under Major-General Hutton, and advanced towards Pretoria on May 1st. We had a 'scrap' on the 3rd and drove the Boers from Brantford, 25 miles from Bloemfontein, and advanced after the enemy. Yesterday we had the severest brush we have had – about four hours' hard fighting, great work being done by the artillery. We finally drove the Boers out, and though they carried away all they could, we found five dead on the field, one wounded (he is with us now), and took several prisoners. I've been out in every fight yet, but as a rule we are not allowed out till the row is over. Lord Roberts is in camp now, and today, without trouble, we occupied this place. We are to move to Kroonstad, the present seat of government, where it is expected the Boers will make a stand. I rather hope they will, as though, from a spectacular point of view, a battle is very fine, yet after the fight, when the poor beggars who have handed in their checks are stretched around, it strikes one as a miserable, sordid way of settling differences in the 1900th year of the Christian era. However, it's no blame of ours, and at present our boys are yarning most amicably with a wounded Boer, whom we are treating like a brother. Poor beggars! From what we've seen, they are a simple, misled people, and are fighting doggedly and well. I am afraid war correspondents are responsible for some awful lies, as, though sometimes a section of the Boers may do some rotten things, as a rule they are not half as black as they are painted. Why, one of them, when they had captured an entire party of about 300, brought in a Britisher to the hospital with the remark, 'I had to plug this chap, and now I've brought him in to you to mend'. We are now under orders to move off, so I will bring this to an end.*

MOORE, Patrick Thomas: *Rank:* Private #93. *Unit:* 'A' Squadron New South Wales Mounted Rifles. *Departed:* 14 November 1899 *SS Langton Grange. Returned:* 8 January 1901 *HMT Orient. Born:* 16 April 1873 Heathcote, Vic. *Parents:* Michael Moore and Mary Kelly. *Occupation:* farmer. *Died:* 19 May 1935 Denman, NSW. *Buried:* Denman Roman Catholic Cemetery. *Spouse:* Mary Doyle. *Married:* 19 May 1935

---

[174] Holman, Richard Charles Frederick 2nd New South Wales Mounted Rifles

Sydney, NSW. *Honours:* Queen's South Africa Medal with 6 clasps. *Memorial:* Wollondilly Heritage Centre, The Oaks.

Moore was a farmer living in Wilton, NSW at the time of enlisting. He saw action in North-West Cape Colony, Free State, Transvaal, Diamond Hill and Elands River Station on 13 June 1900.

MURRAY, James Bernard: *Rank:* Trooper #3108. *Unit:* 2nd New South Wales Mounted Rifles. *Departed:* 15 March 1901 *SS Maplemore* or *SS Custodian*. *Returned:* 3 June 1902 *HMT Aurania*. *Born:* 1879 Wagga Wagga, NSW. *Parents:* William Murray and Mary Ann Ray. *Occupation:* butcher, Picton. *Died:* 1 May 1956 Lidcombe, NSW. *Spouse:* Mary Doyle. *Married:* 1903 Sydney, NSW. *Honours:* Queen's South Africa Medal with 2 clasps. *Memorial:* Wollondilly Heritage Centre, The Oaks.

NETHERY, Robert John: *Rank:* (1) Private #94 (2) Corporal (3) Sergeant. *Unit:* 'A' Squadron New South Wales Mounted Rifles. *Departed:* 16 November 1899 *SS Langton Grange*. *Returned:* 8 January 1901 *HMT Orient*. *Born:* 1875 Kiama, NSW. *Parents:* John Nethery and Margaret Soper. *Died:* 1 August 1947 Kyogle, NSW. *Spouse:* Mary Louisa Dyason. *Married:* 1901 Bathurst, NSW. *Honours:* Queen's South Africa Medal with 5 Clasps.

Camden News
Thursday, 22 February 1900, page 2

THE WAR
New South Wales Mounted Rifles.
THEIR BAPTISM OF FIRE

The following are extracts from a letter from Corporal RJ Nethery, Camden Mounted Rifles:–

We are now camped at a place called Honwater, a watering place on the plains 40 miles from any village. De Aar is the base of operations in Cape Colony, and 608 miles from Cape Town. We spent Christmas there, and a lively one too — dry bread and coffee for breakfast and ship biscuits and tinned beef for dinner.

On December 31 we started on the march for Prieska, a distance of 110 miles. The first day we reached Buxton, 24 miles. The next (New Year's Day) Honwater and the third day at midday Swan's Farm. We had orders to stay there till midnight, when we had to start again for Prieska. The Boer rebels were reported to be looting the town. We reached Prieska at 4 a.m., left our horses just outside the town, and went through the streets ourselves, and found where the rebels camped. The Colonel, who was with us, wanted to fire on them while they were asleep, but Captain Antill would not. He waited till they got up and then called out to them to surrender. As soon as they heard him they started firing on us, but we were too well hidden behind rocks, and none of us were hit, although some shots came pretty close to me. We took eight of them prisoners, and four were buried by their mates. A day after we went over into the enemy's country, and took possession of 13 horses and 1200 sheep and goats, which the rebels had stolen from other people. We have now left Prieska, and are camped about 40 miles from de Aar. Today 200 of the Imperial troops joined us and more are coming tomorrow and next day, when it is supposed we will march across country to Kimberley.

Camden News
Thursday, 5 April 1900, page 8

THE WAR
New South Wales Mounted Rifles
LETTERS FROM THE FRONT

The following extracts are taken from a letter received yesterday (April 4) from Corporal R. J. Nethery of the Mounted Rifles who went to South Africa as a member of the first Contingent by the SS Langton Grange: —

Bankfontein,
Modder River
March 3, 1900

We had a most delightful trip over by sea although there was plenty of hard work attached to it. You have probably known by this time what work we have done during the campaign by reading the papers so there is little need for me describing any of it. I must certainly say that the horrors of war are indescribable on paper. We have had some very trying times here although I never enjoyed better health in my life. We are attached to Lord Roberts' column and have been in the front of each of the seven engagements we have had, with the fortune of having only 3 men wounded, 1 seriously. At present we are camped at Bankfontein (a farm it was before the war, but now a place of ruin) awaiting farther orders. They say that we have very slow work before us now, having done our share previously. The respect shown to us by all other regiments in the field is very great, and Lord Roberts says he never in all his life knew men to be so cool and daring when under fire. I must say we have had some very narrow squeaks when bullets start whistling round [like] hailstones it is enough to make one duck their head. We have had on two occasions the enemy pound us on three sides, and then got away without a scratch. A report came in a few days ago that the first lot of colonial troops were to start for home in seven weeks.

In Corporal Nethery's letter of March 3, which was dated later than Captain Antill's of 21 February and indicated he had been wounded, no mention is made of any injury. Nethery states that he *never enjoyed better health*, so presumably he didn't want to worry his family.

Camden News
Thursday, 26 April 1900, page 1

Letter from the Front

The following are extracts taken from a letter received by a friend in Camden, from Corporal R. J. Nethery, who is now on active service at the front, serving under Captain Antill.

Osfontein,
Modder River,
March 8, 1900

We have been attached to Lord Roberts' column for some time now and have done some good work and daring deeds, but it is needless me describing anything we have taken part in, as you have a chance of watching the papers, and know a great deal more than we really do ourselves.

In the first place a battle field, or on the march, is not all beer and skittles when it comes to sleeping at night for weeks at a time with your great coat for a blanket and helmet for a pillow, one begins to think of the soft little bed he has left behind. It is almost impossible for me to describe the horrors seen on a field the day after a conflict especially with the kind of an enemy which we are dealing with at the present time. We have as our own little lot acted the part of advance guard to Lord Roberts' column for the past month. In the latter part of February we came up to the rear of General Cronje's convoy and kept pushing them on as fast as we could so as to give them little time to make their strongholds as we thought, but they had them made previously. Well we kept on in this way until the 17th February when the real thing itself began. Our orders were to 'go and find Cronje'. This we did, although at a great risk of life to everybody, but orders on a battlefield must be carried out and no shirking. As I said we did find Cronje, but it is a mystery that there is one of our little band left to tell the tale. We were advancing in extended order by troops, when we saw a few mounted men out on a plain. We kept onward, some of our men quite close to the river bank and the outer flank about 300 yards from the foot of a large kopje, we were marching in this manner for about 5 minutes when all at once a shot came whistling along and about ten seconds after, if one bullet passed us 1000 did, and I tell you it didn't take us long to get out of it either. We had bullets coming at us from the right, front and left, some of our chaps being within 150 yards of the enemy's fire, one man being wounded, Private Tweedy,[175] of Forbes MR. We galloped out of range and then rode leisurely back to Colonel Hannay who was in charge of the Royal Horse Artillery. As soon as it was reported he told us to go and have a night's rest and immediately turned round to his own men and said. 'The Australians have done their work, now start and do yours, go and shell that laager by daybreak.' But it wasn't to be done by daybreak, for it took ten days heavy fighting to shift the Boers. It was here where Captain Greeve of NSW Infantry, but here attached to the Black Watch, met his end, that regiment is fairly cut to pieces. General Cronje surrendered here on the anniversary of Majuba Hill, and we, the NSW Mounted Rifles, being the first to find the old General, were the first to enter his old premises. The sight which we beheld was one that I will never forget. Dead horses lying in every direction, rifles and ammunition in every direction, wounded Dutchmen everywhere, and out of some 750 odd wagons only 27 were found to be of any use for transport service, all the remainder being either smashed to pieces or burnt by the explosion of the British shells, especially those of the Naval Brigade, which did the most damage.

Camden News
Thursday, 31 May 1900, page 4

NEWS FROM THE FRONT

Corporal RJ Nethery of the Mounted Rifles, writing to his friends in Camden under date April 29, says: —

We are now camped at Bloemfontein, under canvas, the first time under shelter since the first of the year. For the past four weeks we have been doing outpost and patrol duty near Karree, about 16 miles from here. Now

---
[175] Tweedy, William George #99

we are to stay here for a fortnight for a spell and to get new clothes and so forth. Then I believe we are to march on to Pretoria, and by what I can hear we have some very hard work in front of us yet. I have enjoyed good health, and have got off very lucky so far and live in the hope of going right through now. Fever is very prevalent here; there are no less than 1500 patients in the hospitals around Bloemfontein at the present time.

Since I last wrote we have had some very rough times of it. On the 28th of last month we marched off towards the east from a place called Nell's Drift on the Modder River, and that evening overtook a part of the enemy. We were under the command of Colonel de Lisle, whilst General French had a large column on the opposite side of the kopjes to which we were on. About 2 o'clock in the evening we were marching across the veldt in extended order when suddenly bullets began to fall among us like a shower of hail. We soon put spurs to our horses and made for the side of a kopje about half a mile on our left. We there dismounted and climbed to the top and laid down among a number of stones, occasionally firing a shot when any of the enemy appeared, yet we could very seldom see anyone. The bullets kept whistling very close over us for some time, at last our Vicars Maxim gun began to play on them, and sent them flying in all directions. About an hour after, we returned to our horses and watered them at a pond close by, and halted for a quarter of an hour for rest. Shortly afterwards we got the order to again advance, but had not gone a mile when lead began to come again. We jumped off our horses and ran under cover of ant hills, stones, or anything we could get, along the side of the kopje. It was here that I had my narrowest 'squeak', a bullet passing through my helmet just behind the right ear, and another hitting the ground just in from of me and passing over my left shoulder. A few minutes later I was lying behind a stone about six inches high, I thought it not high enough so put two smaller ones on top, leaving a place between for my rifle, I had no sooner laid my head behind it than a bullet struck the left hand one and turned it right round. That day we had no dinner nor tea at night, next day nothing at all to eat and Good Friday our only meal consisted of fried sheep's liver, which we got that morning. After that meal I was sent out with three others to watch over a party of Boers and the township of Brandford. Our food came in late that night but there was plenty of it, and we have had plenty ever since. Nearly every day I was sent out to patrol the country in the direction of the Boer camps and having the use of Captain Antill's telescope and three good mates there was little danger of our being surprised.

NEWMAN, Joseph: *Rank*: (1) Company Quartermaster-Sergeant #3 (2) Lieutenant. *Unit:* (1) 'A' Squadron New South Wales Mounted Rifles; (2) 2nd New South Wales Mounted Rifles (3) 3rd New South Wales Imperial Bushmen. *Departed: (1)* 16 November 1899 *SS Langton Grange. Returned:* 8 January 1901 *HMT Orient. Departed:(2)* 15 March 1901 *SS Maplemore. Born:* 1868 Campbelltown, NSW. *Parents:* Patrick Paul Newman and Eliza Newman. *Died:* 17 October 1948 Gladesville, NSW. *Honours:* Queen's South Africa Medal with 6 clasps.

Joseph had served with the Camden Half Squadron New South Wales Mounted Rifles prior to the Boer War. Following the end of the war he travelled to England to watch the celebrations surrounding the coronation of King Edward VII.

Camden News
Thursday, 7 February 1900, page 2

Our Boys at the Front
FROM OUR OWN CORRESPONDENT AT THE SEAT OF WAR

We are camped here on a plain with 8000 British troops all waiting for the order 'To the Front'. We had a weary journey in the train from Cape Town. The first night we stopped at a little township called Wellington, very much like the New South Wales Wellington, especially the appearance of the surrounding country. On our arrived there we had a meal, which we needed badly. The station master and his wife were very kind to us (I think they must be Campbelltown people). We were on the train from 2 o'clock on Thursday until 9 on Saturday. Just now things are very quiet in camp, but everyone goes about fully armed and equipped ready to march at a moment's notice, as the Boers are within 15 miles of us.

We were all up before 5 o'clock on Christmas morning listening to the Yorkshire Light Infantry band playing the Christmas hymns, but before getting through their programme the shrill notes of the bugle sounded 'Yorkshire Light Infantry to the front', and with ringing cheers we bade the brave Yorkshires good-bye. I visited the military prison a few days ago and saw two prisoners who were sentenced to be shot on the following day — one was a Boer spy, the other an Englishman. I pitied the poor fellows, notwithstanding they were found guilty of a very serious crime. They were compelled to dig their own graves, and the shooting business had to be done by a company of defaulters. We have 29 mules attached to our regiment and eight drivers. The boss driver is Ned Fitzgerald,[176] and hails from Campbelltown. We had not many luxuries for dinner on Christmas Day: for breakfast, dry bread and coffee, and ditto for dinner. Nevertheless, no men could possibly be in better health and spirits than we are, thank God – every man ready, able, and willing for the fray. We have plenty of muddy water to drink, but nothing to kill the animalcule.[177] Our boys are out every day at field work, and are shaping well. The English officers are greatly pleased with the mounted riflemen from New South Wales, especially their quickness in locating advantageous positions. I was on escort duty at the railway station a few days ago taking wounded men to the hospital, and it was a most pitiful sight to see the way the poor fellows were smashed up. The escort had never seen anything like it, and were consequently much affected as each sufferer was carried out and laid on the platform, but in the midst of it all I had to roar out laughing as we carried a big Dublin Fusilier whose head was nearly severed from his body by a shell that exploded in front of him. When we laid the poor fellow on the platform, he exclaimed, as loud as he was able, 'Be dam bud when am all right I'll go back and brain that blackguard Boer that fired at me from behind the big rock'. But the poor fellow succumbed from the terrible wound he received. With best wishes to all Campbelltown friends.

J Newman

Joseph and William Newman were sons of Patrick Newman who had taught at St. Patrick's Catholic School in Campbelltown from 1864 to 1880. Their father then transferred to Campbelltown Public School as a Headmaster where he remained until he retired in 1901.

---

[176] Fitzgerald, Trooper Edward #3512 2nd New South Wales Mounted Rifles born 1866 Penrith NSW died 17 March 1934 Orange, NSW
[177] Little animals

NEWMAN, William Arthur: *Rank*: Lieutenant. *Unit*: 1st New South Wales Mounted Rifles. *Departed*: 17 January 1900 *HMT Southern Cross*. *Returned*: 8 January 1901 *HMT Orient*. *Born*: 1873 Campbelltown, NSW. *Parents*: Patrick Paul Newman and Eliza Newman. *Died*: 25 August 1931 Grafton, NSW. *Buried*: Grafton General Cemetery.

Newman was one of those given the honour of escorting the captured Boer General Pieter Cronje into exile. He participated in a number of important battles and returned to Australia in January 1901, but, sickened by his war experiences did not re-enlist. His father had been the Headmaster of the Campbelltown Public School but had moved the family to Orange. However, William retained strong ties with Campbelltown.

The Campbelltown Herald
Wednesday, 21 January 1900, page 2

On Board the Troopship Southern Cross
Letters from Volunteers

Mr and Mrs PJ Newman of Campbelltown have received a letter from their son, Lieut. Wm A Newman, who left by the Southern Cross, *written on board that vessel just before leaving Port Phillip Heads. Up to the time of writing Lieut. Newman had enjoyed a really pleasant trip; he was, he said, not the least bit sick, and never felt belter in his life. The send-off at Sydney he considered a trifle too enthusiastic at times, the fighting along the road to get to the boat being anything but pleasant.*

> *'Our squadron (C),' writes Lieut. Newman, 'of which I have been posted as subaltern[178] — also the leader of No. 2 Troop — is a splendid one, the best in the regiment. It includes the following men: T Lees, C Spooner, Wm. Divall (Campbelltown), and F Rudd (Narrandera). Nearly all the Picton, Camden, and Ingleburn men are posted in my troop.'*

Of the cramped accommodation on board, the writer says that in a cabin certified to hold two, four men are placed. After having embarked at Sydney, and just as the boat was about to start, someone passed up a jack-knife with a number of attachments, an inscription reading: 'To Lieut. Newman, from one who never saw him.' His regiment didn't need to send to find him. One of the Corporals (Learmonth) in Lieut. Newman's regiment is said to be worth £100,000 and another man — one Featherstonhaugh[179] — is also reputed to be fabulously rich. The Southern Cross, which is timed to reach Cape Town about February 16th carries 600 horses, including 90 for the Imperial Government.

Private Spooner, on the Southern Cross, *has also written home. He reports a smooth passage to Queenscliff (Vic) and everything OK as regards himself. After leaving Sydney ten stowaways were discovered on the troopship. The writer sends kind regards to all friends.*

---

[178] A British military term for a junior officer. Literally meaning 'subordinate', subaltern is used to describe commissioned officers below the rank of captain
[179] Featherstonhaugh, Cuthbert – Lance-Corporal later Lieutenant-Colonel

The Campbelltown Herald
Wednesday, 28 March 1900, page 2

With the NSW Second South Africa Contingent
Troopship *Southern Cross*, at Sea, Friday, 16th Feb 1900

Though the public demonstration of our embarkation at Woolloomooloo took place on Wednesday, 17th January, it was 8 o'clock the following morning before our troopship was ready to put to sea. Notwithstanding the rather obvious preparations which had been made to ensure our departure at the hour advertised, it was found that the shipping of our regimental baggage and equipment had not been completed. We had therefore to remain in port until this had all been safely stowed aboard. The Southern Cross, *our trooper, is a typical stamp of the regular ocean tramp. She has apparently had a varied experience, her last commission being the transport of a large number of mules from Gibraltar to the Cape. Her rate of progress is particularly slow, in fact at times it becomes extremely monotonous, the record for fast steaming on the present voyage being 235 miles. Her accommodation also is of a most primitive style. In respect of accommodation we are not nearly as fortunate as are our comrades aboard the* Moravian, *but as a prelude to harder times that are to come, we one and all accept our present circumstances in the most philosophic manner imaginable.*

We have aboard the Mounted Infantry Regiment (of about 400 officers and men) and the mounted bearer section of the Army Medical Corps, consisting of 40 of all ranks. There are also about 550 horses, including the Imperial remounts purchased of Major Thompson, the care of which during the voyage across devolves upon our men. Our intention when leaving Sydney was to make Cape Town our first port of call. An outbreak of enteric fever aboard, however, caused our plans to be altered, the condition of one patient, a man named Walker,[180] being considered of sufficient seriousness as to render it necessary for us to land him at Melbourne with a view to his admission to a hospital. In approaching Port Phillip Heads on the Saturday following our departure from Sydney, we signalled for the Port Medical Officer. It was only the matter of a few hours before this official came out to meet us in a pretty little steam yacht which does duty as a pilot boat. We were naturally delighted at the opportunity thus presented of dispatching our hastily-penned home letters and also of hearing the latest cables regarding the progress of the war, which to many of us is an item of even greater importance than it was ere we responded to the Empire's call.

It being the hour devoted to drill, the troops were mustering on their parade decks when the pilot boat came alongside. The sympathetic demeanour shown when witnessing the return home of our first casualty was particularly noticeable. After relieving us of our sick comrade and according us the customary 'cock-a-doodle-doo', with which form of compliment we are, by the way, now fairly familiar, the pilot boat returned to Melbourne and left us to proceed on our long and dreary voyage. From Sydney to Port Phillip Heads our trip was an ideal one — the sea as smooth as glass and the weather perfect. Crossing the Australian Bight it has become usual to expect heavy weather, and in our case there was no exception, the rolling of the boat with its tremendous deck cargo was something to remember. The rough weather we encountered off the South Australian and West Australian coasts was frequently met with during our passage across the Indian Ocean, and we gradually became more and more accustomed to the midnight alarm of 'Stand to your horses' when an exceptionally heavy sea was running.

---

[180] Walker, Private George

It cannot of course be expected that life aboard a trooper is a mass of perfect luxuriance. The regular routine of military duties is carried out to the letter. The reveille sounds at 5.30 a.m., and then follow in order the usual camp duties as on shore, as well as physical exercise and muscle drill, until 'Lights out' is sounded at 9.15 p.m. Much of the officers' time is taken up in the instruction of raw recruits, of whom we appear to have a considerable number. I have been posted as Troop Leader of No. 2 Division of 'C' Squadron, and it will doubtless be of interest to your readers to learn that among the men of my division are the following who hail from our town and district: — Sergeant Vacchini (Picton), Corporal Wallace (Ingleburn), Corporal Anderson (Picton), Lance-Corporal Lees, Privates Divall, Rich,[181] and Spooner, of Campbelltown. Speaking personally, I am indeed gratified at seeing such a fair proportion of our local lads in the division under my command, and it affords me great pleasure in stating that they are without exception the best workers on the boat.

Owing to the method adopted in recruiting our contingent, it contains a strange admixture of all classes of life. Standing side by side with the habitué of Woolloomooloo (who probably learned his horsemanship on the nearest butcher's prad[182]) and the rouseabout from way back will frequently be found men of considerable standing in the community, professional men, station owners, perhaps, and young fellows to whom the everlasting round of duty peculiar to a soldier's life must indeed be a novelty. It is marvellous, nevertheless, to note how quickly the men are being polished into shape. The Mounted Rifle officers aboard, however, viz., Lieutenants Lydiard, Legge, and myself, often regret that Sergt. Majors Daly and Richards are not members of the contingent, as their presence would at times prove invaluable. The 26th of January (Anniversary Day) was celebrated in a truly national manner. The ordinary routine of duty gave place to a programme of sports, which were indulged in with as much vigour as the amount of deck space at our disposal would admit. At night a State dinner was given, and a concert took place on deck. Shortly after clearing the Australian coast, the medical officers aboard (Captains Cortis and Marshall) produced their vaccination appliances and all hands were subjected to this very necessary, though in some cases painful, operation. It was useless to plead that one had been vaccinated — the medical officer's word, aboard a troopship at least, is law. However, in the end most of the cases operated have turned out satisfactorily.

An additional duty altogether unknown on land but which is essential aboard a trooper is the 'keeping of the watch'. Each officer has to take his turn as Officer of the Watch, the duties of which position are of extremely responsible nature. The watches are taken in turns of two hours on duty and four hours off duty, and extends for 24 hours, and as the safety of the whole of the living freight of the troopship entirely depends on the vigilance of the watch officer, it can be realised that the position is at times no sinecure.

The accommodation for the men as well as for the horses aboard the Southern Cross is undoubtedly faulty. A mess room, fitted with fixed tables and seats, has been assigned to each squadron, but the space available is not nearly sufficient for requirements. Each man has a locker allotted to him for storing his kit; and sufficient room is left in front of this locker to swing a hammock, with which each man is provided. Captain Gribben, the Principal Veterinary Surgeon, is accompanying the Contingent in his official capacity, and despite the care and

---

[181] Rich, William Suttor #392
[182] A horse, variant of the Dutch praad and German Pferd.

attention which he has daily and nightly bestowed on his charges, we have lost from various causes ten animals.

We have rather more than the general number of stowaways, but by not making any port of call from Sydney to the Cape no opportunity was given of handing the offenders over to the authorities. The skipper has, however, adopted a more merciful course of compelling them to work their passage, which they are now doing with more or less good grace. The Southern Cross *expects to reach Cape Town tomorrow or the day following. We expect every moment to sight land, which will indeed be a treat after a month's tossing about on the ever-restless sea. On arrival we will most probably go into camp at Green Point, close to where the* SS Thermopylae[183] *was wrecked, in order to give our horses an opportunity of recovering from the effects of the voyage. We will then proceed with as little delay as possible towards Kimberley, where we hope to join our relatives and friends now serving in 'A' Squadron under Captain Antill. In view of our early arrival at Cape Town all hands are kept very busily engaged in arranging kits so as to avoid unnecessary delay in disembarking. Every member of the contingent has already been put through a course of musketry, a beer barrel towed to the stern of the troopship doing duty as a target. The officers' swords and the men's bayonets have all been sharpened to a degree, ready for immediate service, while all the bright metal on our uniforms and horse furniture has been covered with a coating of khaki paint. To observe these preparations for our baptism of fire makes one realise the seriousness of our positions. A more cheerful and contented lot of men, however, would be very difficult to find. An amount of excitement occurred aboard last night when the look-out man reported a vessel in sight – the first we had seen for nearly four weeks. The* Persic, *as the vessel turned out to be, much to our disgust merely signalled her name and destination in answer to our request for news. It was, however, a very pretty sight to watch the effects of the coloured lights and rockets by means of which the messages were exchanged. As this letter has assumed a greater length than I intended, I must now draw it to a close with the hope that my next contribution will contain items of more interest to one and all at home.*

WA Newman

The Campbelltown Herald
Wednesday, 25 April 1900, page 2

With the NSW Mounted Rifles
(FROM OUR CORRESPONDENT)
Bloemfontein, Orange Free State,
South Africa 20/3/00

If I remember rightly, I closed my last contribution as the troopship Southern Cross *was entering Table Bay. It now remains for me to attempt to chronicle the events from that date to the present.*

Anyone approaching Cape Town from the sea for the first time must indeed be struck by the magnificence of the scene. Table Mountain rises almost perpendicularly from the water's edge, and on the day of our arrival was surrounded by a fleecy-looking cloud, which made a very pretty contrast with the lovely blue of the sky. In the Bay, waiting for vacant berths at the wharf, were numbers of troopships, each bearing a distinguishing number, painted on its

---

[183] The *SS Thermopylae* was wrecked off Green Point near the entrance to Table Bay 11 September 1899. All passengers and two racehorses were rescued

bows. Beside one of these enormous vessels the Southern Cross *anchored until our turn for disembarkation arrived. Viewed from the Bay, Cape Town presents a very straggling appearance – an impression which is fully borne out on closer inspection. There are some handsome buildings, but the majority of the structures appear to be very antiquated. An electric tram service runs through the principal streets, and also to most of the suburbs. The cars in use are two-deckers similar to the old cars which were used in Sydney years ago. Almost half the population of Cape Town are Kaffirs [sic.],[184] with a fair sprinkling of Hindus and Lascars. The work of disembarkation, carried out on the lines of the Imperial service, occupied us a very short time, and a move was then made for the cavalry camp, which is situated at Maitland, some five miles out of town. Despite the crowded state of the troopship, our horses arrived in splendid condition, and after two or three days at Maitland we were instructed to proceed at once to the front to join General French's column.*

The journey from Cape Town to Modder River station was extremely tedious, and occupied us 84 hours. A special train was provided for each squadron, and halts were made at regular intervals along the line to feed and water the horses and prepare meals for the men. Before leaving Cape Town, the Mayor and a committee called the Colonial Troops Reception Committee presented each man with a large parcel of fruit and biscuits and a huge bottle of lime-juice. This thoughtful action was indeed appreciated by all. The railway from Cape Town runs for miles through perhaps the most uninteresting country it is possible to imagine, called the Karoo[185] – not a sign of trees or vegetation, excepting here and there patches of scrub resembling salt bush, while rugged looking kopjes, standing out in bold relief, are to be seen in every direction. From the car window would frequently be seen groups of jumbucks and antelopes startled by the train. The southern portion of South Africa has just experienced an exceptionally dry season. This probably accounts for the fact that the rivers are mostly little better than sand beds. At Orange River, on our journey, we first heard of Captain Antill's squadron, from three of its members who were passengers in the ambulance train for Cape Town. The poor fellows had been wounded in action at a place called Priyanka. This little incident brought home very vividly to us the painful realities of war.

On our arrival at Modder River Station, orders were waiting for us to join Lord Roberts' personal staff instead of General French's column. As the commander-in-chief had not yet reached the Modder, we pitched our camp on the site of the Modder River battle to await his arrival. We were thus enabled to have a look over the field where a few months previously the Highland Brigade had suffered such fearful reverses. Numbers of curios and relics of the battle were picked up by us. The construction of the Boer trenches, as well as the barbed wire mazes, were indeed sights of interest. We were, however, not sorry to move forward, as many of our men were commencing to feel the ill effects of the unwholesome atmosphere arising from the hastily made graves of those who fell in the engagements of the previous month. Our course was next directed towards Magersfontein, where we were engaged in making reconnaissances and in outpost duty. From here portion of our regiment proceeded to Paardeberg, where Cronje and his force of 4000 men were surrounded. The remainder of our regiment directed their course towards Kimberley, which was relieved amid general rejoicings a day or so later. After the surrender of Cronje and his army, posts of responsibility in the escort which conveyed him as a prisoner of war to

---

[184] The word kaffir was used in the former South Africa to refer to a black person. Now an offensive ethnic slur, it was formerly a neutral term for South African blacks.
[185] A semi-desert natural region of South Africa

Modder River station, en route to St. Helena, were given to two NSW officers, one of whom was your correspondent. Cronje, who was accompanied by his wife, two sons, and a family physician, occupied a seat in a covered-in wagon, drawn by twelve artillery gun horses – quite an imposing spectacle, and which, it is needless to say, was thoroughly well guarded.

In appearance, the Boer General is a short, stout man, with a full, sandy beard. He wore no uniform, but was dressed in a light tweed suit and a soft, broad-brimmed felt hat, and appeared to be utterly indifferent as to his position. This was in marked contrast to his wife, who appeared to feel her position keenly. The scene of wild excitement which greeted the arrival of the escort at Modder River Station can perhaps be better imagined than described. Having re-joined our regiment at Magersfontein, we were detailed as rear guard of a convoy proceeding on the advance to Bloemfontein. It was at this stage that we experienced our baptism of fire. At a place called Klip Drift, a force of 400 or 500 Boers attacked our convoy. The scouts of our regiment noticed the approaching force, and before many minutes had elapsed we were—most of us for the first time in our lives—under the fire of an enemy. Orders had scarcely been given to dismount before we were saluted by a perfect hail of bullets. Two of our squadrons were ordered to make a frontal attack – one in the firing line, the other in support. Our third squadron, which included my troop, attempted to outflank the Boers, who meanwhile retired to a kopje. Finding our fire rather disconcerting, and apparently miscalculating our strength, the Boers vacated this kopje in favour of one affording better cover, which was situated about a mile to their rear. Our lads appeared to quite enter into the fun of chasing the enemy across the veldt. We were, of course, unable to dislodge them from their second position, but by keeping up our attack we held them in check until nightfall, thus enabling our convoy to arrive at a place of safety.

In this, our first real engagement, our casualties were as follows: killed, nil, wounded, one officer (Lieut Holborow)[186] and seven men. We also had three horses killed. Our regiment was accorded great praise by the commander-in-chief in his report of the affair, and one or two of our officers were specially Mentioned in his Despatch, as it was considered that our prompt action prevented a valuable convoy from falling into Boer hands. It was also an event of importance, inasmuch as it was the first occasion since the commencement of the war on which a colonial regiment, acting independently, had engaged and repulsed the enemy. It was remarkable to note the coolness displayed whilst under fire. It was indeed hard to realise that our men were only recruits and not veterans. The various movements, such as extending under fire, were carried out with almost as much steadiness as if the regiment was on parade and not facing a foe of such magnitude.

Our next battle was Osfontein. We were not under such heavy fire as in our first engagement, it being more of the nature of an artillery duel. Our duty consisted of escorting the guns of the Royal Horse Artillery into action, and when the enemy would be dislodged from a kopje we would follow them up on their retreat and deliver volleys at them. The Osfontein engagement was, however, of interest to us, as it was during the course of the day that we met our 'A' Squadron, under Capt. Antill, who have since been posted to our regiment, under Colonel Knight, with Captain Antill second in command. Among the first to come forward to meet us, and the warmth of whose welcome was undoubted, was the Campbelltown contingent – the Squadron Quartermaster, Sergeant-Major Holman, Privates

---

[186] Holbrow, Lieutenant Grantley Andrew Hillier 1st NSW Mounted Rifles born Richmond, NSW

Axam and Bourke, Private Potts being absent on duty at Modder River, bringing up remounts. We were present with Lord Roberts at the engagement at Poplar Grove some days later, when our casualties were nil but at the Battle of Driefontein, or Abraham's Kraal, we were not so fortunate, as we had one man killed (a fine young fellow named Abrahams,[187] from Bega) one officer (Captain Bennett) and twelve men wounded. We also had three horses killed and five wounded. On occasions such as this the rollcall at the end of the day is indeed pathetic. At this engagement I was detailed as galloper to General Poole-Carew, the officer commanding the guard's brigade, and had of necessity to be under the heaviest of fire throughout the day. The order for the Scots Guards and the Buffs to fix bayonets and charge on the enemy's trenches was conveyed from the General to the respective commanders by me, and as I lingered after carrying out my instructions, I saw a sight such as I hope never to have occasion to see again. The Guards Brigades had previously been lying down, firing independently at the Boers in an adjoining kopje. On the order being given, they leaped into the air and charged the kopje more like maniacs than men. I shall never forget the yells and screams of the Boers as they frantically endeavoured to avoid the bayonet thrusts. In almost less time than it takes to describe it the kopje was taken by the Guards, and an inspection disclosed the most gruesome sight of dead and dying Boers huddled together in the trenches, as evidence to one and all of the terrific effect of a well-directed bayonet charge. The retreating Boers afterwards suffered severely by a charge of the Household Cavalry.

After our victory at Driefontein, Lord Roberts advanced by forced marches, night and day, towards Bloemfontein, the capital of the Orange Free State. The turn of events of the previous week had, however, disconcerted the Free Staters, and instead of encountering a large force, as we expected, we were met outside the city by the chief magistrate, who handed Lord Roberts the keys of the city in quite dramatic style, and implored him not to shell the town. The Commander-in-Chief was only too ready to agree to this arrangement, and after hoisting the British flag with much ceremony on all the public buildings, Lord Roberts took up his quarters in the magnificent house of President Steyn,[188] who had meanwhile fled to Kroonstad, to form a new capital. Our force is now here, enjoying a well-earned rest preparatory to marching on to Pretoria. It is, however, generally recognised that the beginning of the end is at hand, and that before long the flag of liberty and freedom will be flying throughout the Transvaal, as well as over the Orange Free State.

All the Campbelltown boys are very well, and desire to be kindly remembered to their friends at home.

WA NEWMAN, Lieut. NSW MR

OSBORNE, Edmund: *Rank:* Corporal #83. *Unit:* 'A' Squadron NSW Mounted Rifles. *Departed:* 14 November 1899 *SS Langton Grange. Returned:* invalided to Australia 13 September 1900. *Born:* 1873 Concord, NSW. *Parents:* William Osborne and Annie Turner. *Occupation:* orchardist Thirlmere. *Died:* 31 May 1962 Smithfield, NSW. *Buried:* Smithfield Uniting Church cemetery. *Spouse:* Mary Ann Jones. *Married:* 1901 Sydney, NSW. *Honours:* Queen's South Africa Medal with 3 clasps. *Memorial:* Wollondilly Heritage Centre, The Oaks.

Edmund Osborne

---

[187] Abrahams, William John KIA 10 March 1900
[188] Steyn, President Martinus Theunis – Last President of the Orange Free State

Osborne was wounded in the shoulder on 7 May 1900 at Zand River, Orange Free State, South Africa and invalided to Australia.

PEARCE, Wellington Henry: *Rank:* Private #101. *Unit:* 'A' Squadron NSW Mounted Rifles. *Departed:* 14 November 1899 *SS Langton Grange. Returned:* invalided to Australia 3 July 1900. *Born:* 1 November 1878 Richmond, NSW. *Parents:* George Pearce and Emma Jane Maughan. *Occupation:* farmer Cox's River, Burragorang. *Died:* 1976 Five Dock, NSW. *Spouse:* Veronica Graf. *Married:* 1919 Sydney, NSW. *Honours:* Queen's South Africa Medal with 3 clasps. *Memorial:* Wollondilly Heritage Centre, The Oaks.

POTTS, Pembroke: *Rank:* Private #53. *Unit:* 'A' Squadron NSW Mounted Rifles. *Departed:* 3 November 1899 *SS Aberdeen. Returned:* Invalided to Australia 5 May 1900. *Born:* 10 December 1879 Orange, NSW. *Parents:* William Speakman Potts and Matilda Elizabeth Pembroke. *Occupation:* farmer Cox's River, Burragorang. *Died:* 18 November 1952 Concord, NSW. *Spouse:* (1) Elizabeth Isabella Sommerville. *Married:* 7 April 1904 Cape Town, South Africa. (2) Evelyn Marjorie Ellice Flint. *Married*: 1938 North Sydney, NSW. *Honours:* Queen's South Africa Medal with 2 clasps. *Memorial:* Wollondilly Heritage Centre, The Oaks.

Potts was invalided to Australia in May 1900 suffering enteric fever. He also served WWI as a Lieutenant with the 2nd Light Horse Regiment.

REILLY, Philip John: *rank*: Private #95; *unit:* 'A' Squadron New South Wales Mounted Rifles; *departed:* 16 November 1899 *SS Langton Grange*; *occupation:* Farmer; *born:* 21 March 1877 Lacey's Creek, Burragorang, NSW; *parents:* Philip Reilly & Rose O'Reilly; *died:* 30 April 1900 Bloemfontein, South Africa; *buried:* President Brand Cemetery, Bloemfontein, South Africa.

Philip John Reilly

Camden News
Thursday, 18 January 1900, page 1

Transvaal War

The first communication received from the seat of war locally is from Private Philip John Reilly of the NSW Mounted Rifles, son of Mr Reilly, of the Fig Tree Stores, Burragorang. The letter is given in detail, and will doubtless be read with the greatest interest by all: —

Troopship Langton Grange,
Natal, South Africa.
December 13, 1899

Dear Father, Mother, Brothers and Sister —

We arrived here to-day safe and sound and as happy as sand boys. We had rather a bad time coming over, having to look after so many horses, but it did us no harm. I did not get the least bit seasick, and I am putting on condition in a remarkable manner. We have not heard yet what we have to do but I believe we have to go on to Cape Town with the horses.

Nothing worthy of mention happened on the voyage, only a few horses dying. One of our chaps was nearly being shot for going to sleep while on guard, and he has to do three extra watches for the offence, while another was caught smoking among the hay and chaff, and just escaped court martial for endangering the lives of all on board. I have escaped so far.

The harbour here is filled with British ships and is a splendid sight. It was a treat, I can assure you to hear a train whistle and see a town again after being so long a time away from civilisation.

I promised to write to a lot of my Burragorang friends, but I think they will have to wait till I have more time. Tell Mr R I will write to him the first chance. I expected to find it very hot over here but the climate is like old Burragorang. It is anything but pleasant trying to write lying full stretch on the deck. There was about half-a-dozen stowaways on board, and every one of them were seasick, and I can tell you they regretted the day they left sunny New South Wales.

Camden News
Thursday, 22 February 1900, page 2
THE WAR
New South Wales Mounted Rifles.
THEIR BAPTISM OF FIRE

The following letter has been received from Private Philip Reilly, of Burragorang to his parents: —

Prieska, South Africa,
January 9th, 1900

I have been waiting for this opportunity to write to you for the past fortnight. It is a very difficult matter writing letters here, for when you have time to write no note paper can be procured for love or money. The weather is very hot here, we all got a good sun burning the skin peeled off my face from the eyebrows to the bottom of my chin, I did look a pretty object. But as far as health is concerned I never enjoyed such perfect health before. We are staying at a place called Prieska, which is situated on the Orange River. Milk is a great luxury with us chaps, four of us were out the other day doing outpost duty guarding a punt, and some of the farmers were shifting all their sheep and goats across the river into the town we are camped at. You should have seen me and a couple of the other chaps catching the old nannies as they came off the punt. You would have laughed had you seen me holding two nannies by the legs in one hand and one by the horns in the other and the other chaps with their mess tins milking away for all they were worth. It did amuse the Dutch chaps who were watching us. Goats are worth 22s 6d [$2.25] a head, and sheep the same price. Bread is very dear here, 2s [20 cents] a loaf, and very small ones at that. The country is *in a terrible state for want of rain, there is not a blade of grass to be seen anywhere but the sheep and goats are as fat as seals, living on shrubs similar to the salt bush of New South Wales. There are very few English people in this town or in any of the towns we have been in, mostly Dutch and Kaffirs [sic]. It is great fun, trying to make them understand us, but the most of them can speak broken English.*

Our doctor came up from de Aar the other day, about 20 Kaffirs [sic.] came up with him looking for work: we had great fun with them we started them running races for pennies. It was very amusing to see the old fellows about 60 and 70 years and as lame as cats going their best then we had them jumping over a rope not very high. The old men like old Mr. -- would make a devil of a jump at the rope and fall over it. These are the unfortunate people whom the Boers make slaves of.

January 19th, 1900

I do not think it possible for you to imagine how pleased I was to receive a letter from home. We have to fall in about twenty times a day, and it is often done in a careless fashion, but when the word was given to fall in for letters you should have seen us double up. It was laughable to see all the eager faces around Captain Antill waiting to hear our names called out. My letters were nearly the last to be pulled out of the bag, but when my name was called I let them know where to look for me. A good number of our chaps are at de Aar, some sick, and the remainder looking after our sick and crippled horses. Prieska was in possession of a few Dutch rebels, but when we came we soon had possession of the towns, and from that out we used to guard all the crossings of the river, punts, etc. While on guard fowls would come around us to pick up the crumbs; it was laughable to see our chaps running them down. We have fowls baked and boiled and numerous other ways, and also have permission to shoot sheep whenever we feel inclined for mutton. You would hardly know any of us now we are not allowed to shave. Mr W— reminds me of an Irish terrier; I am called 'hairy face', so the whole party looks like a Jewish Sanhedrin.

Camden News
Thursday, July 19, 1900

Death of Private P Reilly, at S. Africa

To the Editor of the Camden News

Sir.— as there seems to be some uncertainty concerning the death of my son, I wish you would publish the enclosed letter which I received from Sergt. Lacey. I have also several other letters from his comrades, all stating that my poor boy died on April 30th last, though it is not yet officially announced;

Yours, etc., P REILLY
Burragorang, July 17, 1900

To Mrs Reilly,

Though you may have heard officially of your poor son's death, I am writing you these few lines. The poor boy had been ailing for some time with fever and dysentery and could not shake it off, though everything was done that could possibly be done by the hospital people he sank and passed away. You will feel this blow very much indeed I know dear Madam, but it's God's will and adds one more to the many that have been lost in this unfortunate war.

Poor Phil was a great favourite with all his mates being universally liked and respected. Poor Phil and I were always having little jokes about our district and wondering when we would get back and, now he is gone poor fellow, and no one knows who will be the next for there is a terrible lot of fever amongst us. I am sincerely sorry for you Madam, for I know how hard you felt the parting, and how little you wanted your son to come, and it makes it doubly hard when a son dies so far away, for everyone who loves him.

Yours sincerely

H. LACEY, Sergt.
Mtd. Infantry
Doorn River, South Africa May 9, 1900

RICHARDS, Robert (Ben): *Rank:* Private #3522. *Unit:* 3rd New South Wales Mounted Rifles. *Departed:* 15 March 1901 *HMT Maplemore*. *Born:* 1872 Bathurst, NSW. *Parents:* Henry Roberts and Mary Ann Bennett. *Died:* 19 February 1902 South Africa. *Buried:* Bayswater Garden of Remembrance, Bloemfontein. *Honours:* Queen's South Africa Medal.

Robert Richards – photo courtesy Australian War Memorial

SCOTT, Jeremiah: *Rank:* Private #20. *Unit:* 3rd Western Australian Bushmen (Citizen) Contingent. *Departed:* 14 March 1900 *SS Maplemore*. *Returned:* 25 May 1901 *HMT Morayshire*. *Born:* 2 December 1871 Narellan, NSW. *Parents:* John Scott and Edith Jones. *Died:* 21 April 1951 Narellan, NSW. *Buried:* St. Thomas' Church of England, Narellan. *Spouse:* Hannah Vera O'Kane. *Honours:* Queen's South Africa Medal.

Scott was wounded on 21 July 1900 at Koster River South Africa but was not invalided home.

SHARPE, Henry: *Rank:* Private #96. *Unit:* 'A' Squadron NSW Mounted Rifles. *Departed:* 14 November 1899 *SS Langton Grange. Returned:* invalided to Australia 5 May 1900 with enteric fever. *Born:* 28 May 1879 Cawdor, NSW. *Parents:* George Sharpe and Sarah Latty. *Died:* 24 May 1955 Marrickville, NSW. *Spouse:* Mary Edith Brown. *Married:* 1904 Tamworth, NSW. *Honours:* Queen's South Africa Medal with 4 clasps. *Memorial:* Wollondilly Heritage Centre, The Oaks.

Henry Sharpe

SHARPE, Robert: *Rank:* Private #97. *Unit:* 'A' Squadron NSW Mounted Rifles. *Departed:* 14 November 1899 *SS Langton Grange. Returned:* invalided to Australia 5 May 1900. *Born:* 18 February 1876 Cawdor, NSW. *Parents:* George Sharpe and Ann Loomes. *Died:* 4 June 1959 Granville, NSW. *Spouse:* Blanche Elizabeth Taber. *Married:* 1903 Petersham, NSW. *Honours:* Queen's South Africa Medal with 4 clasps. *Memorial:* Wollondilly Heritage Centre, The Oaks.

SHAW, William Hamilton Hubert: *Rank:* (1) Lance-Corporal #2033 (2) Sergeant #2033. *Unit:* Roberts'[189] Horse. *Born:* 1857 Scone, NSW. *Parents:* William Shaw and Margaret Innes. *Died:* 27 December 1919 Springwood, NSW. *Spouse:* Elizabeth Stratton. *Married:* 1906 Sydney, NSW.

Robert Sharpe

Shaw from Wedderburn, NSW had gone to South Africa before the war broke out. He was the son of a doctor and when war broke out he joined the South African Light Horse, 2nd Regiment. This regiment would later become known as Roberts' Horse.

***The Campbelltown Herald*
Wednesday, 13 June 1900**

Letter from the Front

TO THE EDITOR *CAMPBELLTOWN HERALD*

Bloemfontein, 31/3/1900. Sir — I thought it might be interesting to your readers to hear a little about one of the irregular corps now fighting the Boers in South Africa. The regiment I belong to is Roberts' Horse. We were recruited at Cape Town in November, and put in a month's training at Rosebank, and then went to de Aar. It seems my squadron to be almost like being in Rookwood camp, as one glance at the men proclaims the land of their birth, and the conversation is mostly about Melbourne and Sydney. In

---

[189] Roberts, Frederick Sleigh, Field Marshall (1st Earl Roberts)

my troop there are thirteen Australians out of twenty-one men. Our lieutenant is an Australian – if not by birth, by adoption. The other three troops in B Squadron are much the same. We journeyed from Cape Town to de Aar by train. It was a weary trip, but, like everything else, it had an ending, and we landed in de Aar at 4.30 on a cold morning. On reaching the camp, I found, to my delight, that there was a small detachment of New South Wales Mounted Rifles there. On enquiry I found that Troopers F Axam and M Burke were with them. Needless to say, we had a regular Australian yarn. I ran across them once since at Orange River. They were then on the eve of leaving for a patrol on the Free State border. They were well and in good spirits. We had a bit of skirmishing between Belmont and the Modder, but our first fight was at Riet River. Our men went into it as coolly as if they were rounding up a mob of fats. We lost on that occasion our second in command (Captain Magney), also several troopers. We were in the relief of Kimberley and in the cordon that surrounded Cronje and his 4000 men in their laager on the banks of the Modder. Whilst waiting at Trouter Drift for Cronje to surrender, we had a little bit of fun on our own. We were holding a kopje about two and a half miles from the Boer laager, when one morning, about nine o'clock, we saw about three hundred Boers sneaking round on adjacent kopjes, evidently trying to escape. We fired on them, and several fell.

We had only our own squadron (85 men), but the captain allowed 40 of us to try and cut them off. We charged, and it was laughable to see those Dutchmen 'scoot'. However, we killed several, wounded four, and captured fourteen, also two wagons and sixteen mules, with the kaffir [sic.] drivers. I got one Boer. He was so frightened that he fired at me at about ten paces and missed me. He then threw up his arms and surrendered. He had a first-class Lee-Metford[190] and 250 rounds. The Boer in the open is a bigger coward than a half-bred dingo. Let him get behind a rock, sniping at us, and he is all there; but on a plain - ugh! As brave as a sheep. After Cronje's surrender, we advanced on Bloemfontein, skirmishing all the way. We got into an ambush one evening, and the squadron nearly lost the number of its mess. The Boers opened fire on us at about 800 yards with shell. We were lucky in only losing a corporal and two men. It was our luck that the Boers were on that occasion bad shots; but the shells came close enough to make things lively. As we had no fieldpiece with us we had to retire, and quick at that. My horse got into a hole, and came down with me, giving me a bit of a shaking. Just then a shell burst forty yards ahead of me. I grabbed my horse, mounted, and shook the dust of that particular portion of the veldt off my feet as quickly as I could. There is no sense in fooling round a 'pom-pom' shell.

I have met a lot of old Australian friends in the course of the last month or two, and they are all holding up their end of the log. In conclusion, I am sorry to say that my squadron has been once more ambushed. We lost 95 men and 8 officers killed and wounded. Out of the 18 of my troop who went out, only eight returned. They were within 200 yards of the hidden Boers. My messmate is a prisoner, and several Australians fell. Our trumpeter was killed. Two of the men have been recommended for the Distinguished Service Medal and one for the VC. All the casualties occurred in a few

---

[190] Bolt action rifle

minutes. After that there was six hours fighting without loss. The Boer shooting was atrocious. —

Yours, etc. WHH Shaw. Corporal B Squadron, Roberts' Horse.

[We regret to say that on Monday last official intelligence was received at Wedderburn to the effect that on May 4th Mr. Shaw was severely wounded. — Ed.]

SMITH, Albert Edward: *Rank:* Private #58. *Unit:* 'A' Squadron NSW Mounted Rifles. *Departed:* 3 November 1899 *SS Aberdeen. Born:* 1876 Penrith, NSW. *Parents:* William Smith and Eliza Groves. *Occupation:* horse breaker. *Died:* 30 May 1900 Bloemfontein, South Africa. *Buried:* President Brand Cemetery, Bloemfontein. *Honours:* Queen's South Africa Medal with 3 clasps. *Memorials:* Parramatta Boer War Memorial, Liverpool, NSW.

SMITH, Carlton: *Rank:* Trooper #1589. *Unit:* 2nd New South Wales Mounted Rifles. *Departed:* 15 March 1901 *SS Maplemore. Returned:* 3 June 1902 *HMT Aurania. Born:* 1876 Penrith, NSW. *Parents:* John Julian Smith and Sophia Jane Gambrill. *Occupation:* landscape gardener. *Died:* 24 April 1919 Newtown, NSW. *Buried:* St. John's Church of England, Camden. *Spouse:* Alice Maud Masters. *Married:* 1903 Granville, NSW. *Honours:* Queen's South Africa Medal with 2 clasps. *Memorial:* Wollondilly Heritage Centre, The Oaks.

Following his return to Australia he tried many avenues of employment including farming at Wyee, storekeeping on the North Shore, and dairy farming in Camden. When his sister, after her marriage, retired from her position as Postmistress at Thirlmere, he became the Postmaster. He built a new Post Office at his own expense as the old one was inadequate, and did shoe repairs on the side to help make ends meet. In 1919 he became seriously ill as a result of an old spinal injury and died on 24 April 1919.

Carlton Smith

SMITH, Charles Roy McIntosh: *Rank:* Saddler #496. *Unit:* 1st New South Wales Mounted Rifles - C Squadron. *Departed:* 17 January 1900 *SS Southern Cross. Returned:* 29 April 1901 *SS Morayshire. Parents:* Charles Roy Smith and Annie McIntosh. *Born:* 1881 Berrima, NSW. *Occupation:* saddler in Camden. *Died:* 8 April 1919 Turramurra, NSW. *Buried:* Field of Mars. *Honours:* Queen's South Africa Medal.

Camden News
Thursday, 28 June 1900, page 2

**THE WAR
A LETTER FROM THE FRONT**

Private CR Smith, of the Mounted Infantry, writes to his father, Mr. C. Smith of Camden, from Winberg under date May 7.

I have been on the march ever since I wrote to you from Naauwpoort; we started a few days after to march to Bloemfontein. We were fourteen days on the road. The hardships are very great, we had to sleep out every night without tents, in fact, I have not seen a tent since I wrote to you last, but on the whole I have been very lucky. I have not had a cold nor an hour's ill health since I landed in Africa. Bloemfontein is the capital of the Orange

Free State, it is a very pretty town and resembles that of Bowral very much, only it is far larger. We stayed in Bloemfontein for two weeks where a large army of 12,000 men was formed to which we were attached, under General Ian Hamilton,[191] to start a general attack on the Boers, driving them northwards, and of course, pushing on towards Pretoria. The division had only been on the road two days when we met the enemy, outside a town called Thaba N'chu. They had taken up a very strong position on a long range of hills outside the town, and were in great numbers, in fact, thousands of them. We were all marching calmly along and when about three miles from the hills the Mounted Infantry in front followed by the artillery and Maxim guns, then the foot infantry. Presently about 7 o'clock in the morning there came a bang from the enemy's guns opening fire on us. The British artillery replied, lodging shell after shell in among the hills. The Boers fought very stubbornly, for seven hours rifle bullets and cannon shell pouring in among us. It was a grand but terrible sight. Some shot dead, others groaning with pain and wounds. Several bullets pinged over my head, others tore up the ground at my feet, but God spared me to come through and I think the bullets from my rifle felled a few of them as I was in a good position and had them well covered. Two of our men New South Wales Mounted Infantry were killed, five wounded and three are missing. One of their names was Smith; I thought you would think it was me. This was the hardest engagement, out of four that I have been in. We then marched on and captured the town of Winberg. I saw the Union Jack hoisted in the town and General Hamilton proclaimed it a British town and the cheers of the people were deafening. We are resting here for a few days as our horses are very weak. Although the Boers have been beaten on every side they are still fighting very stubbornly and I think will fight to the end.

I met young Southey from Mittagong out here. I was pleased to meet him; he is a very nice fellow. I have not had a letter since I left home but, I can quite understand that for the railway communication is all cut off. Give my best wishes to my friends and tell them I am quite safe up to the present.

Camden News
Thursday, 19 January 1901, page 4

Letters from the Front

Mrs. Smith, of Camden, kindly allows the following letter to be published for the information of Private Roy Smith's friends:

*Kroonstad, South Africa,
Dec 10, 1900*

Our column is just passing through Kroonstad. We are chasing a few scattered parties of Boers in the Orange River Colony; all the hard fighting is over but still the work we are doing is very dangerous. We had three men shot last week by snipers, Sergt. Smillie,[192] Privates Robertson[193] and Fulton.[194] The first contingent has left for home. I expect it will be a great

---

[191] General Sir Ian Standish Monteith Hamilton GCB GCMG DSO TD of the British Army
[192] Smillie, Sergeant James 1st New South Wales Mounted Rifles
[193] Robertson, Thomas Cunningham 1st New South Wales Mounted Rifles KIA 21 November 1900 Rhenoster, South Africa
[194] Fulton, Thomas A 1st New South Wales Mounted Rifles KIA 23 November 1900 Kroonstadt, South Africa

day in Camden when they arrive. I would have liked to have gone with them, but expect I will have to spend Christmas on the veldt in Africa. I expect it will be a couple of months or more before the second contingent gets away.

ROY SMITH

SMITH, Reginald Sydney (Rex): *Rank:* Corporal #60, Sergeant #1668, Lieutenant. *Unit:* (1) 'A' Squadron New South Wales Mounted Rifles; (2) 2nd New South Wales Mounted Rifles (3) 3rd New South Wales Imperial Bushmen. *Departed: (1)* 3 November1899 *SS Aberdeen. Returned: (1)* 8 January 1901 *HMT Orient. Departed: (2)* 15 March 1901 *SS Maplemore. Returned: (2)* 11 August 1902 *HMT Drayton Grange. Discharged:* 9 March 1903 Camden, NSW. *Born:* March 1879 Douglas Park, NSW. *Parents:* Luke Smith and Theresa Arnold Guise. *Occupation:* gardener, botanist, teamster. *Died:* Died of wounds 19 Jun 1915 17th General Hospital, Alexandria, Egypt. *Buried:* Alexandria (Chatby) Military and War Memorial Cemetery, Egypt. *Spouse:* Amelia Volkmann. *Married:* 18 March 1903 St. Luke's Church of England, Wilton, NSW. *Honours:* Queen Alexandra Pipe for Gallantry, Queen's South Africa Medal with 5 clasps, King's South Africa Medal with 2 clasps. *Memorials:* St. John's Anglican (Cemetery) Camden; Wollondilly Heritage Centre, The Oaks; Picton War Memorial. *Roll of honour:* Camden, NSW; St. John's Church of England Camden. Rex was promoted to Lieutenant by Lord Kitchener on the recommendation of Colonel Lassetter.

Smith enlisted as Rex and not under his full name. Whilst in South Africa Rex met Amelia Volkmann from Melbourne, Victoria who was in South Africa with her sister. Amelia was the daughter of Colonel Christian Volkmann formerly of Kaiser Franz Joseph's Royal Guard and Cristiana Finger. Rex returned home 11 August 1902 and Amelia followed him to Wilton where they were married on 18 March 1903. After the birth of their daughter Ida Edith in 1905 the family moved to Mount Hunter and Rex purchased his own horse team and carried ore between the Yerranderie Silver Mines and Camden. Later he went on to drive coaches for Butlers between Camden and Burragorang Valley.

Rex served during WWI as a Sergeant #470 but died in Egypt of wounds received at Gallipoli.

December, 1901

Brandfort
April 4, 1900

Dear old Arch,[195]

Just a few lines to let you know that I am all right. I got your letter the day after my birthday. I was very pleased to hear from you. That is the first letter I have had from you and I have had one from Mother. I wish you would both write more often, I look forward to letters out here more than anything.

Well I hope it is right that the Towers[196] *are sold, for it might be better for you all. I hope your shoulder is all right, long enough before you get this. I wish I was with you to go for a good trip but we will have it when I come home. I thought it was a chance if Dar had learnt to ride the bike. Give it an oiling for me so as it won't get too rusted.*

---

[195] Smith, Edward Archibald – brother of Rex
[196] St. Mary's Towers, Douglas Park

Well Archie I will tell you about what we have been doing the last 3 or 4 days. Before we came here we had a fortnight at Bloemfontein. We are now 20 miles from there. We are not in the town that I have headed this letter with, but we are only 4 miles from it, though there will be some hard fighting before we get there. We are the most advanced post in the whole British Army. That is saying a good lot. Each man is on duty every other night. I do all duties and am in every parade, not that I have to, I could stay with the wagons if I wanted to but I think if I knew I was going to be shot I would go out well.

I will tell you about the fight we had the other day. We located the enemy about 9 o'clock and they retired into a splendid position amongst some hills. We made a splash for some hills or a ridge. We were under a very heavy fire until we got behind the hill though no one was hit – our luck as usual. We do not ride in any formation when we are under fire it is every man for himself. Well when we got to the bottom of this hill we dismounted and doubled up onto the hill. The Boers had dashed across the hollow and taken up the next ridge. We got to the ridge and opened fire straight away. I was firing at 10 hundred yards and I can tell you I rattled it into them as fast as I could load. They did not show much of themselves over the ridge so I could not tell how many I got onto.

Well they very soon left that ridge and took up their final position in amongst some hills. There was a lot of infantry who had doubled out on our right. They were right out in an open plain so you can bet I was very much surprised to see about the same number of Boers coming across to meet them. I should say there was about 100 men each side. This was taking place after we had driven the Boers from the second ridge and we were laying there looking at our infantry advancing towards the Boers. Well each side opened fire at about 12 hundred yards our infantry laid into them but the Boers kept on advancing and standing up in line and taking standing shots; they all had Martini-Henry rifles. This went on for some time until the Boers got within about 400 yards then our infantry got up and retired as fast as their legs would carry them and the Boers followed them further only our chaps got a pom-

*Reginald (Rex) Sydney Smith in NSW Mounted Rifles uniform –
photo courtesy Camden Historical Society*

pom onto them which put a round of 1 pound shells right along their line in from of them. This stopped them and they turned and retired in good order and the infantry was satisfied to let them go, I can tell you it was a first rate sight to see; and as for them retiring from the pom-pom I am not surprised at it for we have retired from theirs many a time and every man for himself.

Well we advanced and took up the second ridge that the Boers had left and took shelter behind any bit of cover we could find to get out of the way of the bullets that were flying about. We had a few shots here but the range was too far for our guns though their bullets whistled over head as easily as possible. Well, all we could do was to wait for our guns to shift them out of it. Well we waited there for a long time until the sun was nearly down and we got the order to retire to our horses and we mounted and rode around to the end of our troops and they dismounted out right behind a pom-pom gun that was just going into action, the worst place that they could have put us. Well our gun got into position and opened fire then. There was about a minute passed between the second shell and then the third came right fair in amongst us. I saw something fly through the air and I heard a flop and the third man from me went down onto the ground and I made sure he was killed but he was up in a minute. I was by him in a second. The cannon bullet had struck his haversack which was full of things; raw meat and all kinds of things. It smashed everything into bits and took half of his haversack away and the shell buried itself in the ground about 7 feet away. Bullets had hardly reached the Boer position when a shell from the Boer guns burst about 30 yards to our right and about a minute after another burst about 10 yards from our gun which was right in front of us. We got no order to retire and some of our chaps began to move their horses back but when ordered up into line again our chaps can stand rifle bullets very well that is the biggest part of them, but when shells are bursting around it makes a very different affair of it.

This takes a good while to tell it but it all happened in a few minutes. In about another minute from when the bullet hit his haversack another burst right in front of me and the pieces flew in all directions. This was too much for our chaps; a lot of them mounted their horses and tore away. Others were mounting but were ordered to get off and we got the order to lead our horses away. We had not gone many yards when another came screeching right over my horse. I would not have like to have been on my horse though it might not have hit me it landed on an artillery horse and got him on the side and killed him dead. We hurried off then as fast as we could leading our horses. Three more came screaming overhead and buried themselves in the ground just outside our lines. Our gun retired and fast as it could lick and took up another position about half a mile from the last but another shell came and buried itself in the ground just to the left of it so it retired without firing a shot. The Boers then left their position as they were getting it too hot from the other side for of course we were not the only troops against them we only engaged one portion of them so went and took their position and camped there for the night. The Boers retired into the town that was just in front of them. We went out yesterday morning and took 300 head of cattle, 2000 head of sheep, 100 head of horses and 50 goats. Well that finishes up this bit of performance and I think I have wrote a dashed long letter.

Well old chap I hope it will soon be over. I would like to come home again. Remember me to old Neddy and Tom and Paddy and all the rest of them. Tell mother to keep my clothes and things right, for I will want something decent to put on when I get home.

Well I can't tell you anymore this time, so goodbye old chap.

Love to all from your loving brother, Rex

Sunday,
Bloemfontein, 23 April 1900

Dear old Archie,

I have just received your letter and was pleased to hear from you. You must write every mail. I wrote a letter to Mother the other afternoon, I suppose you will get them both together. I got your other letter and answered, also got one from Andrew Lewis. The only one I haven't got a letter from since I have been out here is Eva. Now Archie I want you to write to her for me and ask her why she doesn't write. Tell her I have sent her some letters and that I have only had one letter from her and that was while I was at Cape Town. If she answers your letter just let me know how she is.

Well old chap we have shifted into Bloemfontein again and not much too soon. We had quite enough of the other place, duty every other night though I don't know if we are much better off now for this place is rotten with fever and our chaps are going away every day to the hospital.

Well our stay here is to be short for we leave here on Tuesday for the front again. They can't do without us though the Lancers get the praise for half the work we do.

Poor old Ben[197] has been in hospital for 6 weeks now and I cannot find out how he is. Heard old Jim Blackwood[198] has had hard luck, he has been in the black troops, he has only been in one fight the one at Bama. To tell the truth he is a bit shaky like a lot more, but as for Ben he is as good a kid as there is out here.

Do you know Reilly[199] of Burragorang, they keep a store at the bottom of the mountain, well he was taken from here yesterday. They carried him to the ambulance from his tent for he could not walk and is that bad he could hardly speak. He has enteric fever and is not expected to live.

I am very sorry for he is one of the best men under fire that I have ever seen and I have taken notice of a lot of them when we are advancing under fire. Ted Cleary[200] is a good kid. Dickie Bateup[201] is a failure and has not been with us since we left Beira. Corporal Osborne[202] is also a failure. Jack Field[203] is also a failure. Reilly is the only good man that came from Picton and although you might not know these men Andrew Lewis will know if you tell him.

Well Archie I have fired a great number of shots at the Boers and I am satisfied that I have hit some but how many I can't say.

The Boers gave our troops a terrible doing at the waterworks the other day; they cleared them off like dust before the wind.

Goodbye old chap

---

[197] Spearing, Benjamin Charles, Private #98 from Wilton, invalided home 2 June 1900
[198] Blackwood, James, Private #86 from Wilton
[199] Reilly, Phillip John, Private #95 from Burragorang died 30 April 1900
[200] Cleary, Edward Thomas, Lance Corporal #90 invalided home 13 August 1900
[201] Bateup, Amos Albert, Corporal #82 invalided to Australia 3 July 1900
[202] Osborne, Edmund, Corporal #83 wounded on 7 May 1900 at Zand River Orange Free State, South Africa and was invalided to Australia
[203] Field, John, Private #102 invalided to Australia 3 July 1900

Remember me kindly to all

Rex

Sunday, Machadodorp
7.10.1900

Dear Archie,

Just a few lines to let you know how I am getting on. Well we are expecting to start for home soon but that does not go for much because we have been expecting to start for home for months past. I hope it is nearly over now though we still have some dangerous work to do yet. We are 180 miles above Pretoria; it is a terrible wild place. We do a lot of patrolling and generally get a few shots at us though we don't get much shooting at them. We went out the other day and burnt a lot of their houses down and turned the women and children out into the veldt and the troops took all they had cot, bed clothing and all. I consider it a disgrace to British troops.

We had a man taken prisoner a few days before we burnt the houses down. Since we burnt the houses we lost one man – he got where the Boers could have taken him prisoner but they shot him dead. The first man they let go but they will let no more go and I do not blame them. If the tables were turned I would do the same as them myself and shoot everyone I could see.

The men are fighting for their rights and they know it. I think that there will be snipers here for the next 12 months.

Well Arch this is only a few lines to say I wrote to you. I haven't had a letter from you for a long time. Goodbye old chap remember me kindly to all at the house.

From your loving brother Rex.

M.R.
Victoria Barracks
23 July 1902

Lieut. Rex Smith
2nd Mtd. Rifles

My dear Rex Smith,

I was very glad to receive your letter and to see that you have been getting on so well as to have been granted a commission in a regiment which has done so well and also to see that Sergt. Wintle has also been promoted.

Naturally, as both of you were two of my old men I take an interest in your welfare apart from the fact that you have both been known to me for so long, and your record has been so good a one, and I sincerely wish you both success if you decide to remain in SA[204] and I hope you will do your best to keep up the credit and good name of your old corps and this regiment. It will be a difficult matter no doubt for you both at first, being moved up to a high position, one in which you have had no experience and this only can be accomplished by reading and keeping your eyes and ears open and your mouth closed as far as you can until you are sure of yourselves. The 2nd MR is back again and practically dispersed and Mr Holman and Wasson back to their old work, but the latter intends to

---

[204] South Africa

return to SA and has resigned from the Staff. I think he will leave very shortly, in one of the empty transports. We have been having a most terrible drought and without rain for about 9 months and there is no prospects of any. All my brother's stock have been trucked to the north where it is not quite so bad, and they have been carting water from Picton for domestic purposes for some time. Hogan is still with me and doing well and I now live at the Glebe the Headquarters having been moved to Sydney. The air is full of retrenchment and things in a military line are very unpromising all round.

My people are quite well and I sent your message to my mother who was glad to get it. Coco is at Jarvisfield as it is too expensive to keep 2 horses in these times with feed £8 ($16) a ton. I shall always be glad to hear from you when you have time to write to me.

With every good wish for your welfare and congratulations on your promotion,

Believe me yours sincerely.

JM Antill

SMITH, Samuel Fairall: *Rank:* Gunner #2410. *Unit:* 'A' Battery Royal Australian Artillery. *Departed:* 3 November 1899 *SS Aberdeen*. *Returned:* invalided to Australia 22 March 1901. *Born:* 26 June 1872 Razorback, NSW. *Parents:* John Smith and Ellen Fairall. *Died:* 23 September 1939 Cawdor, NSW. *Buried:* Cawdor Uniting Church Cemetery. *Honours:* Queen's South Africa Medal. *Memorial:* Wollondilly Heritage Centre, The Oaks.

SOUTHEY, Clifford Melville: *Rank:* Private #103, Lieutenant. *Unit:* (1) New South Wales Infantry E Squadron (2) 3rd New South Wales Imperial Bushmen. *Departed:* 3 November 1899 *SS Aberdeen*. *Returned:* 11 August 1902 *HMT Drayton Grange*. *Born:* 1881 Mittagong, NSW. *Parents:* Henry Edmund Southey and Eliza Renton Phillips. *Died:* 12 February 1955 Mosman, NSW. *Notes:* Slightly wounded, Woolvefontein 20 February 1900.

Southey served during the Boer War and later served as a Major in the Worcestershire Regiment British Army during WWI. He was living in the Mittagong district when he enlisted for the Boer War in the 1st NSW Infantry. This unit was the only Infantry Contingent despatched from NSW and subsequently mounted in South Africa.

Camden News
Thursday, 15 February 1900, page 4

THE WAR
From Private Southey of Bowral

We arrived at the Cape on the 9th and anchored in the harbour. It looks a pretty little town from the water but on landing is rather disappointing. There is no mistake Table Mountain looks very imposing, and in the early morning when the clouds roll over it forms what the sailors call 'spreading the cloth'. We did not land till next morning and then got straight into the train where we remained from Thursday till Sunday night, when we arrived at Enslin. It was too late for us to pitch tents so we camped with the Victorians and South Australians. In the tent I camped in there were eighteen men, and as a tremendous storm came on it added not to the comfort of the scene. Next day however, we pitched our own tents and are now pretty comfortable as things go.

The country out here is very flat. Indeed, from Cape Town right away through there is nothing but a series of plains (veldts) and small and very stony hills called kopjes.[205] *There is not a tree to be seen anywhere for love or money, and the ground is very dry and sandy I can tell you the heat is pretty well unbearable. There is no mistake South Africa is pretty warm. We stayed at de Aar one night and then went on to the Orange River, which is not the river you would imagine it was on perusing the map but merely a chain of dirty, muddy water. We enjoyed a great old storm of rain there and some of the men took the opportunity of getting out of the train and having a shower bath.*

We passed through Belmont where a big fight took place and had tea there. The railway station was riddled through with rifle bullets. We also passed through Grasspan where the British lost three naval officers. The place where we are camped witnessed a pretty hot time. The Boers, numbering about 1500, were fortified on the kopje opposite the railway line where there were a couple of hundred British. The hills they occupied you would have thought could have been held by ten men against a hundred. Anyhow, the British cleared them out with the bayonet and the Boers retreated in double quick time.

From the top of the kopje we saw the English shelling the Boer entrenchments on the Modder River where the present battle is taking place. We get very little news of the fighting. In fact you in Australia get twice as much as we do. The only news we get is from the different detachments of wounded and other troops coming from and going to the front, and they tell as many lies as possible.

The Gordon Highlanders came into camp on Thursday night. The poor beggars had a lively time on the Modder.[206] *Some of them have quite lost the use of their legs as the back of their knees caught the sun, which drew up their sinews. They are a grand body of men. I never thought it would be my luck to see them. The Canadians are also a fine lot of men and very jolly. Of course we have seen most of the Imperial troops and I must say I was rather disappointed in seeing them as most of them are very small. In fact I could look down on most of them. Anyhow they have plenty of go and fight, which is the main thing. I have not seen anything of the Lancers and goodness knows when I will.*

The Victorian Mounted Rifles are great hands at going out on patrol, but I think all they do is to go to some farm and collar all the ducks and geese they can lay their hands on. We do not get any; they keep them for private use. Our routine is get up in the morning between 2 and 3 a.m. stand to arms, and sometimes go into the trenches; wait there till daylight and then come back again. Breakfast consists of coffee and dry bread, sometimes jam; dinner soup, meat and dry bread; tea dry bread and tea, so you can see we don't live in luxury. Sometimes we get a mixture of tea and lime juice which is not too bad when it gets cold. The water is very bad and has to be boiled before we can drink it. I found the medicine I brought out with me very useful, as several of our fellows have been very ill so I dosed them up, and they are now well.

I have had the pleasure of seeing one of the sights of Africa, viz a locust pest, they fly in clouds and as they are of different colours look very pretty. One sees thousands of blacks [sic] *here and don't they love the Dutch. They want the British to arm them and let them have a go at the Boers, who treat them brutally, more like dogs than human beings. I am afraid the vaunted shooting powers and bravery of the Boers are a mere fallacy. No greater coward lives. They won't go*

---

[205] Kopje means stony hill
[206] Short for Modder River

out at night as they are afraid of ghosts, and when they are in battle they get behind the rocks and shoot at random. They are great chaps for sardines. In one place where they had been camping we saw dozens of tins, of sardines (empty) and a few empty Mauser cartridges. They use all sorts of guns, and the sight of a bayonet makes them sick, they are so excessively ticklish that they don't like the feeling of a bayonet.

I think the country we are in is gold-bearing; there is any amount of gold quartz about. It is model country for farming, no clearing to be done and all that the land wants is irrigation and it would grow anything. The Boers are too lazy to do this, and they only cultivate a few acres round their houses and how they subsist I don't know.

Writing is very difficult as pen, ink, and paper are very scarce and my table is a canteen lid. The climate is very funny here, fearfully hot in the daytime and very cold at night. Water is very scarce and scrapers would come in useful to clean us. The Gordons are the cleanest in the camp and are the only fellows who shave. The wild flowers are very beautiful and grow in great variety. Dozens of ostriches are knocking about, and I am going to have a try for some of their feathers or die in the attempt.

SPEARING, Benjamin Charles: *Rank:* Private #98. *Unit:* 'A' Squadron New South Wales Mounted Rifles. *Departed:* 14 November 1899 *SS Langton Grange. Returned:* invalided to Australia 2 June 1900. *Born:* 3 September 1876 Wilton, NSW. *Parents:* Benjamin Spearing and Emma Wanson. *Occupation:* butcher Wilton. *Died:* 1 March 1947 Alstonville, NSW. *Buried:* Alstonville General Cemetery. *Spouse:* Amy Eliza Mildred Harvey. *Married:* 25 March 1903 Picton, NSW. *Honours:* Queen's South Africa Medal with 3 clasps. *Memorial:* Wollondilly Heritage Centre, The Oaks.

Benjamin Charles Spearing

***The Campbelltown Herald*
Wednesday, 4 July 1900, page 3**

Back from the War

Private B. Spearing (a brother of Messrs. Geo. Spearing of Campbelltown, and Edw. Spearing, of Appin) who has been invalided home from South Africa returned to Picton on Saturday. He was met at the railway station by the Mayor and aldermen and a large number of townspeople, and was driven round the town in a four-in-hand drag. The procession was headed by the police, and the Mounted Rifles formed an escort. On arrival at the Post Office, the Mayor (Alderman McQuiggan) read an address of welcome on behalf of the citizens. Private Spearing was then driven to the Great Southern Hotel, where his health was drunk. In the evening he was entertained at a smoke concert.

SPOONER, Charles Greenwood: *Rank:* Private #498. *Unit:* 1st New South Wales Mounted Rifles. *Departed:* 17 January 1900 *SS Southern Cross. Returned:* 8 January 1901 *HMT Orient. Born:* 1879 Manning River, NSW. *Parents:* George Spooner and Caroline Bareham. *Died:* 24 April 1931 Wallsend, NSW.

The Campbelltown Herald
Wednesday, 2 May 1900, page 2

Letters from the Front
TROOPER SPOONER

Writing home under date Ferrari Siding near Bloemfontein, March 18, Trooper C Spooner, one of the Campbelltown men at the Front in South Africa, says:—

Just a few lines to let you know how I am, and that's OK. We are camped outside Bloemfontein at a place called Ferrari Siding, just for a spell for the horses, but not for the men, as they run us about on the plain just as if we were made of steel. The day before yesterday they took the men out to drill, and before they came back at least 20 dropped out. How can they help it! Only fed on biscuits and coffee and one slice of bread a day.

Billy Divall and I took eighteen horses five miles away yesterday to turn out with sore backs, unfit for use, and in coming home Bill came across a Boer camp and found a couple of rugs and a couple of packets of cartridges in one of their trenches. If you could only see their trenches it would amuse you for a couple of hours. I went out driving a Scotch cart with six mules, for wood, and you bet I made them go, over the tufts of grass and into the holes. I tipped one fellow out.

Bill and I are going into town tomorrow if we can get off for a while. All colonial troops are going to hold a review at Bloemfontein on the 30th of this month, and then I would not be surprised if they send us home. I, for one, will not be sorry. When you are having your meals, think of me eating dry biscuits; no sugar or milk.

If you could see us now you would not think it was the same lot that left Sydney on that day so memorable to many a family – sunburnt, dirty faces, torn and ragged and ever on the hunt for tucker.

Yesterday was St. Patrick's Day, but we were not able to enjoy it in any shape or form. They had church here for the Catholics this morning, but the poor Protestants have had to go without from the start, unless they strike up a hymn, as they often do. I think I am in for picket duty tonight, and it is going to be a 'scorcher' – wind and dust, something horrible, a fair southerly buster.

The NSW Lancers are moving into camp, quite near us. We are called troopers now.

The Campbelltown Herald
Wednesday, 23 May 1900, page 4

Letters from the Front
TROOPER SPOONER

Writing home, under date Springfontein, April 3rd Trooper Spooner says:—

Just a few lines to let you know I am OK. We left camp near Bloemfontein on March 28th and marched on through the town to a place called The Glen[207] – about 10 miles. Half the men walked, and some were leading sick horses. We started off in the morning with only a drink of coffee, and went all day, along dusty roads with nothing to eat or drink. We got into a kind

---
[207] Glen Siding

of camp about ten o'clock at night – nothing to eat – and then lay down on the road in our jackets, with only a rifle to keep us warm. We were awake next morning at daybreak, and away again on an empty stomach and dead tired. We proceeded till nearly dinnertime, when we heard the big gun ahead of us at full lick. We then halted, and they gave us a cup of tea and a biscuit, and a tin of bully beef between nine men. We had an hour's rest, and then word came to start again. It took us all day to go about nine miles, over fearfully rough country, till we came to Glen Siding – that is where the Boers blew up the Modder River Bridge. We got into camp about 10 o'clock at night, dead tired, and were up again at daybreak, and started off after we had a cup of coffee. During the morning I commandeered a turkey and cooked it, made some Johnny cakes, and for once in a week felt contented. After dinner we were again on the go, and we marched up to where they were fighting the day before. I just got into camp at Karee[208] when I was told off for outpost. That passed all right, and then again we were on the way until we got here. While passing Karee we came across the KOSB Regiment,[209] and I was told by a Sergeant that they were in the battle the day before. He also showed me where they were burying some thirteen men in one grave. They had over 50 wounded, poor fellows. They 'fell in' terribly in the charge, and there were over 400 casualties on the British side.

We have been at Springfontein four days now. I and two others in charge of Lance-Corporal Lees were sent out on observation this morning, and we are still on duty (at sundown). I suppose we will be relieved at dark by the night outpost. Then we go back and go to bed. This is the best job I have had for about three months – lying down in the shade all day, keeping a look out for Boers. I have not seen any so far today. I think we are going to hold this position till the Modder River Bridge is built again, as they can't get provisions over quick enough for us.

April 5. — I was on fatigue duty yesterday morning, so I could not finish the letter. In the afternoon I did some cooking for Tom and myself. Billy Divall is the cook for the sergeants' mess, so he can live high. I was on outpost last night, and on my going on at first relief, from 10 to 12, I came across the outpost fast asleep and Boers all around us. He was on guard at a pass and held 900 lives in his hands. Only that another young fellow and I pleaded for him, he would no doubt have been court martialled and shot. He is only 16 years old.

Kindly remember me to all kind friends – everyone I know – and tell them that I have no time to write and no place to post, and I should very much like to get a letter from them.

Tom Lees is in the best of health and doing well. He has grown a beard; so has Billy Divall – a real clinker, and you would not know him if you saw him. He is all right. As to myself, well I am a little rough looking. I have a very black beard now, and it does not improve my appearance. I have grown broader, if anything, and a little taller. I have seen Mick Burke and Frank Axam, and they are both in the best of health and doing well. They have also got beards. No more at present.

STEWART, Walter David: *Rank:* Trooper #795. *Unit:* New South Wales Lancers. *Departed:* 3 March 1899 *SS Nineveh* (to UK), 30 November 1899 (to South Africa). *Returned:* 6 December 1901 *HMT Harlech Castle. Born:* 1873 Braidwood, NSW.

---
[208] Karee Siding
[209] The King's Own Scottish Borders Regiment

Parents: David Stewart and Ellenor Jeffrey. *Died:* 8 February 1938 Karratha, WA. *Buried:* Karratha General Cemetery. *Spouse:* Amelia Routley. *Married:* 1893 Goulburn, NSW.

Stewart was a member of the West Camden Half Squadron of the NSW Lancers that went to England in March 1899 as part of the Lancer squadron to train at Aldershot with the British Regular Cavalry. He was living in Western Australia when his son enlisted in WWI.

TAME, Albert Edward: *Rank:* Farrier Sergeant #3618. *Unit:* 3rd NSW Mounted Rifles (absorbed into 3rd New South Wales Imperial Bushmen). *Departed:* 5 April 1901 *SS Antillian. Returned:* 11 August 1902 *HMT Drayton Grange. Born:* 1879 Joadja, NSW. *Parents:* John Ludford Tame and Emily Buckman. *Died:* 5 November 1927 Qld. *Buried:* Drayton and Toowoomba Cemetery, Harristown, Qld. *Spouse:* Ann Hamer. *Married:* 1904 Orange, NSW. *Honours:* Queen's South Africa Medal.

The Campbelltown Herald
Wednesday, 13 November 1901, page 2

A Letter from the Front

Farrier-Sergt. Tame, a member of the Third NSW Bushmen in South Africa writes from Klerksdorp an interesting letter to his friend, Mr Thomas Barrett, of Campbelltown, under date October 2nd. In the course of his remarks he says:

> *Our column has never had a spell since we started out – that was on the 1st of June. It is very monotonous out here, day after day trekking on the veldt, seeing nothing but wild country – no civilisation whatever. If you meet any stranger at all on the veldt, it is a Boer; and if he sees you first, he'll blow your light out if possible. He does his best, anyhow. He is dead to have a couple of shots at you. But as far as war is concerned, it is out of the question now – it is all one-sided. We have all the towns and railways, and all the Boers depend on is the open country. They are always watching us. They wait till we come in sight, and then let drive 50 or 60 rounds, after which they mount and get away for their lives. If we chase them we have to be very careful, for in nine cases out of ten they will lead us into ambush, where we will find about five Boers to every one of us, and then it's either surrender or die. If you surrender they will take your clothes, give you a kick, say something insulting, and tell you to go, and when you are going it is most likely they will have a shot at you. The Boers always use explosive bullets, and if they hit you it is a case. As soon as the bullet strikes it explodes, and the shock kills you, even if you are hit in the arm or leg. You wonder what keeps the war going, but if you were here you would see for yourself. The Boers get on top of the kopjes, and as there is no timber, they can see for miles around. They watch all our movements, and they travel to suit themselves. If they see they haven't any chance they will split up into bunches of 20 or 30, and snipe away at us wherever we go. If on the other hand they find we are not too well represented, it takes them no time to mobilise and sweep down on us — about three to one — when we least expect it.*

> *Last August we came on to two big convoys — one with 40 wagons and 45 men. We took the lot. About a week after we heard of a convoy 21 miles off, so we started at 1 o'clock in the morning. At 9 o'clock we sighted it. We were ordered to gallop. The Boers saw us and fled, but we caught the convoy at*

noon. However, all but 18 of the men escaped; but we captured 120 wagons and oxen and goodness knows how many sheep and horses. It took us all night to get back to camp with our prize, after being in the saddle for 26 hours. We got good praise, the colonel remarking that he was sure the work could not have been done by any other troops in the field; and we were all NSW men!

We have had a few casualties since we've been here, but nothing to speak of. The most painful case was that of a corporal, who was shot on outpost by his own mate. He went outside the line for something, and the sentry, ignorant of the fact, challenged three times. The man could not have heard, or else thought someone else was being halted. Anyway, he did not answer. The sentry fired, and the Corporal fell dead.

This is a great mining place, and the towns over here are well up to date. Before the war, miners got from £1 to 30s per day. There are plenty of vacancies in the railways, but the pay is not too good. Drivers get £1 a day, and guards start at 10s, but this is largely increased with over time. They are also starting electric trams. It costs 30s a week for board, so you see 15s a day here would only equal 10s at home. No more this time.

L-R: Albert Tame; Henry Tame; Walter Tame; Herbert Tame – Photo courtesy Australian War Memorial P03036.001

TAME, Henry: *Rank:* Squadron Quartermaster Sergeant #3616. *Unit:* 3rd NSW Mounted Rifles (absorbed into 3rd New South Wales Imperial Bushmen). *Departed:* 5 April 1901 *SS Antillian. Born:* 1874 Joadja, NSW. *Parents:* John Ludford Tame and Emily Buckman. *Died:* 23 March 1902 Middleburg, South Africa from enteric fever. *Buried:* Middleburg, South Africa. *Honours:* Queen's South Africa Medal.

TAME, Herbert Bernden: *Rank:* Farrier Sergeant #3692. *Unit:* 3rd NSW Mounted Rifles (absorbed into 3rd New South Wales Imperial Bushmen). *Departed:* 5 April 1901 *SS Antillian. Born:* 1884 Joadja, NSW. *Parents:* John Ludford Tame and Emily

Buckman. *Died:* 20 January 1902 Standerton, South Africa from enteric fever. *Buried:* Standerton, South Africa. *Honours:* Queen's South Africa Medal.

TAME, Walter Charles: *Rank:* Private #3617. *Unit:* 3rd NSW Mounted Rifles (absorbed into 3rd New South Wales Imperial Bushmen). *Departed:* 5 April 1901 *SS Antillian*. *Born:* 1882 Joadja, NSW. *Parents:* John Ludford Tame and Emily Buckman. *Died:* 20 October 1901 Standerton, South Africa from enteric fever. *Buried:* Standerton, South Africa. *Honours:* Queen's South Africa Medal.

THOMPSON, Norman Edgar: *Rank:* Private #455. *Unit:* 1st New South Wales Mounted Rifles. *Departed:* 17 January 1900 *SS Southern Cross*. *Born:* 2 November 1863 Camden, NSW. *Parents:* Henry Thompson and Anne Bardwell. *Died:* 4 December 1900 Kroonstad, South Africa from enteric fever. *Buried:* Kroonstad, South Africa.

Camden News
Thursday, 13 December 1900

Obituary

We notice by cables from South Africa that Private Norman Edgar Thompson, fifth son of Mrs. Thompson, of Burwood, and formerly of Camden for many long years, died of enteric fever at Kroonstad, South Africa. The deceased left Australia at the commencement of the war, joining the troop leaving by the Southern Cross, and was in active service at the time of his demise. Mr Thompson was a native of Camden, and was early educated under Mr Reeves, the popular schoolmaster at that time. He was some 34 years of age. Only a few days ago Mr CA Thompson, of Camden, received a letter from his brother, he there stated that he felt out of sorts. Much sympathy is expressed for his mother and relatives.

TREVITT, George Spurway: *Rank:* Private #63. *Unit:* 'A' Squadron NSW Mounted Rifles. *Departed:* 14 November 1899 *SS Langton Grange*. *Returned:* Invalided to Australia 3 July 1900. *Born:* 1876 Bathurst, NSW. *Parents:* George Trevitt and Harriett Elizabeth Smith. *Died:* 1950 Bathurst, NSW. *Spouse:* Eliza Almora Dawson. *Married:* 1905 Bathurst, NSW. *Honours:* Queen's South Africa Medal with 1 clasp.

TURNER, William James: *Rank:* Trooper #815. *Unit:* New South Wales Lancers. *Departed:* 3 March 1899 *SS Nineveh* (to UK), 30 November 1899 (to South Africa). *Returned:* 6 December 1901 *HMT Harlech Castle*. *Born:* 14 September 1876 Ryde, NSW. *Parents:* William Turner and Margaret Saunders. *Died:* 28 January 1952 Parramatta, NSW. *Buried:* Field of Mars. *Spouse:* Margret Humphries. *Married:* 1905, Ryde, NSW. *Honours:* Queen's South Africa Medal with 6 clasps. *Memorial:* New South Wales Lancers Memorial Museum, Parramatta.

Turner was a member of the West Camden Half Squadron of the NSW Lancers that went to England in March 1899 as part of the Lancer squadron to train with British Regular Cavalry at Aldershot.

TWEEDY, William George: *Rank:* Private #99. *Unit:* 'A' Squadron NSW Mounted Rifles. *Departed:* 14 November 1899 *SS Langton Grange*. *Returned:* Invalided to Australia 6 August 1900. *Born:* 1878 Forbes, NSW. *Parents:* William Tweedy and Mary Darcey. *Occupation:* railway employee Picton. *Died:* 26 June 1930. *Buried:* Rookwood General – Roman Catholic.

Tweedy was wounded in action, at Klip Kraal, 17 February 1900, then again wounded in action, at Thaba N'Chu, 30 April 1900. His departure for South Africa was mentioned in *Camden News*. Surname also spelt as Tweedie.

VACCHINI, Caleb Francis: *Rank:* Sergeant #452. *Unit:* 1st New South Wales Mounted Rifles 'C' Squadron. *Departed:* 17 January 1900 *SS Southern Cross*. *Returned:* 8 January 1901 *HMT Orient*. *Born:* 9 May 1870 Sydney, NSW. *Parents:* Tiberio Vacchini and Ann Elizabeth Whitfield. *Occupation:* farm labourer, carpenter. *Died:* 29 October 1947 Concord, NSW. *Spouse:* Louisa Swann. *Married:* 1900 Paddington, NSW. *Honours:* Queen's South Africa Medal with 6 clasps. *Memorial:* Wollondilly Heritage Centre, The Oaks.

Caleb Francis Vacchini

Vacchini was a member of the Picton Half Squadron New South Wales Mounted Rifles and was one of the men to attend Queen Victoria's Diamond Jubilee celebrations. Later in life he became a carpenter but died after falling from a building.

WALSH, Edward: *Rank:* Trooper #677. *Unit:* New South Wales Lancers. *Departed:* 28 October 1899 *HMT Kent*. *Returned:* Invalided, Australia 6 August 1900. *Born:* 1878 Burrawang, NSW. *Parents:* Richard Martin Walsh and Bridget Scahill. *Died:* 7 October 1955 Boorowa, NSW. *Honours:* Queen's South Africa Medal.

Edward Walsh

WALTON, William Joseph: *Rank:* Saddler #1745. *Unit:* 3rd New South Wales Mounted Rifles. *Departed:* 15 March 1901 *SS Maplemore*. *Returned:* 3 June 1902 *HMT Aurania*. *Born:* 1873 Picton. *Parents:* Henry Walton and Mary Gillard. *Occupation:* saddler, railway engine driver. *Died:* 16 May 1944 Picton, NSW. *Buried:* Upper Picton – Roman Catholic. *Spouse:* Matilda Rudolph. *Married:* 1902 St. Peters, NSW. *Honours:* Queen's South Africa Medal.

WARBY, Joseph Hillier: *Rank:* Trooper #790. *Unit:* New South Wales Lancers. *Departed:* 15 March 1901 *SS Maplemore*. *Returned:* 3 June 1902 *HMT Aurania*. *Born:* 1880 St. George, NSW. *Parents:* Walter George Warby and Clara Julie Hillier. *Died:* 4 June 1960 Wentworth Falls, NSW. *Spouse:* Florence Lily Wilson. *Married:* 1908 Burwood, NSW. *Honours:* Queen's South Africa Medal.

WARDROBE, John: *Rank:* Corporal #84. *Unit:* 'A' Squadron NSW Mounted Rifles. *Departed:* 14 November 1899 *SS Langton Grange*. *Returned:* 8 January 1901 *HMT Orient*. *Born:* 17 April 1865 Durham, England. *Parents:* William Wardrobe and Elizabeth. *Occupation:* teamster, storekeeper, alderman. *Died:* 14 November 1945 Hurstville, NSW. *Buried:* Woronora General Cemetery. *Spouse:* Eliza Cracknell. *Married:* 1887 Picton, NSW. *Honours:* Queen's South Africa Medal with 6 clasps. *Memorial:* Wollondilly Heritage Centre, The Oaks.

John Wardrobe

Wardrobe came to NSW aged 16 after the death of his father. During WWI he was a Drill Sergeant stationed in Sydney.

WASSON, John James: *Rank:* (1) Staff Sergeant (2) Warrant Officer (3) Regimental Sergeant-Major #3683. *Unit:* (1) 'A' Squadron New South Wales Mounted Rifles (2) 2nd New South Wales Mounted Rifles. *Departed: (1)* 3 November 1899 *SS Langton Grange*.

Returned: (1) 8 January 1901 *HMT Orient. Departed: (2)* 15 March 1901 *SS Maplemore. Returned: (2)* 11 August 1902 *HMT Drayton Grange. Born:* 2 September 1864 Camden, NSW. *Parents:* Joseph Wasson and Julia Elizabeth Howard. *Died:* 12 March 1949 Randwick, NSW. *Honours:* Distinguished Conduct Medal, Mentioned in Despatches three times 'For Good Work and Bravery in Scouting', Queen's South Africa Medal with 6 Clasps, Kings South Africa Medal. *Memorial:* Bathurst, NSW.

During his second secondment Wasson was engaged in operations against Generals Jacobus Herculaas de la Rey (known as Koos de la Rey); Ferdinandus Jacobus Potgieter and Hendrick Cornelius Wilhelmus Vermaas whilst serving in the Western and Eastern Transvaal.

Wasson was the 2nd Town Clerk for Camden and Inspector of Nuisances from 1890-1892 when he resigned to take a full-time position as Staff Sergeant in the Mounted Rifles. He also served WWI #450 2nd Light Horse Regiment and saw action at Gallipoli and rose to the rank of Lieutenant.

Camden News
Thursday February 1, 1900

Mrs. Wasson senr. of Camden, has received the following letter from her son, Sergt. Major Wasson, of Forbes, now serving with the Mounted Rifles at the Transvaal:

SS Langton Grange
December 18, 1899

Dear Mother: — As we expect to land at Cape Town on the 19th I am sending you word that I am all right. Trusting you and all at home are well.

We have been on the water 34 days. The passage was not a very rough one but rather slow. We did not sight a boat for three weeks. We have on board about 700 horses so there is plenty to do. Most of the lads were seasick but they soon recovered. Our tucker is of the very best and all hands look well. We lost 8 horses, most of them died from pneumonia. Our daily routine consists chiefly in stable duties. The Reveille sounds at 5 a.m. and lights out at 9.15 p.m. We landed 280 horses at Port Natal on December 12, which were immediately entrained to the front. The town of Durban is close by and is rather pretty; we also landed a large quantity of frozen meat. Kaffirs [sic.] were employed, they are a very inferior race – a dirty useless crowd – many of them carry spoons through a hole in their ears with which they take snuff. Leaving Durban on the 14th arrived at East London,[210] 260 miles, on the evening of the 15th. This township is situated on the Buffalo River; it is not a pretty place, but interesting. Both the ports were full of battle ships, gun boats and transports. Troops from England are arriving daily and we are looking forward to a good fight. I think the war will last at least twelve months. The South African coast is very mountainous and will be rough if we have much coast fighting.

December 19 – arrived safely at Cape Town this morning.

---

[210] A city on the east coast of South Africa

WEARNE, Albert Ernest: *Rank:* (1) Private #71 (2) Corporal #71 (3) Lieutenant. *Unit:* (1) 'A' Squadron NSW Mounted Rifles (2) 2nd New South Wales Mounted Rifles (3) 3rd New South Wales Imperial Bushmen. *Departed:* (1) 3 November 1899 *SS Aberdeen*. *Returned:* (1) invalided to Australia 17 August 1900. *Departed:* (2) 15 March 1901 *SS Maplemore*. *Returned:* (2) 11 August 1902 *HMT Drayton Grange*. *Born:* 5 August 1871 Liverpool, NSW. *Parents:* William Carvosso Wearne and Martha Caldwell. *Occupation:* journalist. *Died:* 11 April 1954 Burwood, NSW. *Spouse:* Margery Maud Stevenson. *Married:* 1914 Liverpool, NSW. *Honours:* Queen's South Africa Medal with 3 clasps.

Albert Ernest Wearne

Wearne also served during WWI as a Lieutenant with the 6th Light Horse Regiment and later as a Major. He served in the Middle East and was awarded a Military Cross for conspicuous gallantry on 1 January 1917. He suffered a gunshot wound to the head in April 1917 and was invalided to Australia 15 November 1917.

WHEELER, Robert John: *Rank:* Trooper #66, Trooper #3609. *Unit:* (1) New South Wales Lancers (later 1st Battalion Australian Commonwealth Horse (NSW) 'A' Squadron) (2) 3rd NSW Imperial Bushmen. *Departed: (1)* 16 February 1900 *SS Australian*. *Returned:* 6 December 1901 *HMT Harlech Castle*. *Departed: (2)* 18 February 1902 *SS Custodian*. *Returned: (2)* 11 August 1902 *HMT Drayton Grange*. *Born:* 1861 Redfern, NSW. *Parents:* Robert Wheeler and Maria Elizabeth Miller. *Died:* 17 August 1923 Sydney Hospital, Sydney, NSW. *Spouse:* Annie Chambers. *Married:* 1903 Redfern, NSW. *Honours:* Queen's South Africa Medal.

Wheeler was a member of the West Camden Half Squadron and served under Captain Charles Edward Nicholson.

WINTLE, Alfred: *Rank:* Sergeant #518. *Unit:* 2nd New South Wales Mounted Rifles. *Departed:* 17 March 1901 *SS Custodian or SS Maplemore*. *Returned:* 3 June 1902 *HMT Aurania*. *Born:* 1875 Bermagui, NSW. *Parents:* Walter Robert Wintle and Emily Amelia Mary Gillespie. *Died:* 22 October 1953 Cheltenham, NSW. *Spouse:* Bertha Sawyer. *Married:* 1912 Mosman, NSW. *Honours:* Queen's South Africa Medal with 2 clasps.

He also served WWI #1077 as a Private with the 4th Infantry Battalion.

WINTLE, William Edward (Billy): *Rank:* (1) Private #100 (2) Lieutenant #357. *Unit:* (1) 'A' Squadron New South Wales Mounted Rifles; (2) 3rd New South Wales Imperial Bushmen. *Departed:* 14 November 1899 *SS Langton Grange*. *Returned:* 11 August 1902 *HMT Drayton Grange*. *Born:* 19 September 1875 Glen Hill, The Oaks, NSW. *Parents:* William Augustus Wintle and Diana Elizabeth Gaudry. *Occupation:* miner Yerranderie, NSW. *Died:* 18 June 1963 Beverley Hills, NSW. *Buried:* Camden Catholic Church. *Spouse:* Mary Blanche Carlon. *Married:* 1903 Camden, NSW. *Honours:* Queen Alexandra Pipe for Gallantry, Queen's South Africa Medal with 2 clasps.

William Edward (Billy) Wintle

Wintle was promoted to Lieutenant by Lord Kitchener on the recommendation of Colonel Lassetter.

WONSON, William Edward: *Rank:* Trooper #658. *Unit:* 2nd New South Wales Mounted Rifles. *Departed:* 17 March 1901 *SS Custodian or SS Maplemore*. *Returned:* 3 June 1902 *HMT Aurania*. *Born:* 18 December 1882 Broughton Park, Wilton, NSW.

Parents: William Wonson and Emily Oxenbridge. *Occupation:* labourer for the Water Board. *Died:* 1 April 1918 Garrison Hospital, Victoria Barracks, Paddington, NSW. *Buried:* St. Luke's Church of England, Wilton. *Spouse:* Ethel Irene McMahon. *Married:* 10 March 1906 Sydney, NSW. *Honours:* Queen's South Africa Medal with 3 clasps, King's South Africa Medal with 2 clasps. *Memorial:* Wollondilly Heritage Centre, The Oaks, NSW.

WOODS, Arthur Ernest: *Rank:* Lance Corporal #624. *Unit:* New South Wales Lancers. *Departed:* 3 March 1899 *SS Nineveh* (to UK), 30 November 1899 (to South Africa). *Returned:* 6 December 1901 *HMT Harlech Castle. Born:* 1873 Wollongong, NSW. *Parents:* Edward Woods and Mary Ann McBrien. *Occupation:* Fire Brigade officer. *Died:* 7 May 1947 Kensington, NSW. *Spouse:* Isabella Wylie. *Married:* 1911 Balmain South, NSW. *Honours:* Queen's South Africa Medal.

Woods was a member of the West Camden Half Squadron of the NSW Lancers which went to England in March 1899 as part of the Lancer Squadron to train with the British Regular Cavalry at Aldershot.

ZGLINICKI, Ernest James: *Rank:* Private #111, Sergeant #1750. *Unit*: (1) 'A' Squadron New South Wales Mounted Rifles; (2) 3rd New South Wales Mounted Rifles. *Departed:* (1) 3 November 1899 *SS Aberdeen. Returned: (1)* invalided to Australia arrived 3 July 1900. *Departed: (2)* 15 March 1901 *SS Maplemore. Returned: (2)* 3 June 1902 *HMT Aurania. Born:* 1871 Picton, NSW. *Parents:* Maximilian von Zglinicki and Bridget O'Hare. *Occupation:* compositor. *Died:* 17 March 1941 Liverpool, NSW. *Buried:* Rookwood, Roman Catholic Cemetery. *Spouse:* Martha Bugden. *Married:* 1894 Junee, NSW. *Honours:* Queen's South Africa Medal with 5 clasps, King's South Africa Medal with 2 Clasps.

He also served WWI as Private #3598 with the 6th Machine Gun Company.

Camden News
Thursday, 2 August 1900, page 1

Camden Mounted Riflemen in South Africa

Immediately on the arrival of Private Zglinicki, invalided home from the seat of war, suffering from the effects of enteric fever and dysentery, a representative of the Camden News, *waited on Pt. Zglinicki, the main object being to ascertain the latest particulars as to the health of the several members of the Camden-½-Co. when last he saw or heard of them. Pt. Zglinicki was most pleased to answer the enquiries made.*

Zglinicki, prior to his leaving the seat of war was under the command of Capt. Antill. Zglinicki was taken ill at Brandfort, on the route to Pretoria, and by the command of Lieutenant Onslow was ordered to the field hospital, where he was for some eight weeks prior to his departure to his native home. He received the greatest courtesy from all, and speaks highly of his comrades at arms; also receiving the soldiers' comforts sent by the Australian ladies and were found of the very greatest blessing.

Pt. Zglinicki last saw Capt. Antill and Lieutenant Onslow in May, they were then in good health and very solicitous for the welfare of their men, the slightest trouble is to them a pleasure, so long as the soldiers were well fed and had proper clothing. Many times these officers had given their food to the privates of the squadron.

Sergt. Major Holman was well and proved himself a great administrator, and the Imperial officers considered him an experienced officer.

Sergt. Major Wasson continues in good health and is always at the front when duty calls. Sergt. Major Wasson, Pt. Zglinicki states, is the smartest man in the squadron and one of the right hands under Capt. Antill.

Corporal Nethery when Zglinicki last saw him was at Brandfort looking well. Nethery is a favourite of the squadron – he was always at the front and has undergone great hardships.

Pte. Roy Smith keeps in good health and spirits and was at the front. Naauwpoort was the last place Zglinicki saw him.

Pt. R Sharpe was well, as well, as was Sergt. Major Hawkey, and greatly respected by his comrades. Both these men have been great fighters and have carried their laurels.

Pt. M. Bourke was at Bloemfontein when Pt. Zglinicki was taken ill. Bourke is invalided home and will shortly arrive in Sydney.

Pt. Maxwell, of Burragorang, was last seen at Bloemfontein at the end of May. Maxwell was sent to Kimberley with sick horses. Zglinicki states that Maxwell was subsequently taken ill of the dreaded fever and expected to be invalided home shortly.

In conclusion Pt. Zglinicki was not too communicative but we were anxious to know the health of the many Camden men and their whereabouts.

Camden News
Thursday, 5 September 1901

From South Africa
BY CAMDEN SOLDIER

Only this morning we received the following letter, which will be read with the deepest interest by our local residents. Sergt. Zglinicki is not only a good soldier of the King, but a good descriptive writer. We give prominence to the favoured letter.

> *Sir, — As promised I take the opportunity of a few days halt at Platt Kand to drop you a few lines as to the doings of the 3rd regiment of Mounted Rifles in South Africa.*

> *To commence with we had a splendid trip across, everything going off satisfactorily in connection with the accommodation of the troops. We landed at Port Elizabeth this time instead of Cape Town, the latter place being plague infected. Upon landing we were treated very handsomely by the inhabitants. At about 7 p.m. on day of landing we entrained (or rather trucked), our destination being about 20 miles south of Pretoria. After 11 days of weary travelling in open trucks we arrived at the above place, only to be informed that we were booked for Standerton which meant another day in the trucks. The long journey, however, did not dampen the ardour of the troops, as one could hear by the constant sound of cheering by the men as they passed their British comrades who were stationed on the line of communication to Pretoria. On arrival at Standerton we heard that Major Antill and the 2nd regiment had gone on to Krugersdorp and intended to operate from there. We were indeed in a sorry plight at Standerton that is as regards horses only. All our Australian horses were taken from us and*

a lot of weedy, broken down bus horses handed to us. To look at them one would think we were well mounted but indeed, it was quite the reverse. But there was one thing the Australians had cause to rejoice in, and that was they were placed under the command of Colonel Rimington, who is indeed, a grand soldier. I am sure that he has added to his fame since he has had the 3rd Mounted Regiment under his command, in proof of which I may add that Lord Kitchener has wired in the following terms: 'My thanks to you. Your officers and the men under your command for the splendid work you have done; a continuation of which will lead to a speedy termination of the war.' Since we have commenced operations we have captured no less than four convoys, besides several thousand head of cattle and sheep. It is recognised as a fine piece of work to capture a convoy. But I may tell you that the amount of manoeuvring needed to affect the capture involves a deal of fatigue accompanied by night marches which, at this time of the year, it being intensely cold at night, knock the men and horses about considerably. But to counteract the effect of the cold we have been supplied with warm British coats which are very serviceable. We have secured a large number of prisoners, and also caused a lot of surrender as a result of operations. Despite the hardships incidental to a campaign the men are in good health and do not care for the sleepless nights providing they can have a 'go at the Joes', as the Boers are termed here. The Boers give the Australians credit for being smart men, and I think they will add to it before they are finished with Colonel Rimington and the 3rd Regiment. Since starting this letter we have been out on another night march, and from what I can learn we have been operating against the notorious De Wet [sic.]. Only last night we captured 20 prisoners besides 6 wagons and a few cape carts. All the Camdenites are well, including Corporal Sharpe, Farrier Sergt. Billett, Trooper Walton and also yours truly. Ted Billett is getting on well, in fact he is thought so well of by the officers that he is certain to receive further advancement. He and Harry Sharpe are attached to another squadron to the one I am in but I see them every day. We are under orders tomorrow for a month's hard trek, and as we are pretty busy getting remounts and generally fixing up, with apologies for occupying so much of your valuable space, I beg to remain,

Yours, etc.
SERGEANT ZGLINICKI
Platt Kand
10/07/1901

The following letter from an unnamed soldier was printed in the Campbelltown Herald *and gives some indication of how stoic the soldiers were even when severely injured.*

The Campbelltown Herald
Wednesday, 25 September 1901 page 6

A Peculiar Wound

At Netley there is a very extraordinary case, and in a letter to his brother the wounded man, a private in the Mounted detachment of the West Riding Regiment, says:

The first bullet hit me behind the right ear, passing through my head and knocking my left eye out. I have lost the hearing of my right ear, as the bullet smashed the drum. The second bullet missed the bone, so it is nothing to speak of — only a flesh wound. The third bullet took three nails off on my right hand. I think this is a very lucky shot. It never touched the fingers at all. The doctors think it wonderful that I am alive. The bullet that passed through my head caused my face and mouth to be slightly paralysed, but that is all right now, though at first it caused me to be dumb. You can tell what it meant when I lost 3st. 6 lb in a fortnight, and could not move my mouth at all. I may mention that when I recovered consciousness on the battlefield I found that the Boers had stripped me of everything except my trousers. An officer kindly gave me a shirt otherwise I must have gone to the hospital practically naked.

Australian soldiers also wrote home on the tragedies they encountered.

The Campbelltown Herald
Wednesday, 14 February 1900

A Pitiful Incident

A pathetic incident at Elandslaagte is described in a letter from one of the bearer company: —

We were out looking after the wounded at night, after the fight was over, when I came across an old white-bearded Boer. He was lying behind a bit of rock supporting himself on his elbows. I was a bit wary of the old fellow at first, so I kept my eye on him, but when I got nearer I saw he was too far gone to raise his rifle. He was gasping hard for breath, and I saw he was not long for this world. He motioned me that he wanted to speak, and I bent over him. He asked me to go and find his son – a boy thirteen years old, who had been fighting by his side when he fell. Well, I did as he asked me (continues the writer), and under a heap of wounded I found the poor lad, stone dead, and I carried him back to his father. Well, you know I'm not a chicken-hearted sort of fellow. I have seen a bit of fighting in my time, and that sort of thing knocks all the soft stuff out of a chap; but I had to turn away when the old Boer saw his dead lad. He hugged the dead boy to him and moaned over it, and carried on in a way that fetched a big lump in my throat. Until that moment I never thought how horrible war is. I never wanted to see another shot fired. And when I looked round again the old Boer was dead, clasping the body of his dead boy.

Britain introduced a 'scorched earth' policy and interred the Boer civilian populations in concentration camps. As the war dragged on the suffering of the Boer civilians disenchanted Australians. When Lieutenant Harry (Breaker) Morant and Lieutenant Peter Handcock were convicted of murdering twelve Boer prisoners and executed on 27 February 1902 the Australian public were angered and support for the war was eroded. Lieutenants Morant and Handcock maintained in their defence that they were following the orders of the British command.

On 31 May 1902 the Treaty of Vereeniging was signed and all Boers became British subjects. However, even today the descendants of the Boers bear a grudge against

Britain. It has been said that 'the Boers might have lost the war, but their determined resistance won them the peace'.[211]

As the Boer War continued many in Australia and England began to express their concern for the women and children caught up in the conflict. Soldiers such as Rex Smith wrote home of their disgust at the way women and children were being treated. To deny the Boers access to food, shelter and intelligence Lord Kitchener had ordered the British Army and the Colonials to sweep the veldt clean. Farms were burnt, stock was taken or destroyed and women and children forced into concentration camps. Kitchener referred to these camps as 'refugee camps' but they were far from that. The women and children were given no choice – they were herded into inadequate camps. Epidemics broke out – measles, pneumonia and enteric fever. Sanitation was inadequate and the quality of water and food bordered on starvation rations. Basic necessities such as clothing, bedding, soap etc. were unavailable. Up to 12 people would share a single small tent.

Kitchener believed that the hardships faced by the women and children would force the Boers to surrender. However, his ruthless methods were self-defeating. The treatment of the civilians added to the bitterness and resolve of the Boers and undoubtedly extended the duration of the war. Between 20,000 and 28,000 civilians died in the camps, including one in five children. The British public were appalled by the holocaust. Organisations like the Quakers began to appeal for donations to ease the suffering.

Camden News
Thursday, 31 October 1901

The Sad War in South Africa
AN APPEAL BY THE SOCIETY OF FRIENDS

Dear Christian Friends — The terrible suffering caused by the war in South Africa, particularly to the women and children, many of whom are British, seems to us a loud call on all Christian people to do what they can to relieve the widespread distress.

The Society of Friends (Quakers), in England, and others, have taken the matter up, and have already sent over 20,000 garments besides material for making into clothing and comforts to South Africa, where Quaker women, and others connected with them, are now distributing what they have already received to those in need, independent of race or party.

The death rate in many of the camps, during the month of July especially, was enormous, particularly amongst the children. In the camp for which returns are available, there were in Orange River Colony, 86,696 people, of which number 20,132 were children, deaths 488; in the Transvaal 54,129, of which 24,462 were children, deaths 917, this affects only the two States mentioned.

From a private source we hear of a large number of British refugees in Durban also in dire distress. Miss Hobhouse[212] *who has visited many of those camps, and who is now in England telling her sad story, and appealing for help, says, amongst many things of a similar kind: —*

---

[211] Laband, J., Why the Boers Lost the War, *African Studies Review* Vol 49, Number 3, December 2006 pp. 97-98 | 10.1353/arw.2007.0045
[212] Hobhouse, Emily

> *'I call this camp system a wholesale cruelty, it presses hardest on the children who drop in the terrible heat, and with the insufficient, unsuitable food, whatever the authorities do, and they are, I believe doing their best, with very limited means; it is all only a miserable patch on a great ill.*
>
> *'I can't describe what it is to see these children lying about in a state of collapse. It is just exactly like faded flowers thrown away, and one has to stand and look on at such misery, and be able to do almost nothing. When it rains at night, as often, it drips on them all night and makes little pools on their beds, no wonder children sicken and die.*
>
> *'A nice-looking woman with a very white face, spoke to us, she had been travelling two days, and had no food given and the children were crying with hunger.'*

While Miss Hobhouse was holding her meetings in England in July, the frightful mortality mentioned above was going on in South Africa caused principally by measles with pneumonia supervening through the intense cold and privations.

Would the ladies of each household give one or more new garments (woollen preferably), blankets, rugs, knitted caps of various sizes for women and children, and cases furnished with needles, buttons, tapes etc., it would in the aggregate, go far to alleviate the present need.

The committee, in connection with the Society of Friends (or Quakers) in Sydney would be glad to receive parcels which may be sent to W. Cooper, Cadbury Bros. Ltd., 267 George Street, Sydney, or WJ Baber, Cutler, Hunter Street, Sydney, for transmission to South Africa.

Articles sent for this purpose are allowed to enter South Africa free of duty. The sanction and sympathy of the British Government are with this movement.

Note — To prevent any misconception of this object, it may be mentioned that our desire is to alleviate the vast amount of suffering among women and children of all classes while, irrespective of nationality, occasioned by the prolongation of the war. We have nothing to do with one side or the other in this disastrous conflict, but it is our desire to assist as far as possible its myriad of innocent victims.

Hobhouse's comments saw her labelled in Britain as pro-Boer, but she was not alone in her condemnation of the concentration camps. Members of Parliament such as Lloyd-George,[213] Ellis[214] and Scott[215] attacked the camp system, in Parliament, as being barbaric. In April 1900, American pro-Boers sent a special message of sympathy to the President of the Transvaal, Paul Kruger, on behalf of 22,000 American born children.

The British public had originally expected the war in South Africa to be over by Christmas 1899. However, it has been said 'it proved to be the longest (two and three-quarter years), and the costliest (over £200 million), and the bloodiest (at least 22,000 British, 25,000 Boer and 12,000 African lives) and the most humiliating war that Britain fought between 1815 and 1914.'[216] Following the end of the Boer War both the Transvaal and the Orange Free State became part of the colony of South Africa. South Africa would not obtain its independence from Britain until 1934.

---

[213] Lloyd-George, David – 1st Earl Lloyd-George of Dwyfor (a Liberal Party politician)
[214] Ellis, John (a Labour Party politician)
[215] Scott, Charles Prestwich – (journalist, publisher and Liberal Party politician)
[216] Pakenham, T, *The Boer War* (Random House, London 1979)

BOXER REBELLION

The Boxer Rebellion took place at the beginning of the 20th Century, but no Camden residents appear to have been involved in the naval and military campaign instigated by Great Britain.

Today it seems ironic that during the 19th Century Great Britain and the major European powers compelled the reluctant Chinese Empire to start trading with them. The Chinese government was very reluctant to undertake trade with the West. However, at the time there was a strong demand for opium among the population of China. During what became known as the Opium Wars of 1839–1842 and 1856– 1860, Britain forced China to accept the import of opium in return for Chinese goods, and trading centres were established at major ports. The largest trading centre was Shanghai, where French, German, British, and American merchants demanded large tracts of land in which they asserted 'extra-territorial' rights, meaning they were subject to the laws of their own country, not China.

The Boxer Rebellion or Yihetuan Movement was an anti-imperialist uprising which took place in China towards the end of the Qing dynasty between 1899 and 1901. It was initiated by the Militia United in Righteousness (Yihetuan), known in English as the 'Boxers', and was motivated by proto-nationalist sentiments and opposition to foreign imperialism and associated Christian missionary activity. International tensions and domestic unrest led to the violent uprising. Boxer aggression against foreign missionaries and their Chinese converts, including the massacre of many, led to retaliation by British and European forces.

FEDERATION

From 1899 the war in South Africa was not the only topic of interest to Camden residents. Correspondents to the *Camden News* (Frederick William Arthur Downes, Stephen Pegum etal) expressed varying support to the concept of federation, the major advantages being the abolition of border taxes between the various Australian states and the impetus it would provide to a burgeoning manufacturing industry. Numerous meetings were held around the district with speakers such as Frederick William Arthur Downes, Alfred Denison Little, Patrick Kilmartin, JO Moore, James Downie Rankin, John Kidd, James William Macarthur-Onslow and George Edward Young enthusiastically supporting Federation. However, gentlemen such as John Edward Moore of Ellenville, Glenmore, Stephen Pegum and John Alexander Porter were opposed to the Bill and also organised rallies to engender support for their cause.

Referendums held in June 1899 in the colonies of NSW, Queensland, Victoria, South Australia and Tasmania voted in favour of Federation. A referendum was not held in the colony of Western Australia until 1900. Following majority support in that state the Bill was forwarded to Britain for ratification.

On 1 January 1901 Australia became an independent nation but remained part of the British Commonwealth.

DEATH OF QUEEN VICTORIA
22 January 1901

The *Camden News* of Thursday, 24 January 1901 announced the death of the monarch at 6:30 p.m. on Tuesday 22 January. On Saturday 2 February 1901 (the date of the Queen's funeral) all shops in Camden were closed from 10:30 a.m. to 4:00 p.m. as a sign of respect.

DUKE and DUCHESS OF YORK'S VISIT

It had originally been intended that Prince Albert Edward (the Duke of York) and his Duchess visit Australia in the spring of 1901 to open the first Australian Parliament. The death of Queen Victoria required the Duke of York's presence in Britain in preparation for his coronation the following year. As a consequence the uncrowned King sent his son George (Duke of Cornwall and York) with his wife Princess Victoria Mary of Teck.

After opening the parliament in Melbourne the Royal couple travelled by train to Sydney. Whilst the royal visitors did not come to Camden members of the NSW Mounted Rifles attended the ceremonies in Melbourne and Sydney.

CORONATION OF KING EDWARD VII
9 August 1902

King Edward VII reigned from 22 January 1901 to 6 May 1910 as King of the United Kingdom and the British Dominions and Emperor of India. Several of the troops who were in South Africa when the war ended took the opportunity to travel to London to see the celebrations. Members of the New South Wales Mounted Rifles were chosen as official representatives at the ceremonies.

Camden News
Thursday, 24 April 1902

It has been decided to send six men from the NSW Mounted Rifles to take part in the Coronation. Trooper Axam has been chosen to represent the Camden squadron. The appointment has given entire satisfaction as he is a popular member of the local squadron. Trooper Axam was a member of the first contingent of Mounted Rifles who volunteered for active service in South Africa, thus winning the honour bestowed on him. We wish Trooper Axam a very pleasant and enjoyable trip.

Trooper RJ Nethery late of Camden and now of Bathurst has received the honour of being selected as one of the NSW Mounted Rifles to visit London during the coronation ceremonies. Trooper Nethery goes to London with the rank of Corporal. He was also a member of the first contingent who volunteered for active service in South Africa. During his military career Trooper Nethery has done good work. He rose to the rank of Sergeant while on active service, on his return home he was appointed as an Instructor to the Imperial Draft Contingent and on their departure for the war he was temporarily appointed to the position of Staff Sergeant Major to the Bathurst Mounted Rifles.

On 22 May 1902 the men of the NSW Mounted Rifles en route for the Coronation departed on the *SS Columbian* under the leadership of Colonel James William Macarthur-Onslow.

The Coronation had originally been organised for 26 June 1902 but had to be postponed when the King became ill and had to be operated on for perityphlitis (appendicitis).

CORONATION OF KING GEORGE V
22 June 1911

On 6 May 1910 King Edward VII died and the throne passed to his son King George V. No official representatives from Camden appear to have been sent to England to participate in the celebration of the Coronation of King George V, although a number of residents took the opportunity to visit England and Francis William Axam of Campbelltown also attended. However, a contingent of New South Wales Cadets under Wynne was sent to participate in the celebration. Amongst them was Frederick James Buttenshaw from Narellan. The young cadets were also given the opportunity to visit the battlefields of the Boer War. Buttenshaw would later serve as a Private with the 41st Infantry Battalion during World War I.

Also amongst those in England at the time was Elizabeth Macarthur-Onslow. Whether she had intended to participate in the celebrations is unclear, however she had been in London for some months. Her health started to fail whilst she was in England and in August Camden was saddened to hear of her passing on 2 August 1911 in London. Elizabeth was buried in the churchyard at Send, Surrey, England.

BIBLIOGRAPHY

A Short History of New South Wales Mounted Rifles 1888–1913, Marchant & Co (Sydney 1914)

Ballyn, S., Jean Baptiste Lehimas de Arrieta: The First Spanish Settler *La Trobe Journal,* No 68, Spring 2001 p.43

Bateson, C., 'Hall, James (1784 - 1869)', *Australian Dictionary of Biography, Volume 1*, (Melbourne University Press, 1966), p. 503

Cobley, Dr. J., *Sydney Cove 1788: The First Year of the Settlement of Australia*; Hodder and Stoughton Ltd., (London 1962)

Cohen, L., *Elizabeth Macquarie: Her Life and Times*, Wentworth Books Pty. Ltd., (Sydney 1979)

Hine, Janet D., 'Clark, Ralph (1762-1794)', *Australian Dictionary of Biography*, National Centre of Biography, Australian National University

Laband, J., 'Why the Boers Lost the War' – *African Studies Review Vol 49, Number 3*, (December 2006) pp. 97–98 | 10.1353/arw.2007.0045

Macarthur-Onslow, A., 'From the Old to New South Wales: the Life of Astley John Onslow Thompson'; *Camden History: Journal of the Camden Historical Society Inc.* (March 2015), Volume 3, Number 9 Special Issue

Menpes, M., *War Impressions: Being a Record in Colour; Messrs. Carl Hentschel, Limited*, (London 1901)

Munro, J. and McGill, J., *Campbelltown and the Boer War, 1899–1902* Campbelltown & Airds Historical Society (Campbelltown, 1997)

Murray, Lieut.-Colonel P.L. R.A.A. (Ret.); *Official Records of the Australian Military Contingents to the War in South Africa* Government Printer (Melbourne 1911)

Nairn, B., 'Lassetter, Henry Beauchamp (1860–1926)', *Australian Dictionary of Biography*, National Centre of Biography, Australian National University, Vol 5, (MUP), 1974

Noad, KB., 'Douglass, Henry Grattan (1790–1865)', *Australian Dictionary of Biography, Volume 1* (Melbourne University Press, 1966) pp. 314–316

Packenham, T., *The Boer War*, Weidenfeld and Nicolson (London1979)

Parsons, V., 'Howe, William (1777–1855)', *Australian Dictionary of Biography*, National Centre of Biography, Australian National University, Vol 1, (MUP), 1966

Perry, T. M., 'Hovell, William Hilton (1786–1875)', *Australian Dictionary of Biography*, National Centre of Biography, Australian National University, Vol 1, (MUP), 1966

Litherland, AR. and Simkin, BT., *Spink's Standard Catalogue of British and associated Orders Decorations & Medals*, Spink (UK 1990)

Sproule, C., *From Picton to Pretoria: The Forgotten Men of a Forgotten War*. The Oaks Historical Society (The Oaks, 1996)

Turner & Henderson, *The New South Wales Contingents to South Africa, From October, 1899 to March, 1900 with a 'Roll Call of Honour' being the names of our officers and men at the front. Compiled from official and other sources.* (Sydney 1900)

Walsh, G. P., 'Huon de Kerilleau, Gabriel Louis Marie (1769–1828)' *Australian Dictionary of Biography*, National Centre of Biography, Australian National University, Vol 1 (MUP), 1996

Wilcox, C., *Australia's Boer War: The War in South Africa 1899–1902* Oxford University Press (Melbourne, Vic 2002)

Wright, C., *Wellington's Men in Australia – Peninsular War Veterans and the Making of Empire 1820–40* (Basingstoke, Hampshire, Great Britain 2011)

Young, A., *Ripe for Harvest* Angela Young (Moss Vale, NSW 1980)

Newspapers

Australian Town & Country Journal 1871–1919

Camden News 1895–1959

Campbelltown Herald 1899–1959

Picton Post 1900–1959

Sydney Gazette 1803–1842 *Sydney*

Morning Herald 1850–1959 *The*

Argus (Melbourne) 1933

The Carcoar Chronicle 1900

Western Champion 1900

Index

1st NSW Mounted Rifles 52, 131, 133, 139, 142, 144, 159, 172, 181, 186, 187
1st Royal Scots Regiment............ 34
2nd NSW Mounted Rifles 112, 114, 130, 135, 137, 139, 142, 143, 154, 157, 187, 189
3rd NSW Imperial Bushmen 129, 130, 157, 174, 179, 184-186, 189
6th Light Horse Regiment............ 52, 134, 189
8th Portsmouth Company, Royal Marines 22
11th (North Devonshire) Regiment of Foot......... 43
11th Hussars (Prince Albert's Own)............ 55
16th (The Queen's) Lancers 150
18th (Royal Irish) Regiment of Foot............ 27
38th (1st Staffordshire) Regiment of Foot 52, 143
42nd (Royal Highlanders) Regiment of Foot...... 10
46th (South Devonshire) Regiment of Foot......... 25
47th (Lancashire) Regiment of Foot 38
48th (Northamptonshire) Regiment of Foot...11, 40-41, *60,* 61, 143, 147
57th (The West Middlesex) Regiment of Foot 14, 38, 39, 46, 48
58th (Rutlandshire) Regiment of Foot 41-42, *43*
59th Regiment of Foot............ 14
60th (King's Royal Rifles) Regiment............ 35, 55-56, 59, 100, 151
68th (Durham) Regiment of Foot............ 9
80th (South Staffordshire) Regiment of Foot..... .... 41, 42, 52, 66, 68, 143
94th Regiment of Foot............ 25, 104
98th (Prince of Wales) Regiment of Foot........... 8-9
99th (Lanarkshire) Regiment of Foot............ 41-43
102nd Regiment............ 4, 7-9

'A' Squadron NSW Mounted Rifles............ ....114, 120, 127-133, 137-139, 142, 148, 151-157, 162-166, 170-174, 181, 186-190
Abbott, Captain Edward 7
Abraham's Kraal 120, 125, 165
Abrahams, William John............ 120
Akers, Stanley Ernest............ 111-112
Aldershot.94, 100-112, 129-130, 184-186, 190
American Revolutionary War aka American War of Independence 9, 14
Anderson, William Samuel 112
Anniversary Day, 26 January............ 161
Antill, Edward Augustus............ 113, *113*
Antill, Henry Colden 1, 24
Antill, John Macquarie 74, 77, 114-120, *114,* 165, 191
Antill, Robert Henry............ 27
Appin Massacre 6
Artillery Colonial Military Forces (NSW) 51-52
Australian Commonwealth Horse 111, 128, 131, 140, 151-152, 189
Axam, Francis William 107, 120-126, *121,* 148, 152, 165, 171, 183, 197-198

Baird, Major General Sir David 25
Baker, William............ 5
Bankfontein 155
Bateup, Amos Albert ... 107, 120, 127-128, 177
Bathurst, Earl Henry............ 28
Battle of
　Aboukir 26
　Albuera 11, 14, 38
　Alma............ 14, 44
　Camperdown............ 35
　Driefontein 77, 142, 165
　Elandslaagte 193
　Inkerman 14
　Magersfontein 118, 136
　Montmartre (Paris)............ 32
　Paardeberg ... 77, 112, 114, 120, 123-124, 131, 136, 140
　Saran Star............ 60-61
　Seringapatam............ 10, 14, 23-25, 56
　the Nile............ 25
　Talavera 11
　Toulouse 11, 15, 32-34
　Trafalgar............ 1, 36
　Waterloo............ 10, 16, 38-42
Bechuanaland Expedition 104, 140
Beckhaus, Frederick............ 128, *128*
Bell, George Lawluck 128
Belmont Station 129-130
Bigge, Commissioner John Thomas............ 34
Billett, John Ernest Edward (Ted)......... 128, 192
Blackwood, James............ 107, 128, 129, 177
Blencowe, Arthur William............ 129
Bligh, Governor William 9
Bloemfontein. 145-146, 152, 165, 171-172
Boer ....
　　fighting ... 117, 153, 164, 171, 175, 184
　　history 103, 194
Bollard, Albert John............ 98, 107, 129
Bonaparte, Napoleon............ 33, 149
Bourke, Governor Sir Richard............ 37
Brandfort 126, 190-191
Breaker Morant............ 193
Bresnahan, Patrick 129-130
Breton, Henry William............ 2, 16-17, *16*
Brew, Phillip Carvell 130
Bridges, William Frederick............ 130
Brisbane, Governor Sir Thomas 26, 29-30
Britstown 116-117
Broughton, Bishop William Grant............ 37
Buffalo River 188
Buffs (Royal East Kent) Regiment .. 51-52, 133, 165
Bull, Edward Canute............ 130-131
Burke, Michael Joseph............ 131, *131,* 171
Bushmen's Contingent............ 110
bushrangers 12, 15, 89, 94
Butler, Arthur Albert............ 131-132
Buttenshaw, Frederick James............ 198

Cambridgeshire Militia............ 44

201

Camden Mounted Rifles 80-81
Camden Park.. 7, 40
Cape Colony... 103, *103*
Cape Town 121-122, 162-163, 180
Carnarvon, Lord... 62
Carrington, Lord Charles Robert 66, 93
Chauvel, Henry George (Harry)........................71
Chisholm, James... 8
Christmas dinner..158
Clark, Ralph...2-3
Cleary, Edward Thomas....... 107, 132-133, 177
Clifford, George 108, 133
Colesberg 129-130
Collins, Lieutenant-Governor David.....................9
Corbett, Edward.. 3
Cornwallis, Sir William 35
Cornwell, William Charles............................ 51, *51*
Corps of Permanent Mounted Infantry.............. 66
Cowpastures..............................2-3, *19*, 23, 26
Cowper, William Robert.....................................64
Cox, Charles Frederick............... 111-112, 133
Crimean War *45*
Cronje, General Pieter Arnoldus 112,
 118-119, 124, 144, 146, 148, *149,* 156, 164
Cross, Ephraim Snr....................................... 44-45
Crowe, William 10-11
Culshaw, Richard Matthew Wyoming 133

Darling, Governor Sir Ralph................................ 38
Davey, Lazarus 26
Davey, Walter George.............. 51-52, 133, *133*
Davis, Edward... 15
Dawes, William Lieutenant................................. 22
de Aar 112-123, 154, 168, 170-171, 180
de Arrieta Jean (John) Baptiste Lehimas 26-27
de la Rey, General Jacobus Herculaas 128, 188
de Lisle, Colonel Sir Henry de Beauvoir 157
de Witt, Christiaan.. 132
Dharawal.. 6-7
Diamond Hill 140
Die Hards 14, 38, 46
Divall, William 52, 133-134, 183
Donahoe, John (Bold Jack) 15
Doornkloof... 138
Douglass, Henry Grattan 27-31, *27, 29*
Downes, Frederick William Arthur 64
Duff Challenge Cup 71, 74-75
Dunbar, Frederick 135
Dunk, Jesse 2, 31-33, *32*
Durban 131, 141, 188, 195
Dwyer, Thomas John 98

Elizabeth Farm 8, 10, 40
Ellis, John 195
English, Herbert Thomas.................................... 79
English, James Joseph 80
Enslin 136, 147, 180
enteric fever................ 120, 127, 131, 133, 160,
 166, 177, 186
Erskine, Colonel James 40
Eustace, Isaac.. 4-5

Fairley, Edward James 98-99
Farrell, Edward Nicholas................... 135, *135*

Fenwick, George Thomas 135-137, *136*
Ferrari Siding..182
Ferris, John Dabinett.. 99
Fidden, Charles William 52, 137
Field, John 137
Fighting 29 ....129-130, 136
First Fleet 3-4, 22
Fitzgerald, Edward (Ned) 158
Forbes, Charles..2, 16
Forster, George Brooke 137, *137*
Fourth Fleet 4
French, General John 87, 124, 163
Fryer, Richard 21

Gandangara... 7
Geary, Edmund 137-138
Gibson, James 43
Gipps, Governor Sir George................................ 30
Glen Siding.. 183
Gordon, Major-General Charles George............. 50
Gordon Highlanders............................ 61, 180-181
Graham, Alfred Adolphus Doran 138
Gregory, John Jervis 17-18
Griqualand 122
Grootveld 149

Hall, Dr. James... 29
Hannay, Colonel Ormelie Campbell......120, 156
Hawkey, John Martin...99-100, *106,* 138, *138,*
 191
Hayes, Frederick St. Leger 139, *139*
Heilbron 77, 149
Hepburn, Robert William (James) 33-34
Higgins, Robert... 7
Hilder, Henry 52
Hill, William..139
Historical Records 2nd ALHR Coy Mounted Rifles
 ....65, *65*
Hobart Town 9, 26, 42-43
Holman, Richard Charles Frederick 65, 69,
 100, 104, 116, 139-140, *139,* 191
horses
 Boer Wars................. 108, 115, 160, 192
 Jubilee detachment 83, 91, 94
Hovell, William Hilton 2
Howe, Robert..30
Howe, William 34
Huckstepp, George Edwin.......................140-142
Huer, Edward Theodore George............ 142, *142*
Hughes, Ellen Rosetta 39
Hughes, James Terry 37
Hughes, John Samuel 142
Humphries, Frederick James (Frank. 142, *142*
Huon de Kerilleau, Gabriel Louis Marie 8
Hutton, Major-General Edward Thomas Henry
 126, 153
Hutton Shield 71, 74-75, 78

India 10
indigenous people 3, 5-7, 11
Inglis, Colonel.. 14

Jacobsdal.. 119, 124

Jervois, Sir William Francis Drummond. 62-63
Jessop, Joseph 142
Johannesburg 77, 131-132, 136, 140, 142, 150
Johnston, Colonel George 23
Jones, Walter 61, 143

Kelly-Kenny, General Sir Thomas 118
Kemp, Captain Anthony Fenn 8
Kennedy, John 6
Khartoum 50-52, 100
Khedive's Star 52, *52*, 134, 143
Kidd, John 45, 111, 196
Kilmartin, Patrick 196
Kimberley 104, 112, 117, 124, 144, 171
King, Philip Gidley 3, 18
King, William Henry 143
Kitchener, Lord Horatio Herbert
 .... 53, 118, 148, 194
Klerksdorp 129, 184
Klip Drift 164
Klip Kraal 187
Knight, Isaac 22-23
Kroonstad 132, 140, 153, 165, 173, 186

Lacey, Henry Noel 69, 123, 168-169
Langverwagt 133
Larkin, Captain Willie 108-111
Lassetter, Henry Beauchamp 51-52, 66-71,
 87, 91, 93, 96, *97*, 100, 143-144
Lawson, William 29
Laycock, Thomas William 8-9
Le Mesurier, Lieutenant-Colonel Haviland 128
Lees, Thomas James (Tom) 144-147, 183
Lewis, George 61, 147
Little, Alfred Denison 196
Lloyd, William George 148
Lloyd-George, David, 1st Earl Lloyd-George of
 Dwyfor 195
Loader, Charles Arthur Clarendon 148
Lockhart, General Sir William 61
Lyster, James Sanderson 141

MacAlister, Lachlan 2, 11-12
Macarthur, Edward 35, *35*
Macarthur, Elizabeth nee Veale 8, 46, 55,
 101, 148, 150-151, 198
Macarthur, Hannibal Hawkins 29-30, 37
Macarthur, James 40
Macarthur, John 1, 9-10, 12, *9*
Macarthur, William 8, 12, 16
Macarthur-Onslow, Annette 79
Macarthur-Onslow, Arthur John (Jack) ... 101,
 148, *148*
Macarthur-Onslow, Arthur William 150, *150*
Macarthur-Onslow, Elizabeth 198
Macarthur-Onslow, Francis Arthur 150, *150*
Macarthur-Onslow, James William .. 55-59, *55*,
 76, *81*, 98, 101, 125-126, 151, *151*, 191
McBaron, Matthew Montgomery (Monty) 152,
 152
McDonald, Colonel MM 70-71
McEwen, James Fraser 152-153
McIntyre, Lieutenant 61

Mackay, Lieutenant-Colonel James Alexander
 Kenneth 128
MacKenzie, Lieutenant-Colonel John Kenneth
 16
Macleay, Alexander 46
Macleay, William 46
Macquarie, Governor Lachlan 6-7, 10, 18,
 24, 28
Majuba Hill 156
Maori Wars 42-43
Marden, John 14
Maritime strike, Sydney 1890 69
Marsden, Rev. Samuel 29-30
Martin, Alexander 2, 35-38, *35*
Maxwell, Alfred Ernest 151
Maxwell, John Cornelius 151, 191
measles 141
Messina, Marshall Andre 33
Methuen, Lord Paul Sanford 129-130, 140
Military Cross 138
Mitchell, Major William 12
Modder River 112, 120, 122, 163
Molle, George James 2, 25, *25*
Moore, John Edward 196
Moore, Patrick Thomas 153-154
Muggleston, John 15
Murray, James Bernard 154
Mysore Wars 10, 23

Naauwpoort 112, 172, 191
Napoleonic Wars 1, 9, 11, 15-16, 20, 34, 38
Nelson, Admiral Lord 25, 36
Nethery, Robert John 154-157, 191, 198
NSW Corps 4, 22
NSW Lancers (1st ALHR) 52, 111, 129, 133
NSW Mounted Police 15-16
NSW Mounted Rifles (2nd ALHR) 52, 64, 69-70,
 90, 94, 95, 96, 97, 107-108, *119*, 131, 139,
 139
NSW Police 20
New Zealand 10, 14, 41-43, 130, 135, 150
Newman, Joseph 157-158
Newman, William Arthur 159-165
Nile Expedition 52
Noonan, Timothy 6
Norfolk Island 3, 7, 15, 21
North-West Indian Frontier 60

O'Brien, William Edward 100
Onslow, Arthur Alexander Walton 46, *46*, 53
Onslow, Harry Hamilton 53
Orange Free State 165
Orange River 163, 180
Osborne, Edmund 165, *165*
Osfontein 164
Ottoman Empire 44
Oxley, John Joseph William Molesworth ... 1,
 18, *18*

Paardeberg 112
Parkes, Sir Henry 66, 70
Paterson, Andrew Barton (Banjo) 148
Pearce, Wellington Henry 166
Pegum, Stephen 63-64

Peninsular War 11, 26, 33, 38
Peshawar...55-60
Philipstown 138
Phillip, Governor Arthur............................3
Pitt, William Moreton............................. 26
Poole, John William............................41-42
Poplar Grove 77, 165
Port Albert 13
Port Dalrymple *now Launceston*........... 9, 12
Porter, Frederick Stanley...................... 145
Porter, John Alexander......................... 196
Potgieter, Ferdinandus Jacobus.........114, 188
Potts, Pembroke 166
Prieska 116, 154, 168
Prince of Wales *94*

Quakers (Society of Friends) 194-195
Queen Victoria..... 54, 68, 75, 95, 99-100, 129, 139, 143, 187
Queensland Police 20

Ramah or Ramah Spring 117, 120
Rankin, James Downie........................ 98, 196
Read's Drift.. 138
Reilly, Philip John............... 166-169, *166*, 177
Rhodesia...128, 138
Richards, Robert (Ben) 169, *169*
Richards, Staff Sergeant-Major Thomas Robert
.... 69, 107
Richardson, Major-General John Soame.......... 68
Rimington, Sir Michael Frederic 133, 147, 192
Roberts' Horse 170
Roberts, Lord Frederick 95, *96*, 118, 140, 145
Robertson, Thomas Cunningham............. 173
Ross, Lieutenant Robert 3
Royal Marines 3, 49
Royal Navy 35, 46
Royal Regiment of Artillery 55
Royal Veteran Regiment 4
Russia 44, 54

S.S. *Thermopylae*....................................162
Schaw, Henry (Major-General) 66
Scots Brigade 25
Scott, Charles Prestwich 195
Scott, James 3, 22
Scott, Jeremiah 169
Scott, John (Surgeon-General) 3
Scratchley, Lieutenant-Colonel Sir Peter Henry
....62
Second Fleet 10
Seringapatam 10
Sevastopol................................... 14, 44, 46
Shadforth, Henry Tudor......................... 14
Shadforth, Thomas (jnr.)............38, 46-49, *48*
Shadforth, Thomas (snr) 2, 38-39, *39*
Sharpe, George 49-50
Sharpe, Henry (Harry) *106,* 170, *170,* 192
Sharpe, Richard..................................... *106*
Sharpe, Robert 170, *170*
Shaw, William Hamilton Hubert............ 170-172
Shoobridge, William............................... 39

Short History of NSW Mounted Rifles 1888–1913
.... *65,* 91
Small, James 101
Smillie, Sergeant James........................ 173
Smith, Albert Edward 172
Smith, Carlton 172, *172*
Smith, Charles Roy McIntosh 172-174, 191
Smith, Reginald Sydney (Rex) ... 132, 174-179, *175*
Smith, Samuel Fairall 179
Soult, Marshall Jean-de-Dieu.............. 33-34
Southern Cross (Troopship) 160
Southey, Clifford Melville 173, 179-181
Sparrow, Captain Henry Glendower Bodycham
.... 66-67, 71
Spearing, Benjamin Charles 181, *181*
Spearing, James Stares 26, 30
Spooner, Charles Greenwood 159, 181-183
Springfontein 183
Standerton 144, 146, 186, 191-192
Starr, William 39
Stewart, Walter David.....................183-184
Steyn, President Martinus Theunis 165
Sudan *53*
Sullivan, Mary...5
Swan, Charles 19-20
Swan's Farm 154

Table Bay 103, 121, 162-163
Tame, Albert Edward 184, *185*
Tame, Henry 185, *185*
Tame, Herbert Bernden 185, *185*
Tame, Walter Charles 186, *185*
Taplin, Henry Edwin 101-102
Taylor, Elizabeth 30
Tench, Watkin Captain 22
Terry, Samuel 26-27
Third Fleet 8, 21
Thompson, Astley John Onslow 65, 77-79, *79,* 92, 102, *102*
Thompson, Norman Edgar 186
Tipoo 23, *24*
Townson, Lieutenant John 21
Transvaal 104, 151, 167
Trevitt, George Spurway 186
Turner, William James......................... 186
Tweedy, William George 156, 186-187

uniforms 67
    Diamond Jubilee........................... 85-86
    Mounted Rifles 1894 .... 71-73, *73*

Vacchini, Caleb Francis....... 102, 145, 187, *187*
van Diemen's Land..................... 8, 9, 12
Vaughan, Alfred Edward 102
Vermaas, Hendrick Cornelius Wilhelmus.... 188
Volunteer Regulation Act.........................63

Walker, William 27
Walsh, Edward 187, *187*
Walton, William Joseph....................... 187
War of 1812 .... 9, 32, 38

Warburton, James 16
Warby, Joseph Hillier 187
Wardrobe, John 187, *187*
Warren, Richard Benson 64
Wasson, John James 187-188, 191
Waxted, James 6
Wearne, Albert Ernest 189, *189*
Wellington, Duke of 11, 39
Wentworth, William Charles 30-32, 37
Wheeler, Jonathan 40
Wheeler, Robert John 189
Wild, John Henry 40, *40*
Wilkinson, Walter John 26
Wintle, Abraham Joseph 41
Wintle, Alfred 189
Wintle, William Edward (Billy) 108, 189, *189*

Wolseley, General Garnet Joseph 50-51, 52, 94, 100
Wonson, William Edward 189-190
Woods, Arthur Ernest 190
Woore, Thomas 2, 18-19
Worgan, Charles Bouchier 4

York, Duke of 77
Young, George Edward 196

Zand River 127, 151, 166
Zglinicki, Ernest James 190-192
Zglinicki, Maximilian von 20-21
Zulu Wars 104

www.ingramcontent.com/pod-product-compliance
Lightning Source LLC
Chambersburg PA
CBHW080855010526
44107CB00057B/2583